SELECTED ANTITRUST CASES

Landmark Decisions in Federal Antitrust

SELECTED ANTITRUST CASES

LANDMARK DECISIONS IN FEDERAL
ANTITRUST

By IRWIN M. STELZER, PH.D.

ECONOMIC CONSULTANT, BAYSIDE, NEW YORK

1955

RICHARD D. IRWIN, INC.

HOMEWOOD, ILLINOIS

First Printing, September, 1955

Library of Congress Catalogue Card No. 55–11466

TO

ELAINE

PREFACE

The purpose of this book is to provide students in economics, government, and business administration with an opportunity to obtain a clear understanding of our antitrust laws. Teachers in these fields are almost uniform in their agreement that there is no substitute for an actual reading of the case material, in order to facilitate an understanding of the legal and economic issues raised by our antitrust laws, and to provide the student with concrete "real-world" problems which by their very nature are the most interesting. However, students can rarely be required to read lengthy court opinions in addition to a standard text. Consequently, I undertook the task of compiling a list of the leading decisions in this area, and of editing them to manageable proportions, taking care, at the same time, to preserve all that is of lasting significance in the opinions. In every instance the original language of the court has been retained; and the deletions made were not permitted to interfere with the smooth flow of thought and language of these judicial opinions.

A word about the selection of cases is, I believe, in order. Only those which represent truly landmark opinions have been included. An attempt has been made to select cases so that the student will have both an understanding of the law as it now stands, and a knowledge of the historical development of the attitude of the courts on the various legal-economic issues. Furthermore, although each section of the book is self-contained in the sense that it covers an issue or problem in its entirety, the various sections are definitely interrelated. Thus, for example, the first section provides a rather thorough treatment of court attitudes towards monopoly, while the second section deals with the legal and economic issues raised by direct price-fixing agreements. The cases in these portions of the book were also selected so that the student might easily *compare* court attitudes towards proprietary consolidations and monopoly, on the one hand, and loose-knit confederations on the other. In this way the concept of the "double standard" in federal antitrust is made more readily understandable.

Although final responsibility for the selection of cases remains my own, I would like to thank Joel Dirlam, of the University of Connecticut, Alfred E. Kahn of Cornell University, George W. Stocking of Vanderbilt University, and Simon N. Whitney of the Twentieth Century Fund for their many helpful suggestions. Others whose advice I would like to acknowledge include M. A. Adelman of Massachusetts Institute of Technology; Aaron Director of the University of Chicago; Jesse W. Markham of Princeton University; Clair Wilcox of Swarthmore College; and William V. Wilmot, Jr. of the University of Wisconsin. Last, but far from least, I would like to acknowledge the invaluable assistance rendered by my wife, Elaine, in this project.

IRWIN M. STELZER

BAYSIDE, NEW YORK
June 1955

CONTENTS

CHAPTER   PAGE

PART I. PROPRIETARY CONSOLIDATIONS AND MONOPOLY

1. CLOSE-KNIT COMBINATIONS AND MONOPOLY   3
   Standard Oil of New Jersey and the Adoption of the Rule of Reason.
   Application of the Rule in United States Steel. Alcoa and the "New
   Sherman Act." Rational Oligopoly Behavior and the Sherman Act—
   American Tobacco. Integration and the Law—Yellow Cab and Para-
   mount Pictures. A Modified Rule of Reason—The Shoe Machinery
   Case. Economic Performance and the Law—the Cellophane Case.

2. INTERCORPORATE STOCKHOLDING AND MERGERS   60
   Thatcher Manufacturing Company and the Emasculation of Section 7
   of the Clayton Act. Mergers and the Sherman Act—Columbia Steel.
   Revival of Antimerger Policy—Pillsbury Mills and the Amended Clayton Act.

PART II. LOOSE-KNIT CONFEDERATIONS

3. DIRECT PRICE-FIXING AGREEMENTS   79
   The "Reasonableness" of Price-Fixing Agreements—Addyston Pipe and
   Trenton Potteries. Market Power, Distress Conditions and the Law—
   Appalachian Coals and Socony-Vacuum.

4. TRADE ASSOCIATION ACTIVITIES   95
   Trade Associations and the Elimination of Competition—American Col-
   umn and Lumber. Permissible Activities—Sugar Institute and Tag Manufacturers.

5. DELIVERED PRICE SYSTEMS   111
   The Single Basing Point System and Price Discrimination—Corn Prod-
   ucts. Basing Point Pricing and the Good Faith Meeting of Competition
   —Staley. The Cement Case—the Multiple Basing Point System as an
   Unfair Method of Competition. Triangle Conduit and Conscious Paral-
   lelism.

PART III. TRADE PRACTICES

6. EXCLUSIVE DEALING ARRANGEMENTS   135
   Standard Fashion—Exclusive Dealing and the Incipiency of the Threat
   to Competition. Standard Stations and the Substantiality of the Commerce Affected. The Permissible Area of Exclusive Dealing—The Case
   case.

7. TYING DEVICES   147
   American Can and the Use of Monopoly "Leverage." Tied Sales without Monopoly Power—Times-Picayune.

CHAPTER	PAGE
8. PRICE DISCRIMINATION	161

The Reasonable Possibility of Competitive Injury—Morton Salt. Price Discrimination in Good Faith—Standard of Indiana.

PART IV. LEGAL MONOPOLIES UNDER FEDERAL ANTITRUST

9. PATENTS—THE RIGHT AND ITS LIMITS	173

Patent Pools, Cross—Licensing and the Problem of Adequate Remedy —Hartford-Empire. Tied Sales and the Patent Right—International Salt.

10. COPYRIGHTS AND TRADEMARKS	183

The Copyright and Price-Fixing—Interstate Circuit. Block-Booking and the Copyright—Paramount Pictures.

PART V. FOREIGN COMMERCE AND INTERNATIONAL AGREEMENTS

11. CARTELS	191

The Use of Patents to Restrain Foreign Commerce—National Lead. The "Joint Venture" Concept. The Reasonableness of Cartel Agreements—Timken Roller Bearing.

APPENDIX

APPENDIX: EXCERPTS FROM ANTITRUST STATUTES	203

INDEX

INDEX OF CASES	209

PART I

Proprietary Consolidations and Monopoly

Chapter 1

CLOSE-KNIT COMBINATIONS AND MONOPOLY

Since the enactment of the antitrust laws, enforcement officials and the courts have traditionally been called upon to apply them to two types of combines—the so-called close-knit combination, formed by trust, holding company, merger or consolidation, and the loose-knit confederation to be discussed in Part II. The cases presented below trace the development of court attitudes since the adoption of the "rule of reason" in the Standard Oil decision of 1911. This doctrine, which required the courts to examine the circumstances surrounding the formation of a combination as well as the pattern of its business behavior in an attempt to discover an intent to monopolize, gave rise to the corollary statement in the United States Steel case that the law does not make mere size an offense. Critics of the rule of reason professed to see the emergence of a "New Sherman Act" from the Alcoa case, and received further encouragement from the American Tobacco decision. Whether these decisions did in fact mark the gutting of the rule of reason, or merely its intelligent application, it is generally agreed that these two cases greatly increased the effectiveness of antitrust policy.[1] The two Yellow Cab cases and the Paramount Pictures cases are of interest for the light they shed on the problems created by vertical integration. The first Yellow Cab case was taken by many to indicate a much sterner judicial view of the dangers inherent in vertical integration, and by some to indicate that virtually all such integration had been declared unlawful. Both the Paramount Pictures and second Yellow Cab cases, however, indicated the Court's continued reliance on "intent," with the former decision evidencing the manner in which an intent to monopolize may be inferred from various restrictive practices. The dissent in the second Yellow Cab case has been included to highlight the divergent views concerning the necessity of proving "intent to monopolize" in order to establish a Section 2 Sherman Act violation. The Shoe Machinery case represents an attempt to apply a rule of reason modified to account for the Alcoa decision. Finally, the Cellophane case represents an attempt by the judiciary

[1] For an incisive discussion of these points see Joel B. Dirlam and Alfred E. Kahn, *Fair Competition: The Law and Economics of Antitrust Policy* (Ithaca: Cornell University Press, 1955), chapters 3 and 5.

to apply the economist's concepts of workable or effective competition to antitrust problems by a broad assessment of the economic performance of an alleged violator of the law.

Standard Oil Company of New Jersey v. United States
221 U.S. 1 (1911)

Note: Mr. Chief Justice White delivered the opinion of the Court, the legal reasoning of which is abstracted below. The findings of fact, too lengthy to be set forth in detail here, were essentially as follows: Standard of Ohio, organized by John D. and William Rockefeller in 1870, had by 1872 acquired all but 3 or 4 of the 35 to 45 refineries in Cleveland. By obtaining preferential rates and large rebates from the railroads the combination was able to force competitors to join it or be driven out of business. As a result, the combine obtained control of 90 per cent of the petroleum industry, a dominance which enabled it to fix the price of both crude and refined petroleum. In 1899 Standard Oil of New Jersey was established as a holding company to replace the Ohio trust. The new organization continued to obtain preferential treatment from railroads, engaged in several unfair practices against competing pipelines so as to obtain control of that means of transportation as well, engaged in local price cutting to suppress competition, set up bogus independents, engaged in industrial espionage, and earned enormous profits. The Court continued:

. . . [*T*]*he text of the* [*Sherman*] *Act and its meaning.* . . . *The* debates . . . conclusively show . . . that the main cause which led to the legislation was the thought that it was required by the economic conditions of the times; that is, the vast accumulation of wealth in the hands of corporations and individuals, the enormous development of corporate organization, the facility for combination which such organization afforded, the fact that the facility was being used, and that combinations known as trusts were being multiplied, and the widespread impression that their power had been and would be exerted to oppress individuals and injure the public generally. . . .

There can be no doubt that the sole subject with which the first section deals is restraint of trade as therein contemplated, and that the attempt to monopolize and monopolization is the subject with which the second section is concerned. It is certain that those terms, at least in their rudimentary meaning, took their origin in the common law, and were also familiar in the law of this country prior to and at the time of the adoption of the act in question.

We shall endeavor, then first, to seek their meaning . . . by making a very brief reference to the elementary and indisputable conceptions of both the English and American law on the subject prior to the passage of the antitrust act. . . .

Without going into detail, and but very briefly surveying the whole field, it may be with accuracy said that the dread of enhancement of prices and of other wrongs which it was thought would flow from the undue limitation on competitive conditions caused by contracts or other acts of individuals or corporations led, as a matter of public policy, to the prohibition or treating as illegal all contracts or acts which were unreasonably restrictive of competitive conditions, either from the nature or character of the contract or act, or where the surrounding circumstances were such as to justify the conclusion that they had not been entered into or performed with the legitimate purpose of reasonably forwarding personal interest and developing, trade, but, on the contrary, were of such a character as to give rise to the inference or presumption that they had been entered into or done with the intent to do wrong to the general public and to limit the right of individuals, thus restraining the free flow of commerce and tending to bring about the evils such as enhancement of prices, which were considered to be against public policy. It is equally true to say that the survey of the legislation in this country on this subject from the beginning will show, depending, as it did, upon the economic conceptions which obtained at the time when the legislation was adopted or judicial decision was rendered, that contracts or acts were at one time deemed to be of such character as to justify the inference of wrongful intent which were at another period thought not to be of that character. But this again, as we have seen, simply followed the line of development of the law of England.

Let us consider the language of the 1st and 2d sections, guided by the principle that where words are employed in a statute which had at the time a well-known meaning at common law or in the law of this country, they are presumed to have been used in that sense unless the context compels to the contrary.

As to the 1st section. . . . [A]s the contracts or acts embraced in the provision were not expressly defined, since the enumeration addressed itself simply to classes of acts, those classes being broad enough to embrace every conceivable contract or combination which could be made concerning trade or commerce or the subjects of such commerce, and thus caused any act done by any of the enumerated methods anywhere in the whole field of human activity to be illegal if in restraint of trade, it inevitably follows that the provision necessarily called for the exercise of judgment which required that some standard should be resorted to for the purpose of determining whether the prohibition contained in the statute had or had not in any given case been violated. Thus not specifying, but indubitably contemplating and requiring a standard it follows that it was intended that the standard of reason which had been applied at the common law in this country in dealing with subjects of the character embraced by the statute was intended to be the measure used for the purpose of determining whether, in a given case, a particular act had or had not brought about the wrong against which the statute provided.

And a consideration of the text of the 2d section serves to establish that it was intended to supplement the 1st, and to make sure that by no possible guise could the public policy embodied in the 1st section be frustrated or evaded. . . .

In other words, having by the 1st section forbidden all means of monopolizing trade, that is, unduly restraining it by means of every contract, combination, etc., the 2d section seeks, if possible, to make the prohibitions of the act all the more complete and perfect by embracing all attempts to reach the end prohibited by the 1st section, that is, restraints of trade, by any attempt to monopolize, or monopolization thereof, even although the acts by which such results are attempted to be brought about or are brought about be not embraced within the general enumeration of the 1st section. And, of course, when the 2d section is thus harmonized with and made, as it was intended to be, the complement of the 1st, it becomes obvious that the criteria to be resorted to in any given case for the purpose of ascertaining whether violations of the section have been committed is the rule of reason guided by the established law and by the plain duty to enforce the prohibitions of the act, and thus the public policy which its restrictions were obviously enacted to subserve. And it is worthy of observation, as we have previously remarked concerning the common law, that although the statute, by the comprehensiveness of the enumerations embodies in both the 1st and 2d sections, makes it certain that its purpose was to prevent undue restraints of every kind or nature, nevertheless by the omission of any direct prohibition against monopoly in the concrete, it indicates a consciousness that the freedom of the individual right to contract, when not unduly or improperly exercised, was the most efficient means for the prevention of monopoly, since the operation of the centrifugal and centripetal forces resulting from the right to freely contract was the means by which monopoly would be inevitably prevented if no extraneous or sovereign power imposed it and no right to make unlawful contracts having a monopolistic tendency were permitted. In other words, that freedom to contract was the essence of freedom from undue restraint on the right to contract. . . .

The facts and the application of the statute to them. . . . Giving to the facts . . . the weight which it was deemed they were entitled to, in the light afforded by the proof of other cognate facts and circumstance, the court below held that the acts and dealings established by the proof operated to destroy the "potentiality of competition" which otherwise would have existed to such an extent as to cause the transfers of stock which were made to the New Jersey corporation and the control which resulted over the many and various subsidiary corporations to be a combination or conspiracy in restraint of trade, in violation of the 1st section of the act, but also to be an attempt to monopolize and monopolization bringing about a perennial violation of the 2d section.

We see no cause to doubt the correctness of these conclusions . . . for the following reasons:

a) Because the unification of power and control over petroleum and its products which was the inevitable result of the combining in the New Jersey corporation by the increase of its stock and the transfer to it of the stocks of so many other corporations, aggregating so vast a capital, gives rise, in and of itself, in the absence of countervailing circumstances, to say the least, to the prima facie presumption of intent and purpose to maintain the dominancy over the oil industry, not as a result of normal methods of industrial development, but by new means of combination which were resorted to in order that greater power might be added than would otherwise have arisen had normal methods been followed, the whole with the purpose of excluding others from the trade, and thus centralizing in the combination a perpetual control of the movements of petroleum and its products in the channels of interstate commerce.

b) Because the prima facie presumption of intent to restrain trade, to monopolize and bring about monopolization, resulting from the act of expanding the stock of the New Jersey corporation and vesting it with such vast control of the oil industry, is . . . conclusive. . . .

[W]e think no disinterested mind can survey the period in question without being irresistibly driven to the conclusion that the very genius for commercial development and organization which it would seem was manifested from the beginning soon begot an intent and purpose to exclude others which was frequently manifested by acts and dealings wholly inconsistent with the theory that they were made with the single conception of advancing the development of business power by usual methods, but which, on the contrary, necessarily involved the intent to drive others from the field and to exclude them from their right to trade, and thus accomplish the mastery which was the end in view. . . . The exercise of the power which resulted from that organization fortifies the foregoing conclusions, since the development which came, the acquisition here and there which ensued of every efficient means by which competition could have been asserted, the slow but resistless methods which followed by which means of transportation were absorbed and brought under control, the system of marketing which was adopted by which the country was divided into districts and the trade in each district in oil was turned over to a designated corporation within the combination, and all others were excluded, all lead the mind up to a conviction of a purpose and intent which we think is so certain as practically to cause the subject not to be within the domain of reasonable contention. . . .

The remedy to be administered. It may be conceded that ordinarily where it was found that acts had been done in violation of the statute, adequate measure of relief would result from restraining the doing of such acts in the future. . . . But in a case like this, where the condition which has been brought about in violation of the statute, in and of itself is not only a continued attempt to monopolize, but also a monopolization, the duty to enforce the statute requires the application of broader and more controlling remedies. . . .

In applying remedies for this purpose, however, the fact must not be overlooked that injury to the public by the prevention of an undue restraint on, or the monopolization of, trade or commerce, is the foundation upon which the prohibitions of the statute rest, and moreover that one of the fundamental purposes of the statute is to protect, not to destroy, rights of property. . . .

So far as the decree held that the ownership of the stock of the New Jersey corporation constituted a combination in violation of the 1st section and an attempt to create a monopoly or to monopolize under the 2d section, and commanded the dissolution of the combination, the decree was clearly appropriate. . . .

Our conclusion is that the decree below was right and should be affirmed, except as to the minor matters concerning which we have indicated the decree should be modified. Our order will therefore be one of affirmance, with directions, however, to modify the decree in accordance with this opinion. The court below to retain jurisdiction to the extent necessary to compel compliance in every respect with its decree.

And it is so ordered.

Mr. Justice Harlan concurred in part and dissented in part. . . .

United States v. United States Steel Corporation et al.

251 U.S. 417 (1920)

Mr. Justice McKenna delivered the opinion of the Court.

Suit against the Steel Corporation and certain other companies which it directs and controls by reason of the ownership of their stock, it and they being separately and collectively charged as violators of the Sherman Antitrust Act.

It is prayed that it and they be dissolved because engaged in illegal restraint of trade and the exercise of monopoly.

Special charges of illegality and monopoly are made and special redresses and remedies are prayed, among others, that there be a prohibition of stock ownership and exercise of rights under such ownership, and that there shall be such orders and distribution of the stock and other properties as shall be in accordance with equity and good conscience and "shall effectuate the purpose of the Antitrust Act." General relief is also prayed.

The Steel Corporation is a holding company only; the other companies are the operating ones, manufacturers in the iron and steel industry, 12 in number. There are, besides, other corporations and individuals more or less connected in the activities of the other defendants, that are alleged to be instruments or accomplices in their activities and offendings, and that these activities and offendings (speaking in general terms) extend from 1901 to 1911, when the bill was filed. . . .

The case was heard in the District Court by four judges. They agreed that the bill should be dismissed; they disagreed as to the reasons for it. . . . One opinion (written by Judge Buffington and concurred in by Judge McPherson) expressed the view that the Steel Corporation was not formed with the intention or purpose to monopolize or restrain trade, and did not have the motive or effect "to prejudice the public interest by unduly restricting competition or unduly obstructing the course of trade." The corporation, in the view of the opinion, was an evolution, a natural consummation of the tendencies of the industry on account of changing conditions. . . . And the concentration of powers (we are still representing the opinion) was only such as was deemed necessary, and immediately manifested itself in improved methods and products and in an increase of domestic and foreign trade. . . .

Not monopoly, therefore, was the purpose of the organization of the corporation, but concentration of efforts, with resultant economies and benefits.

All considerations deemed pertinent were expressed and their influence was attempted to be assigned and, while conceding that the Steel Corporation after its formation in times of financial disturbance, entered into informal agreements or understandings with its competitors to maintain prices, they terminated with their occasions, and, as they had ceased to exist, the course was not justified in dissolving the corporation.

The other opinion, by Judge Woolley and concurred in by Judge Hunt . . . , was in some particulars, in antithesis to Judge Buffington's. The view was expressed that neither the Steel Corporation nor the preceding combinations, which were in a sense its antetypes, had the justification of industrial conditions, nor were they or it impelled by the necessity for integration, or compelled to unite in comprehensive enterprise because such had become a condition of success under the new order of things. On the contrary, that the organizers of the corporation and the preceding companies had illegal purpose from the very beginning, and the corporation became "a combination of combinations by which, directly or indirectly, approximately 180 independent concerns were brought under one business control," which, measured by the amount of production, extended to 80 percent or 90 percent of the entire output of the country, and that its purpose was to secure great profits which were thought possible in the light of the history of its constituent combinations, and to accomplish permanently what those combinations had demonstrated could be accomplished temporarily, and thereby monopolize and restrain trade.

The organizers, however, (we are still representing the opinion) underestimated the opposing conditions and at the very beginning the corporation instead of relying upon its own power sought and obtained the assistance and the cooperation of its competitors (the independent companies). In other words, the view was expressed that the testimony did "not show that the corporation in and of itself ever possessed or exerted sufficient power when acting alone to control prices of the products of the industry." Its power was efficient only when in cooperation with its competitors, and hence it concerted with them in the expedients of pools, associations, trade meetings, and finally in a system of dinners inaugurated in 1907 by the president of the company, E. H. Gary, and called "the Gary Dinners." The dinners were congregations of producers and "were nothing but trade meetings," successors of the other means of associated action and control through such action. They were instituted first in "stress of panic," but their potency being demonstrated they were afterwards called to control prices "in periods of industrial calm." "They were pools without penalties" and more efficient in stabilizing prices. But it was the further declaration that "when joint action was either refused or withdrawn the corporation's prices were controlled by competition."

The corporation, it was said, did not at any time abuse the power or ascendency it possessed. It resorted to none of the brutalities or tyrannies that the cases illustrate of other combinations. . . . It combined its power with that of its competitors. It did not have power in and of itself, and the control it exerted was only in and by association with its competitors. Its offense, therefore, such as it was, was not different from theirs and was distinguished from "theirs only in the leadership it assumed in promulgating and perfecting the policy." This leadership it gave up and it had ceased to offend against the law before this suit was brought. It was hence concluded that it should be distinguished from its organizers and that their intent and unsuccessful attempt should not be attributed to it, that it "in and of itself is not now and has never been a monopoly or a combination in restraint of trade," and a decree of dissolution should not be entered against it.

This summary of the opinions . . . indicate that the evidence admits of different deductions as to the genesis of the corporation and the purpose of its organizers, but only of a single deduction as to the power it attained and could exercise. Both opinions were clear and confident that the power of the corporation never did and does not now reach to monopoly, and their review of the evidence, and our independent examination of it, enables us to elect between their respective estimates of it, and we concur in the main with that of Judges Woolley and Hunt. And we add no comment except, it may be, that they underestimated the influence of the tendency and movement to integration, the appreciation of the necessity or value of the continuity of manufacture from the ore to the finished product. . . .

In other words, our consideration should be of, not what the corporation had power to do or did, but what it has now power to do and is doing, and what judgment shall be now pronounced—whether its dissolution, as the government prays, or the dismissal of the suit, as the corporation insists.

The alternatives are perplexing, involve conflicting considerations, which, regarded in isolation, have diverse tendencies. . . . Monopoly . . . was not achieved, and competitors had to be persuaded by pools, associations, trade meetings, and through the social form of dinners, all of them, it may be, violations of the law, but transient in their purpose and effect. They were scattered through the years from 1901 (the year of the formation of the corporation) until 1911, but, after instances of success and failure, were abandoned nine months before this suit was brought. There is no evidence that the abandonment was in prophecy of or dread of suit; and the illegal practices have not been resumed, nor is there any evidence of an intention to resume them, and certainly no "dangerous probability" of their resumption. . . .

What, then can now be urged against the corporation? Can comparisons in other regards be made with its competitors and by such comparisons guilty or innocent existence be assigned it? It is greater in size and productive power than any of its competitors, equal or nearly equal to them all, but its power over prices was not and is not commensurate with its power to produce.

It is true there is some testimony tending to show that the corporation had such power, but there was also testimony and a course of action tending strongly to the contrary. The conflict was by the judges of the District Court unanimously resolved against the existence of that power, and in doing so they gave effect to the greater weight of the evidence. It is certain that no such power was exerted. On the contrary, the only attempt at a fixation of prices was, as already said, through an appeal to and confederation with competitors, and the record shows besides that when competition occurred it was not in pretense, and the corporation, declined in productive powers—the competitors growing either against or in consequence of the competition. If against the competition we have an instance of movement against what the government insists was an irresistible force; if in consequence of competition, we have an illustration of the adage that "competition is the life of trade" and is not easily repressed. The power of monopoly in the corporation under either illustration is an untenable accusation. . . . [C]ompetitors, dealers, and customers of the corporation testify in multitude that no adventitious interference was employed to fix or maintain prices, and that they were constant or varied according to natural conditions. Can this testimony be minimized or dismissed by inferring that, as intimated, it is an evidence of power, not of weakness, and power exerted, not only to suppress competition, but to compel testimony, is the necessary inference, shading into perjury, to deny its exertion? The situation is indeed singular, and we may wonder at it, wonder that the despotism of the corporation, so baneful to the world in the representation of the government, did not produce protesting victims.

But there are other paradoxes. . . . In one, competitors (the independents) are represented as oppressed by the superior power of the corporation; in the other, they are represented as ascending to opulence by imitating that power's prices, which they could not do, if at disadvantage from the other conditions of competition, and yet confederated action is not asserted. If it were, this suit would take on another cast. The competitors would cease to be the victims of the corporation, and would become its accomplices. And there is no other alternative. The suggestion that lurks in the government's contention that the acceptance of the corporation's prices is the submission of impotence to irresistible power is, in view of the testimony of the competitors, untenable. They, as we have seen, deny restraint in any measure or illegal influence of any kind. The government, therefore, is reduced to the assertion that the size of the corporation, the power it may have, not the exertion of the power, is an abhorrence to the law, or, as the government says, "the combination embodied in the corporation unduly restrains competition by its necessary effect . . . , and therefore is unlawful regardless of purpose.". . . To assent to that, to what extremes should we be led? . . .

We have pointed out that there are several of the government's contentions which are difficult to represent or measure, and the one we are now considering—that is, the power is "unlawful regardless of purpose" —is another of them. It seems to us that it has for its ultimate principle and justification that strength in any producer or seller is a menace to the public interest and illegal, because there is potency in it for mischief. The regression is extreme but short of it the government cannot stop. The fallacy it conveys is manifest . . .

The corporation is undoubtedly of impressive size, and it takes an effort of resolution not to be affected by it or to exaggerate its influence. But we must adhere to the law, and the law does not make mere size an offense, or the existence of unexerted power an offense. It, we repeat, requires overt acts, and trusts to its prohibition of them and its power to repress or punish them. It does not compel competition, nor require all that is possible. . . .

We have seen whatever there was of wrong intent could not be executed; whatever there was of evil effect was discontinued before this suit was brought, and this, we think, determines the decree. We say this in full realization of the requirements of the law. It is clear in its denunciation of monopolies, and equally clear in its direction that the courts of the nation shall prevent and restrain them (its language is "to prevent and restrain violations of" the act); but the command is necessarily submissive to the conditions which may exist and the usual powers of a court of equity to adapt its remedies to those conditions. In other words, it is not expected to enforce abstractions, and do injury thereby, it may be, to the purpose of the law. It is this flexibility of discretion—indeed, essential function—that makes it value in our jurisprudence—value in this case as in others. We do not mean to say that the law is not its own measure, and that it can be disregarded, but only that the appropriate relief in each instance is remitted to a court of equity to determine, not, and let us be explicit in this, to advance a policy contrary to that of the law, but in submission to the law and its policy, and in execution of both. And it is certainly a matter for consideration that there was no legal attack on the corporation until 1911, 10 years after its formation and the commencement of its career. We do not, however, speak of the delay simply as to its time, or say that there is estoppel in it because of its time, but on account of what was done during that time—the many millions of dollars spent, the development made, and the enterprises undertaken; the investments by the public that have been invited and are not to be ignored. And what of the foreign trade that has been developed and exists? . . .

The government, however, tentatively presents a proposition which has some tangibility. It submits that certain of the subsidiary companies are so mechanically equipped and so officially directed as to be released and remitted to independent action and individual interests and the competition to which such interests prompt, without any disturbance to business. . . . They are fully integrated, it is said—possess their own supplies, facilities of transportation, and distribution. They are subject to the Steel Corporation, is in effect the declaration, in nothing but its control of their prices. We may say parenthetically that they are defendants in the suit and charged as offenders, and we have the strange circumstance of violators of the law being urged to be used as expedients of the law.

But let us see what guide to a procedure of dissolution of the corporation and the dispersion as well of its subsidiary companies, for they are asserted to be illegal combinations, is prayed. And the fact must not be overlooked or underestimated. The prayer of the government calls for, not only a disruption of present conditions, but the restoration of the conditions of 20 years ago, if not literally, substantially. . . .

In conclusion, we are unable to see that the public interest will be served by yielding to the contention of the government respecting the dissolution of the company or the separation from it of some of its subsidiaries; and we do see in a contrary conclusion a risk of injury to the public interest, including a material disturbance of, and, it may be serious detriment to, the foreign trade. And in submission to the policy of the law and its fortifying prohibitions the public interest is of paramount regard.

We think, therefore, that the decree of the District Court should be affirmed.

So ordered.

Mr. Justice McReynolds and Mr. Justice Brandeis took no part in the consideration or decision of the case.

Mr. Justice Day, dissented. . . .

United States v. *Aluminum Company of America*[2]

148 F.2d 416 (1945)

Before L. Hand, Swan, and Augustus N. Hand, Circuit Judges. L. Hand, Circuit Judge. . . .

For convenience we have divided our discussion into four parts: (1) whether "Alcoa" monopolized the market in "virgin" aluminum ingot; (2) whether "Alcoa" was guilty of various unlawful practices, ancillary to the establishment of its monopoly; (3) whether [Aluminum] "Limited" and "Alcoa" were in an unlawful conspiracy; and whether, if not, "Limited" was guilty of a conspiracy with foreign producers; (4) what remedies are appropriate in the case of each defendant who may be found to have violated the Act.

I. "Alcoa's" Monopoly of "Virgin" Ingot. . . .

There are various ways of computing "Alcoa's" control of the aluminum market—as distinct from its production—depending upon what one regards as competing in that market. The judge [in the District Court] figures its share—during the years 1929–1938, inclusive—as only about thirty-three percent; to do so he included "secondary," and excluded that part of "Alcoa's" own production which it fabricated and did not therefore sell as ingot. If, on the other hand, "Alcoa's" total production, fabricated and sold, be included, and balanced against the sum of imported "virgin" and "secondary," its share of the market was in the neighborhood of sixty-four percent for that period. The percentage we have already mentioned—over ninety—results only if we both include all "Alcoa's" production and exclude "secondary." That percentage is enough to constitute a monopoly; it is doubtful whether sixty or sixty-four percent would be enough; and certainly thirty-three percent is not. Hence it is necessary to settle what he shall treat as competing in the ingot market. That part of its production which "Alcoa" itself fabricates, does not of course ever reach the market as ingot; and we recognize that it is only when a restriction of production either inevitably affects prices, or is intended to do so, that it violates Section 1 of the Act. . . . However even though we were to assume that a monopoly is unlawful under Section 2 only in case it controls prices, the ingot fabricated by "Alcoa," necessarily had a direct effect upon the ingot market. All ingot—with

---

[2] Because the Supreme Court was unable to obtain a quorum to review the District Court's opinion in this case, the issue was sent to the Circuit Court of Appeals for final decision. IMS.

trifling exceptions—is used to fabricate intermediate, or end, products; and therefore all intermediate, or end, products which "Alcoa" fabricates and sells, pro tanto reduce the demand for ingot itself. . . . We cannot therefore agree that the computation of the percentage of "Alcoa's" control over the ingot market should not include the whole of its ingot production.

As to "secondary,". . . we can say nothing more definite than that, although "secondary" does not compete at all in some uses (whether because of "sales resistance" only, or because of actual metallurgical inferiority), for most purposes it competes upon a substantial equality with "virgin." On these facts the judge found that "every pound of secondary or scrap aluminum which is sold in commerce displaces a pound of virgin aluminum which otherwise would, or might have been, sold." We agree: so far as "secondary" supplies the demand of such fabricators as will accept it, it increases the amount of "virgin" which must seek sale elsewhere; and it therefore results that the supply of that part of the demand which will accept only "virgin" becomes greater in proportion as "secondary" drives away "virgin" from the demand which will accept "secondary." (This is indeed the same argument which we used a moment ago to include in the supply that part of "virgin" which "Alcoa" fabricates; it is not apparent to us why the judge did not think it applicable to that item as well.) At any given moment therefore "secondary" competes with "virgin" in the ingot market; further, it can, and probably does, set a limit or "ceiling" beyond which the price of "virgin" cannot go, for the cost of its production will in the end depend only upon the expense of scavenging and reconditioning. It might seem for this reason that in estimating "Alcoa's" control over the ingot market, we ought to include the supply of "secondary," as the judge did. Indeed, it may be thought a paradox to say that anyone has the monopoly of a market in which at all times he must meet a competition that limits his price. We shall show that it is not.

In the case of a monopoly of any commodity which does not disappear in use and which can be salvaged, the supply seeking sale at any moment will be made up of two components: (1) the part which the putative monopolist can immediately produce and sell, and (2) the part which has been, or can be, reclaimed out of what he has produced and sold in the past. By hypothesis he presently controls the first of these components; the second he has controlled in the part, although he no longer does. During the period when he did control the second, if he was aware of his interest, he was guided, not alone by its effect at that time upon the market, but by his knowledge that some part of it was likely to be reclaimed and seek the future market. That consideration will to some extent always affect his production until he decides to abandon the business, or for some other reason ceases to be concerned with the future market. Thus, in the case at bar "Alcoa" always knew that the future supply of ingot would be made up in part of what it produced at the time, and, if it was as farsighted as it proclaims itself, that consideration must have had its share in determining how much to produce. How accurately it could forecast the effect of present production upon the future market is another matter. Experience, no doubt, would help; but it makes no difference that it had to guess; it is enough that it had an inducement to make the best guess it could, and that it would regulate that part of the future supply, so far as it should turn out to have guessed right. The competition of "secondary" must therefore be disregarded, as soon as we consider the position of "Alcoa" over a period of years; it was as much within "Alcoa's" control as was the production of the "virgin" from which it had been derived. . . .

We conclude therefore that "Alcoa's" control over the ingot market must be reckoned at over ninety percent; that being the proportion which its production bears to imported "virgin" ingot. . . .

Was this a monopoly within the meaning of Section 2? The judge found that, over the whole half century of its existence, "Alcoa's" profits upon capital invested, after payment of income taxes, had been only about ten percent, and, although the plaintiff puts this figure a little higher, the difference is negligible. . . . This assumed, it would be hard to say that "Alcoa" had made exorbitant profits on ingot, if it is proper to allocate the profit upon the whole business proportionately among all its products—ingot, and fabrications from ingot. A profit of ten percent in such an industry, dependent, in part at any rate, upon continued tariff protection, and subject to the vicissitudes of new demands, to the obsolescence of plant and process—which can never be accurately gauged in advance —to the chance that substitutes may at any moment be discovered which will reduce the demand, and to the other hazards which attend all industry; a profit of ten percent, so conditioned, could hardly be considered extortionate.

There are however, two answers to any such excuse; and the first is that the profit on ingot was not necessarily the same as the profit of the business as a whole, and that we have no means of allocating its proper share to ingot. . . . But the whole issue is irrelevant anyway, for it is no excuse for "monopolizing" a market that the monopoly has not been used to extract from the consumer more than a "fair" profit. The Act has wider purposes. Indeed, even though we disregarded all but economic considerations, it would by no means follow that such concentration of producing power is to be desired, when it has not been used extortionately. Many people believe that possession of unchallenged economic power deadens initiative, discourages thrift and depresses energy; that immunity from competition is a narcotic, and rivalry is a stimulant, to industrial progress; that the spur of constant stress is necessary to counteract an inevitable disposition to let well enough alone. Such people believe that competitors, versed in the craft as no consumer can be, will be quick to detect opportunities for saving and new shifts in production, and be eager to profit by them. In any event the mere fact that a producer, having command of the domestic market, has not been able to make more than a "fair" profit, is no evidence that a "fair" profit could not have been made at lower prices. . . . True, it might have been thought adequate to condemn only those monopolies which could not show that they had exercised the highest possible ingenuity, had adopted every possible economy, had anticipated every conceivable improvement, stimulated every possible demand. No doubt, that would be one way of dealing with the matter, although it would imply constant scrutiny and constant supervision, such as courts are unable to provide. Be that as it may, that was not the way that Congress chose; it did not condone "good trusts" and condemn "bad" ones; it forbade all. Moreover, in so doing it was not necessarily actuated by economic motives alone. It is possible, because of its indirect social or moral effect, to prefer a system of small producers, each dependent for his success upon his own skill and character, to one in which the great mass of those engaged must accept the direction of a few. These considerations, which we have suggested only as possible purposes of the Act, we think the decisions prove to have been in fact its purposes.

It is settled, at least as to Section 1, that there are some contracts restricting competition which are unlawful, no matter how beneficent they may be; no industrial exigency will justify them; they are absolutely forbidden. . . . Starting, however, with the authoritative premise that all contracts fixing prices are unconditionally prohibited, the only possible difference between them and a monopoly is that while a monopoly necessarily involves an equal, or even greater, power to fix prices, its mere existence might be thought not to constitute an exercise of that power. That distinction is nevertheless purely formal; it would be valid only so long as the monopoly remained wholly inert; it would disappear as soon as the monopoly began to operate; for, when it did—that is, as soon as it began to sell at all—it must sell at some price and the only price at which it could sell is a price which it itself fixed. Thereafter the power and its exercise must needs coalesce. Indeed it would be absurd to condemn such contracts unconditionally, and not to extend the condemnation to monopolies; for the contracts are only steps toward that entire control which monopoly confers: They are really partial monopolies.

But we are not left to deductive reasoning. Although in many settings it may be proper to weigh the extent and effect of restrictions in a contract against its industrial or commercial advantages, this is never to be done when the contract is made with intent to set up a monopoly. . . . Perhaps, it has been idle to labor the point at length; there can be no doubt that the vice of restrictive contracts and of monopoly is really one, it is the denial to commerce of the supposed protection of competition. To repeat, if the earlier stages are proscribed, when they are parts of a plan, the mere projecting of which condemns them unconditionally, the realization of the plan itself must be proscribed.

We have been speaking only of the economic reasons which forbid monopoly; but as we have already implied, there are others, based upon the belief that great industrial consolidations are inherently undesirable, regardless of their economic results. . . . Throughout the history of these [antitrust] statutes it has been constantly assumed that one of their purposes was to perpetuate and preserve, for its own sake and in spite of possible cost, an organization of industry in small units which can effectively compete with each other. We hold that "Alcoa's" monopoly of ingot was of the kind covered by Section 2.

It does not follow because "Alcoa" had such a monopoly, that it "monopolized" the ingot market: it may not have achieved monopoly; monopoly may have been thrust upon it. If it had been a combination of existing smelters which united the whole industry and controlled the production of all aluminum ingot, it would certainly have "monopolized" the market. . . . We may start therefore with the premise that to have combined ninety percent of the producers of ingot would have been to "monopolize" the ingot market; and, so far as concerns the public interest, it can make no difference whether an existing competition is put an end to, or whether prospective competition is prevented. . . . Nevertheless, it is unquestionably true that from the very outset the courts have at least kept in reserve the possibility that the origin of a monopoly may be critical in determining its legality. . . . This notion has usually been expressed by saying that size does not determine guilt; that there must be some "exclusion" of competitors; that the growth must be something else than "natural" or "normal"; that there must be a "wrongful intent," or some other specific intent; or that some "unduly" coercive means must be used. At time there has been emphasis upon the use of the active verb, "monopolize," as the judge noted in the case at bar. . . . What engendered these compunctions is reasonably plain; persons may unwittingly find themselves in possession of a monopoly, automatically so to say; that is, without having intended either to put an end to existing competition, or to prevent competition from arising when none had existed; they may become monopolists by force of accident. . . . A single producer may be the survivor out of a group of active competitors, merely by virtue of his superior skill, foresight and industry. . . . The successful competitor, having been urged to compete, must not be turned upon when he wins. . . .

It would completely misconstrue "Alcoa's" position in 1940 to hold that it was the passive beneficiary of a monopoly, following upon an involuntary elimination of competitors by automatically operative economic forces. . . . This increase and this continued and undisturbed control did not fall undesigned into "Alcoa's" lap; obviously it could not have done so. It could only have resulted, as it did result, from a persistent determination to maintain the control, with which it found itself vested in 1912. There were at least one or two abortive attempts to enter the industry, but "Alcoa" effectively anticipated and forestalled all competition, and succeeded in holding the field alone. True, it stimulated demand and opened new uses for the metal, but not without making sure that it could supply what it had evoked. . . . It was not inevitable that it should always anticipate increases in the demand for ingot and be prepared to supply them. Nothing compelled it to keep doubling and redoubling its capacity before others entered the field. It insists that it never excluded competitors; but we can think of no more effective exclusion than progressively to embrace each new opportunity as it opened, and to face every newcomer with new capacity already geared into a great organization, having the advantage of experience, trade connections and the elite of personnel. Only in case we interpret "exclusion" as limited to manoeuvres not honestly industrial, but actuated solely by a desire to prevent competition, can such a course, indefatigably pursued, be deemed not "exclusionary." So to limit it would in our judgment emasculate the Act; would permit just such consolidations as it was designed to prevent.

We disregard any question of "intent". . . . By far the greatest part of the fabulous record piled up in the case at bar, was concerned with proving such an intent. The plaintiff was seeking to show that many transactions, neutral on their face, were not in fact necessary to the development of "Alcoa's" business, and had no motive except to exclude others and perpetuate its hold upon the ingot market. Upon that effort success depended in case the plaintiff failed to satisfy the court that it was unnecessary under Section 2 to convict "Alcoa" of practices unlawful of themselves. The plaintiff has so satisfied us, and the issue of intent ceases to have any importance. . . . In order to fall within Section 2, the monopolist must have both the power to monopolize, and the intent to monopolize. . . . [N]o monopolist monopolizes unconscious of what he is doing. So here, "Alcoa" meant to keep, and did keep, that complete and exclusive hold upon the ingot market with which it started. That was to "monopolize" that market, however innocently it otherwise proceeded. So far as the judgment held that it was not within Section 2, it must be reversed. . . .

II. "ALCOA'S UNLAWFUL PRACTICES.

[Since it was found that Alcoa had monopolized the ingot market, the question of its unlawful practices would, according to the Court, be moot. But war-wrought changes in the ingot market made consideration of these charges necessary to the proper framing of a decree.] . . .

In spite of the prolixity of the evidence, the challenged practices can be divided into three classes: . . .

(a) *"Pre-emption" of Bauxite and Water-Power.* The plaintiff attempted to prove, and asserts that it did prove, that "Alcoa" bought up bauxite deposits . . . in excess of its needs, and under circumstances which showed that the purchases were not for the purpose of securing an adequate future supply, but only in order to seize upon any available supply and so assure its monopoly. The very statement of this charge shows that it depends upon "Alcoa's" intent, for, if the purchases provided for the future needs of the business, or for what "Alcoa" honestly believed were its future needs, they were innocent. . . . The judge . . . overruled all the plaintiff's contentions . . . [and] we should be unwarranted in declaring these findings "clearly erroneous."

(*b*) *Suppression of Competitors in Seeking to Invade the Ingot Market.* [Alcoa's purchases of various potential competitors were treated by the court in the same manner as its purchases of bauxite and water power sites, i.e., the finding of the lower court that these acquisitions did not evidence an intent to suppress competition was upheld.]

(*c*) *"Alcoa's" Domination of the Fabricating Fields.* The last of "Alcoa's" supposedly unlawful practices was its infiltration into, and manipulation of, some of the markets for fabricated goods. These were three kinds: (1) buying an interest in the Aluminum Castings Company, and Aluminum Manufactures, Inc.; (2) the "Price Squeeze"; (3) the "Piston Patent Pool."

(1) "Castings" were one of the earliest uses of aluminum. . . . Five of these [casting producers] combined in . . . [1909] to form the Aluminum Castings Company, of whose shares "Alcoa" received fifty percent in exchange for advances made. . . .

The Aluminum Goods Manufacturing Company makes cooking and other utensils out of aluminum. . . . At the trial thirty-one percent of the shares were held by "Alcoa" and its officers. . . . [T]here was nothing to support the conclusion that here was a practice or manoeuvre merely to suppress or exclude competitors. . . .

(2) The "Price Squeeze." The plaintiff describes as the "Price Squeeze" a practice by which, it says, "Alcoa" intended to put out of business the manufacturers of aluminum "sheet" who were its competitors; for "Alcoa" was itself a large—in fact much the largest—maker of that product. . . .

The plaintiff's theory is that "Alcoa" consistently sold ingot at so high a price that the "sheet rollers," who were forced to buy from it, could not pay the expenses of "rolling" the "sheet."

. . . [W]e think that the plaintiff made out a prima facie case that "Alcoa" had been holding ingot at a price higher than a "fair price," and had reduced the price only because of pressure [resulting from a Department of Justice investigation into the complaints of several "sheet" makers]. If this was not so, it should have rebutted the inference.

In spite of this evidence the judge found that in these years [1925–1932] "Alcoa" had not intended to monopolize the "sheet" market; or to exclude others; or to fix discriminatory prices, or prices of any kind; or to sell below the cost of production, measuring ingot price as part of the cost. . . . That is indeed hard to believe. . . . That it was unlawful to set the price of "sheet" low and hold the price of ingot so high, seems to us unquestionable, provided, as we have held, that on this record the price of ingot must be regarded as higher than a "fair price." True, this was only a consequence of "Alcoa's" control over the price of ingot, and perhaps it ought not to be considered as a separate wrong; moreover, we do not use it as part of the reasoning by which we conclude that the monopoly was unlawful. But it was at least an unlawful exercise of "Alcoa's" power after it had been put on notice by the "sheet rollers' " complaints; and this is true, even though we assent to the judge's finding that it was not part of an attempt to monopolize the "sheet" market. . . .

(3) The Piston Patent Situation. The plaintiff charges "Alcoa" with three kinds of misuses of patents: (1) an unlawful limitation of the production of licensees of its own patents; (2) accepting a license agreement from another patentee that unlawfully limited its own production; (3) using its own patents to force the purchase of ingot upon licensees. [The court held that in two instances the evidence was not sufficient to establish unlawfulness, while in the third, expiration of the patents involved made it unnecessary for the court to pass upon the agreement.]

III. "LIMITED."

[In this portion of its decision the court found that cartel arrangements between Limited, a Canadian firm, and Alliance, a Swiss concern, affected imports into the United States and therefore violated the Sherman Act. It was held, however, that "Alcoa" had not participated in the cartel, and therefore could not be held responsible for the import restrictions.]

IV. THE REMEDIES.

Nearly five years have passed since the evidence was closed; during that time the aluminum industry . . . has been revolutionized by the nation's efforts in a great crisis. That alone would make it impossible to dispose of the action upon the basis of the record as we have it. . . .

[I]t is impossible to say what will be "Alcoa's" position in the industry after the war. . . . Dissolution is not a penalty but a remedy; if the industry will not need it for its protection, it will be a disservice to break up an aggregation which has for so long demonstrated its efficiency. . . .

But there is another, and even more persuasive, reason why we should not now adjust a dissolution of any kind. The Surplus Property Act of 1944 provides [that the disposal agencies shall dispose of government properties in such a manner as] . . . "to give maximum aid in the reestablishment of a peacetime economy of free independent private interprise" . . . [and] "to discourage monopolistic practices and strengthen the competitive position of small business concerns in an economy of free enterprise. . . ." [If the disposal authorities fail to reestablish competitive conditions, it will then be necessary for the District Court to act.]

[An injunction was then issued against resumption of the "price squeeze," and "Limited" was enjoined from entering into any agreement covering imports into this country.]

Judgment reversed, and cause remanded for further proceedings not inconsistent with the foregoing.

American Tobacco Company v. United States

328 U.S. 781 (1946)

Mr. Justice Burton delivered the opinion of the Court.

The petitioners are The American Tobacco Company, Liggett and Myers Tobacco Company, R. J. Reynolds Tobacco Company, American Suppliers, Inc., a subsidiary of American, and certain officials of the respective companies who were convicted by a jury, in the District Court of the United States for the Eastern District of Kentucky, of violating Sections 1 and 2 of the Sherman Antitrust Act. . . .

Each petitioner was convicted on four counts: (1) conspiracy in restraint of trade, (2) monopolization, (3) attempt to monopolize, and (4) conspiracy to monopolize. Each count related to interstate and foreign trade and commerce in tobacco. No sentence was imposed under the third count as the Court held that count was merged in the second. Each petitioner was fined $5,000 on each of the other counts, making $15,000 for each petitioner and a total of $255,000. . . .

The Circuit Court of Appeals for the Sixth Circuit . . . affirmed each conviction. . . . This opinion is limited to the convictions under Section 2 of the Sherman Act. . . .

The issue . . . emphasized in the order allowing certiorari and primarily argued by the parties has not been previously decided by this Court. It is raised by the following instructions which were especially applicable to the second count but were related also to the other counts under Section 2 of the Sherman Act:

Now, the term 'monopolize' as used in Section 2 of the Sherman Act, as well as in the last three counts of the Information, means the joint acquisition or maintenance by the members of the conspiracy formed for that purpose, of the *power to control and dominate interstate trade and commerce in a commodity to such an extent that they are able, as a group, to exclude actual or potential competitors from the field, accompanied with the intention and purpose to exercise such power.*

The phrase 'attempt to monopolize' means the employment of methods, means and practices which would, if successful, accomplish monopolization, and which, though falling short, nevertheless approach so close as to create a dangerous probability of it, which methods, means and practices so employed by the members of and pursuant to a combination or conspiracy formed for the purpose of such accomplishment.

It is in no respect a violation of the law that a number of individuals or corporations, each acting for himself or itself, may own or control a large part, or even all of a particular commodity, or all the business in a particular commodity.

An essential element of the illegal monopoly or monopolization charged *in this case is the existence of a combination or conspiracy to acquire and maintain the power to exclude competitors to a substantial extent.*

Thus you will see that *an indispensable ingredient of each of the offenses charged in the Information is a combination or conspiracy.* (Italics supplied [by the Supreme Court].)

. . . The trial court's instructions did not call for proof of an "actual exclusion" of competitors on the part of the petitioners. For the purposes of this opinion, we shall assume, therefore, that an actual exclusion of competitors by the petitioners was not claimed or established by the prosecution. Simply stated the issue is: Do the facts called for in the trial court's definition of monopolization amount to a violation of Section 2 of the Sherman Act?

. . . To support the verdicts it was not necessary to show power and intent to exclude *all* competitors, or to show a conspiracy to exclude *all* competitors. The requirement stated to the jury and contained in the statute was only that the offenders shall "monopolize any part of the trade or commerce among the several States, or with foreign nations." This particular conspiracy may well have derived special vitality, in the eyes of the jury, from the fact that its existence was established, not through the presentation of a formal written agreement, but through the evidence of widespread and effective conduct on the part of petitioners in relation to their existing or potential competitors. . . .

First of all, the monopoly found by the jury to exist in the present cases appears to have been completely separable from the old American Tobacco Trust which was dissolved in 1911. The conspiracy to monopolize and the monopolization charged here do not depend upon proof relating to the old tobacco trust but upon a dominance and control by petitioners in recent years over purchases of the raw material and over the sale of the finished product in the form of cigarettes. The fact, however, that the purchases of leaf tobacco and the sales of so many products of the tobacco industry have remained largely within the same general group of business organizations for over a generation, inevitably has contributed to the ease with which control over competition within the industry and the mobilization of power to resist new competition can be exercised. . . . The verdicts indicate that practices of an informal and flexible nature were adopted and that the results were so uniformly beneficial to the petitioners in protecting their common interests as against those of competitors that, entirely from circumstantial evidence, the jury found that a combination or conspiracy existed among the petitioners from 1937 to 1940, with power and intent to exclude competitors to such a substantial extent as to violate the Sherman Act as interpreted by the trial court.

The position of the petitioners in the cigarette industry from 1931 to 1939 is clear. . . . [A]lthough American, Liggett and Reynolds gradually dropped in their percentage of the national domestic cigarette production from 90.7% in 1931 to 73.3%, 71% and 68%, respectively, in 1937, 1938 and 1939, they have accounted at all times for more than 68%, and usually for more than 75%, of the national production. The balance of the cigarette production has come from six other companies. No one of these six ever has produced more than 10.6% once reached by Brown and Williamson in 1939. . . . [W]hile the percentage of cigarettes produced by American, Liggett and Reynolds in the United States dropped gradually from 90.7% to 68%, their combined volume of production actually increased. . . .

The further dominance of American, Liggett and Reynolds within their special field of burley blend cigarettes, as compared with the so-called "10-cent cigarettes," is also apparent. In 1939, the 10-cent cigarettes constituted about 14½% of the total domestic cigarette production. Accordingly, the 68% of the total cigarette production enjoyed by American, Liggett and Reynolds amounted to 80% of that production within their special field of cigarettes. . . . In addition . . . they also produced over 63% of the smoking tobacco and over 44% of the chewing tobacco. They never were important factors in the cigar or snuff fields of the tobacco industry.

The foregoing demonstrates the basis of the claim of American, Liggett and Reynolds to the title of the "Big Three.". . . Without adverse criticism of it, comparative size on this great scale inevitably increased the power of these three to dominate all phases of their industry. . . . An intent to use this power to maintain a monopoly was found by the jury in these cases.

The record further shows that . . . in . . . each of the years 1937, 1938 and 1939, American, Liggett and Reynolds expended a total of over $40,000,000 a year for advertising. Such advertising is not here criticized as a business expense. Such advertising may benefit indirectly the entire industry, including the competitors of the advertisers. Such tremendous advertising, however, is also a widely published warning that these companies possess and know how to use a powerful offensive and defensive weapon against new competition. New competition dare not enter such a field, unless it be well supported by comparable national advertising. Large inventories of leaf tobacco, and large sums required for payment of federal taxes in advance of actual sales, further emphasize the effectiveness of a well financed monopoly in this field against potential competitors if there merely exists an intent to exclude such competitors. Prevention of all potential competition is the natural program for maintaining a monopoly here, rather than any program of actual exclusion. "Prevention" is cheaper and more effective than any amount of "cure." . . .

The verdicts show that the jury found that petitioners conspired to fix prices and to exclude undesired competition against them in the purchase of the domestic types of flue-cured tobacco and of burley tobacco. These are raw materials essential to the production of cigarettes of the grade sold by the petitioners and also, to some extent, of the 10-cent grade of cigarettes which constitutes the only substantial competition to American, Liggett and Reynolds in the cigarette field of the domestic tobacco industry. . . . The petitioners purchased a combined total of between 50% and 80% of the domestic flue-cured tobacco . . . [and] from 60% to 80% of the annual crop of burley.[3] . . .

The Government introduced evidence showing . . . that petitioners refused to purchase tobacco on these [auction] markets unless the other petitioners were also represented thereon. There were attempts made by others to open new tobacco markets but none of the petitioners would participate in them unless the other petitioners were present. Consequently, such markets were failures due to the absence of buyers. . . . In this way the new tobacco markets and their locations were determined by the unanimous consent of the petitioners and, in arriving at their determination, the petitioners consulted with each other as to whether or not a community deserved a market.

The Government presented evidence to support its claim that, before the markets opened, the petitioners placed limitations and restrictions on the prices which their buyers were permitted to pay for tobacco. None of the buyers exceeded these price ceilings. Grades of tobacco were formulated in such a way as to result in the absence of competition between the petitioners. There was manipulation of the price of lower grade tobaccos in order to restrict competition from manufacturers of the lower priced cigarettes. Methods used included the practice of petitioners of calling their respective buyers in, prior to the opening of the annual markets, and giving them instructions as to the prices to be paid for leaf tobacco in each of the markets. These instructions were in terms of top prices or price ranges. The price ceilings thus established for the buyers were the same for each of them. . . .

Where one or two of the petitioners secured their percentage of the crop on a certain market or were not interested in the purchase of certain offerings of tobacco, their buyers, nevertheless, would enter the bidding in order to force the other petitioners to bid up to the maximum price. The petitioners were not so much concerned with the prices they paid for the leaf tobacco as that each should pay the same price for the same

---

[3] Flue-cured, or bright tobacco, takes its name from the fact that it is cured in barns heated by a system of flues. Burley tobacco is produced largely in Kentucky and Tennessee, and is cured by exposing the leaves to the air, without heat. IMS.

grade and that none would secure any advantage in purchasing tobacco. . . .

At a time when the manufacturers of lower priced cigarettes were beginning to manufacture them in quantity, the petitioners commenced to make large purchases of the cheaper tobacco leaves used for the manufacture of such lower priced cigarettes. No explanation was offered as to how or where this tobacco was used by petitioners. The composition of their respective brands of cigarettes calling for the use of more expensive tobaccos remained unchanged during this period of controversy and up to the end of the trial. The Government claimed that such purchases of cheaper tobacco evidenced a combination and a purpose among the petitioners to deprive the manufacturers of cheaper cigarettes of the tobacco necessary for their manufacture, as well as to raise the price of such tobacco to such a point that cigarettes made therefrom could not be sold at a sufficiently low price to compete with petitioners' more highly advertised brands.

The verdicts also show that the jury found that the petitioners conspired to fix prices and to exclude undesired competition in the distribution and sale of their principal products. The petitioners sold and distributed their products to jobbers and to selected dealers who bought at list prices, less discounts. . . . The list prices charged and the discounts allowed by petitioners have been practically identical since 1923 and absolutely identical since 1928. Since the latter date, only seven changes have been made by the three companies and those have been identical in amount. The increases were first announced by Reynolds. American and Liggett thereupon increased their list prices in identical amounts.

The following record of price changes is circumstantial evidence of the existence of a conspiracy and of a power and intent to exclude competition from cheaper grade cigarettes. . . . 1931 . . . was one of the worst years of financial and economic depression in the history of the country. On June 23, 1931, Reynolds, without previous notification or warning to the trade or public, raised the list price of Camel cigarettes, constituting its leading cigarette brand, from $6.40 to $6.85 a thousand. The same day, American increased the list price of Lucky Strike cigarettes, its leading brand, to the identical price of $6.85 a thousand. No economic justification for this raise was demonstrated. The president of Reynolds stated that it was "to express our own courage for the future and our own confidence in our industry." The president of American gave as his reason for the increase, "the opportunity of making some money.". . . The officials of Liggett claimed that they thought the increase was a mistake . . . but they contended that unless they also raised their list price for Chesterfields, the other companies would have greater resources to spend in advertising and thus would put Chesterfield cigarettes at a competitive disadvantage. This general price increase soon resulted in higher retail prices and a loss in volume of sales. Yet in 1932, in the midst of the national depression with the sales of the petitioners' cigarettes falling off greatly in number, the petitioners still were making tremendous profits as a result of the price increase. Their net profits in that year amounted to more than $100,000,000. This was one of the three biggest years in their history.

. . . [A]fter the above described increase in list prices of the petitioners in 1931, the 10-cent brands made serious inroads upon the sales of the petitioners. These cheaper brands of cigarettes were sold at a list price of $4.75 a thousand and from 1931 to 1932 the sales of these cigarettes multiplied 30 times, rising from 0.28% of the total cigarette sales of the country in June, 1931, to 22.78% in November, 1932. In response to this threat of competition . . . the petitioners . . . cut the list price of their three leading brands . . . to $5.50 a thousand. The evidence tends to show that this cut was directed at the competition of the 10-cent cigarettes. . . . Following the . . . price cut by petitioners, the sales of 10-cent brands fell off considerably. . . . When the sale of the 10-cent brands had dropped from 22.78% of the total cigarette sales in November, 1932, to 6.43% in May, 1933, the petitioners, in January, 1934, raised the list price of their leading brands from $5.50 back up to $6.10 a thousand. During the period that the list price of $5.50 a thousand was in effect, Camels and Lucky Strikes were being sold at a loss by Reynolds and American. Liggett at the same time was forced to curtail all of its normal business activities and cut its advertising to the bone in order to sell at this price. [Subsequent increases brought the price to $6.53 by 1940.] . . .

Certain methods used by the petitioners to secure a reduction in the retail prices of their cigarettes were in evidence. Reynolds and Liggett required their retailers to price the 10-cent brands at a differential of not more than 3 cents below Camel and Chesterfield cigarettes. They insisted upon their dealers correcting a greater differential by increasing the retail price of the 10-cent brands to 11 cents with petitioners' brands at 14 cents a package, or by requiring that petitioners' brands be priced at 13 cents with the lower priced cigarettes at 10 cents a package. . . . After the list price reductions were made and at the height of the price war, the petitioners commenced the distribution of posters advertising their brands at 10-cents a package and made attempts to have dealers meet these prices. . . . In addition to the use of . . . inducements, petitioners also used threats and penalties to enforce compliance with their retail price program. . . . There was evidence that when dealers received an announcement of the price increase from one of the petitioners and attempted to purchase some of the leading brands of cigarettes from the other petitioners at their unchanged prices before announcement of a similar change, the latter refused to fill such orders until their prices were also raised, thus bringing about the same result as if the changes had been precisely simultaneous.

It was on the basis of such evidence that the Circuit Court of Appeals found the verdicts of the jury were sustained by sufficient evidence on each count. The question squarely presented here by the order of this Court in allowing the writs of certiorari is whether actual exclusion of competitors is necessary to the crime of monopolization in these cases under Section 2 of the Sherman Act. We agree with the lower courts that such actual exclusion of competitors is not necessary to that crime in these cases and that the instructions given to the jury, and hereinbefore quoted, correctly defined the crime. A correct interpretation of the statute and of the authorities makes it the crime of monopolizing, under Section 2 of the Sherman Act, for parties, as in these cases, to combine or conspire to acquire or maintain the power to exclude competitors from any part of the trade or commerce among the several states or with foreign nations, provided they also have such a power that they are able, as a group, to exclude actual or potential competition from the field and provided that they have the intent and purpose to exercise that power. See United States *v.* Socony-Vacuum Oil Co. . . .

It is not the form of the combination or the particular means used but the result to be achieved that the statute condemns. It is not of importance whether the means used to accomplish the unlawful objectives are in themselves lawful or unlawful. Acts done to give effect to the conspiracy may be in themselves wholly innocent acts. Yet, if they are part of the sum of the acts which are relied upon to effectuate the conspiracy which the statute forbids, they come within its prohibition. No formal agreement is necessary to constitute an unlawful conspiracy. Often crimes are a matter of inference deduced from the acts of the person accused and done in pursuance of a criminal purpose. Where the conspiracy is proved, as here, from the evidence of the action taken in concert by the parties to it, it is all the more convincing proof of an intent to exercise the power of exclusion acquired through that conspiracy. The essential combination or conspiracy in violation of the Sherman Act may be found in a course of dealing or other circumstances as well as in an exchange of words. . . . Where the circumstances are such as to warrant a jury in finding that the conspirators had a unity of purpose or a common design and understanding, or a meeting of minds in an unlawful arrangement, the conclusion that a conspiracy is established is justified. Neither proof of exertion of the power to exclude nor proof of actual exclusion of existing or potential competitors is essential to sustain a charge of monopolization under the Sherman Act. . . .

[The Court then took this opportunity to endorse the key portions of Judge Learned Hand's decision in United States *v.* Aluminum Company of America, 148 F.2d 416.]

In the present cases, the petitioners have been found to have conspired to establish a monopoly and also to have the power and intent to establish and maintain the monopoly. To hold that they do not come within the prohibition of the Sherman Act would destroy the force of that Act. Accordingly, the instructions of the trial court under Section 2 of the Act are approved and the judgment of the Circuit Court of Appeals is affirmed.

Mr. Justice Frankfurter entirely agrees with the judgment and opinion in these cases. He, however, would have enlarged the scope of the orders allowing the petitions for certiorari so as to permit consideration of the alleged errors in regard to the selection of the jury.

Mr. Justice Reed and Mr. Justice Jackson took no part in the consideration or decision of these cases.

Mr. Justice Rutledge concurred. . . .

United States v. Yellow Cab Company

332 U.S. 218 (1947)

Mr. Justice Murphy delivered the opinion of the Court.

The United States filed a complaint in the federal district court below pursuant to Section 4 of the Sherman Antitrust Act, . . . to prevent and restrain the appellees from violating Sections 1 and 2 of the Act. . . . The complaint alleged that the appellees have been and are engaged in a combination and conspiracy to restrain and monopolize interstate trade and commerce (1) in the sale of motor vehicles for use as taxicabs to the principal cab operating companies in Chicago, Pittsburgh, New York City and Minneapolis, and (2) in the business of furnishing cab services for hire in Chicago and vicinity. The appellees moved to dismiss the complaint for failure to state a claim upon which relief might be granted. That motion was sustained. . . . The case is now here on direct appeal by the United States. . . .

The alleged facts, as set forth in the complaint, may be summarized briefly. In January, 1929, one Morris Markin and others commenced negotiations to merge the more important cab operating companies in Chicago, New York and other cities. Markin was then president and general manager, as well as the controlling stockholder, of the Checker Cab Manufacturing Corporation (CCM). That company was engaged in the business of manufacturing taxicabs at its factory in Kalamazoo, Michigan, and shipping them to purchasers in various states.

Parmelee Transportation Company (Parmelee) was organized in April, 1929, with 62% of its stock being owned by CCM. It promptly took over the business of operating special unlicensed cabs to transport passengers and their luggage between railroad stations in Chicago, pursuant to contracts with railroads and railroad terminal associations. It then acquired a controlling interest in the Chicago Yellow Cab Company, Inc. (Chicago Yellow). This latter company holds all the capital stock of Yellow Cab Company (Yellow), the owner and operator of "Yellow" cabs in Chicago and vicinity. Yellow presently holds 53% of the taxicab licenses outstanding in Chicago. In addition, Parmelee acquired or organized subsidiary companies which now hold 100% of the taxicab licenses outstanding in Pittsburgh, 58% of those in Minneapolis, and 15% of those in New York City. . . .

Thus, by the end of 1932, Markin had gained control of the three largest taxicab companies operating in Chicago and, through Parmelee, had substantial footholds in the taxicab business in New York City, Pittsburgh, and Minneapolis.

Yellow and Checker have consistently held a vast majority of the Chicago taxicab licenses.[4] . . .

Such is the nature of the facts set forth in the complaint. Those facts allegedly give rise to a combination and conspiracy on the part of the appellees (Yellow, Chicago Yellow, Parmelee, Cab Sales, Checker, CCM and Markin) in violation of the Sherman Act. The problems thereby raised can best be considered in relation to the purported terms of this combination and conspiracy. For present purposes, of course, we must assume, without deciding or implying, that the various facts and allegations in the complaint are true.

It is said that the appellees have agreed to control the operation and purchase of taxicabs by the principal operating companies in Chicago, New York City, Pittsburgh and Minneapolis, insisting that they purchase their cabs exclusively from CCM. This excludes all other manufacturers of taxicabs from 86% of the Chicago market, 15% of the New York City market, 100% of the Pittsburgh market and 58% of the Minneapolis market. At the same time, the trade of the controlled cab companies is restrained since they are prevented from purchasing cabs from manufacturers other than CCM. The result allegedly is that these companies must pay more for cabs than they would otherwise pay, their other expenditures are increased unnecessarily, and the public is charged high rates for the transportation services rendered.

The commerce which is asserted to be restrained in this manner has a character that is undeniably interstate. . . .

But the amount of interstate trade thus affected by the conspiracy is immaterial in determining whether a violation of the Sherman Act has been charged in the complaint. Section 1 of the Act outlaws unreasonable restraints on interstate commerce, regardless of the amount of the commerce affected. . . . And Section 2 of the Act makes it unlawful to conspire to monopolize "any part" of interstate commerce, without specifying how large a part must be affected. Hence it is enough if some appreciable part of interstate commerce is the subject of a monopoly, a restraint or a conspiracy. The complaint in this case deals with interstate purchases of replacements of some 5,000 licensed taxicabs in four cities. That is an appreciable amount of commerce under any standard. . . .

[4] These firms held 2595 of the 3000 licenses outstanding in 1946. IMS.

Likewise irrelevant is the importance of the interstate commerce affected in relation to the entire amount of that type of commerce in the United States. The Sherman Act is concerned with more than the large, nation-wide obstacles in the channels of interstate trade. It is designed to sweep away all appreciable obstructions so that the statutory policy of free trade might be effectively achieved. . . .

Nor can it be doubted that combinations and conspiracies of the type alleged in this case fall within the ban of the Sherman Act. By excluding all cab manufacturers other than CCM from that part of the market represented by the cab operating companies under their control, the appellees effectively limit the outlets through which cabs may be sold in interstate commerce. . . . In addition, by preventing the cab operating companies under their control from purchasing cabs from manufacturers other than CCM, the appellees deny those companies the opportunity to purchase cabs in a free, competitive market. The Sherman Act has never been thought to sanction such a conspiracy to restrain the free purchase of goods in interstate commerce. . . .

The fact that these restraints occur in a setting described by the appellees as a vertically integrated enterprise does not necessarily remove the ban of the Sherman Act. The test of illegality under the Act is the presence or absence of an unreasonable restraint on interstate commerce. Such a restraint may result as readily from a conspiracy among those who are affiliated or integrated under common ownership as from a conspiracy among those who are otherwise independent. Similarly, any affiliation or integration flowing from an illegal conspiracy cannot insulate the conspirators from the sanctions which Congress has imposed. The corporate interrelationships of the conspirators, in other words, are not determinative of the applicability of the Sherman Act. That statute is aimed at substance rather than form. . . .

It is said that the appellees have agreed that Yellow and Cab Sales will not compete with Parmelee for contracts with railroads or railroad terminal associations to transport passengers and their luggage between railroad stations in Chicago. . . .

Only Parmelee is free to attempt to procure such contracts; Yellow and Cab Sales are forbidden to compete for such contracts, despite the fact that they conceivably might provide the same transportation service at lower cost to the railroads. . . .

Moreover, the fact that the competition restrained is that between affiliated corporations cannot serve to negative the statutory violation where, as here, the affiliation is assertedly one of the means of effectuating the illegal conspiracy not to compete.

Finally, it is said that the appellees have conspired to control the principal taxicab operating companies in Chicago and to exclude others from engaging in the transportation of interstate travelers to and from Chicago railroad stations. . . .

We hold, however, that such transportation is too unrelated to interstate commerce to constitute a part thereof within the meaning of the Sherman Act. . . .

For the reasons set forth in Parts I and II of this opinion,[5] the complaint does state a cause of action under the Act, entitling the United States to a trial on the merits. Since the portion of the complaint dealt with in Part III of this opinion is defective, appropriate steps should be taken to delete the charges in relation thereto. With that understanding, we reverse the judgment of the District Court and remand the case for further proceedings consistent with this opinion.

Reversed.

Mr. Justice Black and Mr. Justice Rutledge agree with Parts I and II of this opinion but dissent from the holding in Part III.

Mr. Justice Burton concurs in Part III of this opinion. However, he believes that the complaint as a whole fails to state a cause of action and that, therefore, the judgment of the District Court dismissing it should be affirmed.

Mr. Justice Douglas took no part in the consideration or decision of this case.

United States v. Paramount Pictures, Inc., et al.

334 U.S. 131 (1948)

Mr. Justice Douglas delivered the opinion of the Court.

These cases are here on appeal from a judgment of a three-judge District Court holding that the defendants have violated Section 1 and Section 2 of the Sherman Act . . . , and granting an injunction and other relief. . . .

The defendants fall into three groups: (1) Paramount Pictures, Inc., Loew's, Incorporated, Radio-Keith-Orpheum Corporation, Warner Bros. Pictures, Inc., Twentieth Century–Fox Film Corporation, which produce motion pictures, and their respective subsidiaries or affiliates which distribute and exhibit films. These are known as the five major defendants or exhibitor-defendants. (2) Columbia Pictures Corporation and Universal Corporation, which produce motion pictures, and their subsidiaries which distribute films. (3) United Artists Corporation, which is engaged only in the distribution of motion pictures. The five majors, through their subsidiaries or affiliates, own or control theatres; the other defendants do not.

The complaint charged that the producer defendants had attempted to monopolize and had monopolized the production of motion pictures. The District Court found to the contrary and that finding is not challenged

[5] Part I was presented above. Part II held transportation between Chicago stations to be part of interstate commerce. Part III held the transportation of interstate travelers to and from Chicago stations to be unrelated to interstate commerce. IMS.

here. The complaint charged that all the defendants, as distributors, had conspired to restrain and monopolize and had restrained and monopolized interstate trade in the distribution and exhibition of films by specific practices which we will shortly relate. It also charged that the five major defendants had engaged in a conspiracy to restrain and monopolize, and had restrained and monopolized, interstate trade in the exhibition of motion pictures in most of the larger cities of the country. It charged that the vertical combination of producing, distributing, and exhibiting motion pictures by each of the five major defendants violated section 1 and section 2 of the Act. It charged that each distributor-defendant had entered into various contracts with exhibitors which unreasonably restrained trade. Issue was joined; and a trial was had.

First. Restraint of Trade—(1) Price Fixing. No film is sold to an exhibitor in the distribution of motion pictures. The right to exhibit under copyright is licensed. The District Court found that the defendants in the licenses they issued fixed minimum admission prices which the exhibitors agreed to charge, whether the rental of the film was a flat amount or a percentage of the receipts. It found that substantially uniform minimum prices had been established in the licenses of all defendants. Minimum prices were established in master agreements or franchises which were made between various defendants as distributors and various defendants as exhibitors and in joint operating agreements made by the five majors with each other and with independent theatre owners covering the operation of certain theatres.[6] By these later contracts minimum admission prices were often fixed for dozens of theatres owned by a particular defendant in a given area of the United States. Minimum prices were fixed in licenses of each of the five major defendants. The other three defendants made the same requirement in licenses granted to the exhibitor-defendants. . . .

The District Court found that two price-fixing conspiracies existed— a horizontal one between all the defendants, a vertical one between each distributor-defendant and its licensees. The latter was based on express agreements and was plainly established. The former was inferred from the pattern of price-fixing disclosed in the record. We think there was adequate foundation for it too. It is not necessary to find an express agreement in order to find a conspiracy. It is enough that a concert of action is contemplated and that the defendants conformed to the arrangement.

On this phase of the case the main attack is on the decree which en-

[6] A master agreement is a licensing agreement or "blanket deal" covering the exhibition of features in a number of theatres, usually comprising a circuit.

A franchise is a licensing agreement, or series of licensing agreements, entered into as part of the same transaction, in effect for more than one motion picture season and covering the exhibition of features released by one distributor during the entire period of the agreement.

An independent as used in these cases means a producer, distributor, or exhibitor, as the context requires, which is not a defendant in the action, or a subsidiary or affiliate of a defendant.

joins the defendants and their affiliates from granting any license, except to their own theatres, in which minimum prices for admission to a theatre are fixed in any manner or by any means. . . . [It] is argued that if the patentee can fix the price at which his licensee can sell the patented article, the owner of the copyright should be allowed the same privilege. It is maintained that such a privilege is essential to protect the value of the copyrighted films.

We start, of course, from the premise that so far as the Sherman Act is concerned, a price-fixing combination is illegal *per se*. . . . We recently held . . . that even patentees could not regiment an entire industry by licenses containing price-fixing agreements. . . . Certainly the rights of the copyright owner are no greater than those of the patentee.

Nor can the result be different when we come to the vertical conspiracy between each distributor-defendant and his licensees. The District Court stated in its findings . . . : "In agreeing to maintain a stipulated minimum admission price, each exhibitor thereby consents to the minimum price level at which it will compete against other licensees of the same distributor whether they exhibit on the same run or not. The total effect is that through the separate contracts between the distributor and its licensees a price structure is erected which regulates the licensees' ability to compete against one another in admission prices."

That consequence seems to us to be incontestable. . . .

(2) Clearances and Runs. Clearances are designed to protect a particular run of a film against a subsequent run.[7] The District Court found that all of the distributor-defendants used clearance provisions. . . .

The Department of Justice maintained below that clearances are unlawful *per se* under the Sherman Act. But this is a question we need not consider, for the District Court ruled otherwise and that conclusion is not challenged here. In its view their justification was found in the assurance they give the exhibitor that the distributor will not license a competitor to show the film either at the same time or so soon thereafter that the exhibitor's expected income from the run will be greatly diminished. A clearance when used to protect that interest of the exhibitor was reasonable, in the view of the court, when not unduly extended as to area or duration. Thus the court concluded that although clearances might indirectly affect admission prices, they do not fix them and that they may be reasonable restraints of trade under the Sherman Act.

The District Court held that in determining whether a clearance is unreasonable, the following factors are relevant:

---

[7] A clearance is the period of time, usually stipulated in license contracts, which must elapse between runs of the same feature within a particular area or in specified theatres.

Runs are successive exhibitions of a feature in a given area, first-run being the first exhibition in that area, second-run being the next subsequent, and so on, and include successive exhibitions in different theatres, even though such theatres may be under a common ownership or management.

(1) The admission prices of the theatres involved, as set by the exhibitors;

(2) The character and locations of the theatres involved, including size, type of entertainment, appointments, transit facilities, etc.;

(3) The policy of operation of the theatres involved, such as the showing of double features, gift nights, give-aways, premiums, cut-rate tickets, lotteries, etc.;

(4) The rental terms and license fees paid by the theatres involved and the revenues derived by the distributor-defendant from such theatres;

(5) The extent to which the theatres involved compete with each other for patronage;

(6) The fact that a theatre involved is affiliated with a defendant-distributor or with an independent circuit of theatres should be disregarded; and

(7) There should be no clearance between theatres not in substantial competition.

It reviewed the evidence in light of these standards and concluded that many of the clearances granted by the defendants were unreasonable. . . . The evidence is ample to show . . . that many of the clearances had no relation to the competitive factors which alone could justify them. The clearances which were in vogue had, indeed, acquired a fixed and uniform character and were made applicable to situations without regard to the special circumstances which are necessary to sustain them as reasonable restraints of trade. The evidence is ample to support the finding of the District Court that the defendants either participated in evolving this uniform system of clearances or acquiesced in it and so furthered its existence. That evidence, like the evidence on the price-fixing phase of the case, is therefore adequate to support the finding of a conspiracy to restrain trade by imposing unreasonable clearances. . . .

(3) *Pooling Agreements; Joint Ownership.* The District Court found the exhibitor-defendants had agreements with each other and their affiliates by which theatres of two or more of them, normally competitive, were operated as a unit, or managed by a joint committee or by one of the exhibitors, the profits being shared according to prearranged percentages. Some of these agreements provided that the parties might not acquire other competitive theatres without first offering them for inclusion in the pool. The court concluded that the result of these agreements was to eliminate competition *pro tanto* both in exhibition and in distribution of features,[8] since the parties would naturally direct the films to the theatres in whose earnings they were interested.

The District Court also found that the exhibitor-defendants had like agreements with certain independent exhibitors. Those alliances had, in its

---

[8] A feature is any motion picture, regardless of topic, the length of the film of which is in excess of 4,000 feet.

view, the effect of nullifying competition between the allied theatres and of making more effective the competition of the group against theatres not members of the pool. . . . The District Court required the dissolution of existing pool agreements and enjoined any future arrangement of that character.

These provisions of the decree shall stand. The practices were bald efforts to substitute monopoly for competition and to strengthen the hold of the exhibitor-defendants on the industry by alignment of competitors on their side. Clearer restraints of trade are difficult to imagine.

There was another type of business arrangement that the District Court found to have the same effect as the pooling agreements just mentioned. Many theatres are owned jointly by two or more exhibitor-defendants or by an exhibitor-defendant and an independent. The result is, according to the District Court, that the theatres are operated "collectively rather than competitively." And where the joint owners are an exhibitor-defendant and an independent the effect is, according to the District Court, the elimination by the exhibitor-defendant of "putative competition between itself and the other joint owner, who otherwise would be in a position to operate theatres independently." The District Court found these joint ownerships of theatres to be unreasonable restraints of trade within the meaning of the Sherman Act.

The District Court ordered the exhibitor-defendants to disaffiliate by terminating their joint ownership of theatres; and it enjoined future acquisitions of such interests. . . . This dissolution and prohibition of joint ownership as between exhibitor-defendants was plainly warranted. . . .

The District Court also ordered disaffiliation in those instances where theatres were jointly owned by an exhibitor-defendant and an independent. . . . This phase of the decree is strenuously attacked. . . . The argument is that the findings show no more than the existence of joint ownership of theatres by exhibitor-defendants and independents. The statement by the District Court that the joint ownership eliminates "putative competition" is said to be a mere conclusion without evidentiary support. . . .

It is conceded that the District Court made no inquiry into the circumstances under which a particular interest had been acquired. . . . In this we think it erred.

We have gone into the record far enough to be confident that at least some of these acquisitions by the exhibitor-defendants were the products of the unlawful practices which the defendants have inflicted on the industry. . . . [But] Some [cases of joint ownership] apparently involve no more than innocent investments by those who are not actual or potential operators. If in such cases the acquisition was not improperly used in furtherance of the conspiracy, its retention by defendants would be justified absent a finding that no monopoly resulted. [This portion of the case was thereupon remanded for further findings.]

[Section (4) of the decision dealt with formula deals, master agreements and franchises, and is of little interest in the present context. Section (5) dealt with block-booking, and is presented in Chapter 10, below. Section (6) dealt with discriminations against small independent exhibitors. The Court resumed. . . .]

Second. Competitive Bidding. The District Court concluded that the only way competition could be introduced into the existing system of fixed prices, clearances and runs was to require that films be licensed on a competitive bidding basis. . . .

At first blush there is much to commend the system of competitive bidding. The trade victims of this conspiracy have in large measure been the small independent operators. They are the ones that have felt most keenly the discriminatory practices and predatory activities in which defendants have freely indulged. They have been the victims of the massed purchasing power of the larger units in the industry. It is largely out of the ruins of the small operators that the large empires of exhibitors have been built. Thus it would appear to be a great boon to them to substitute open bidding for the private deals and favors on which the large operators have thrived. But after reflection we have concluded that competitive bidding involves the judiciary so deeply in the daily operation of this nation-wide business and promises such dubious benefits that it should not be undertaken.

. . . Columbia [Pictures Corp.] puts these pertinent queries: "No two exhibitors are likely to make the same bid as to dates, clearance, method of fixing rental, etc. May bids containing such diverse factors be readily compared? . . ."

The question as to who is the highest bidder involves the use of standards incapable of precise definition because the bids being compared contain different ingredients. Determining who is the most responsible bidder likewise cannot be reduced to a formula. . . .

We mention these matters merely to indicate the character of the job of supervising such a competitive bidding system. It would involve the judiciary in the administration of intricate and detailed rules governing priority, period of clearance, length of run, competitive areas, reasonable return, and the like. . . . The judiciary is unsuited to affairs of business management. . . .

The system [competitive bidding] uproots business arrangements and established relationships with no apparent overall benefit to the small independent exhibitor. If each feature must go to the highest responsible bidder, those with the greatest purchasing power would seem to be in a favored position. Those with the longest purse—the exhibitor-defendants and the large circuits—would seem to stand in a preferred position. . . . If a premium is placed on purchasing power, the court-created system may be a powerful factor towards increasing the concentration of economic power in the industry rather than cleansing the competitive system of unwholesome practices. . . .

. . . In light of these considerations we conclude that the competitive bidding provisions of the decree should be eliminated so that a more effective decree may be fashioned.

. . . [T]his alteration in the decree leaves a hiatus or two which will have to be filled on remand of the case. . . . But out of an abundance of caution we add this additional word. The competitive bidding system was perhaps the central arch of the decree designed by the District Court. Its elimination may effect the cases in ways other than those which we expressly mention. Hence on remand of the cases the freedom of the District Court to reconsider the adequacy of decree is not limited to those parts we have specifically indicated.

Third. Monopoly, Expansion of Theatre Holdings, Divestiture. . . . The controversy over monopoly relates to monopoly in exhibition and more particularly monopoly in the first-run phase of the exhibition business.

The five majors in 1945 had interests in somewhat over 17 percent of the theatres in the United States—3,137 out of 18,076. Those theatres paid 45 percent of the total domestic film rental received by all eight defendants.

In the 92 cities of the country with populations over 100,000 at least 70 percent of all the first-run theatres are affiliated with one or more of the five majors. . . . In 38 of those cities there are no independent first-run theatres. . . .

In cities between 25,000 and 100,000 populations the majors have interests in 577 of a total of 978 first-run theatres or about 60 percent. In about 300 additional towns, mostly under 25,000, an operator affiliated with one of the five majors has all of the theatres in town. . . .

The District Court did . . . enjoin the five majors from expanding their present theatre holdings in any manner. It refused to grant the request of the Department of Justice for total divestiture by the five majors of their theatre holdings. . . .

It is clear, so far as the five majors are concerned, that the aim of the conspiracy was exclusionary, i.e., it was designed to strengthen their hold on the exhibition field. In other words, the conspiracy had monopoly in exhibition for one of its goals, as the District Court held. . . .

It is, therefore, not enough in determining the need for divestiture to conclude with the District Court that none of the defendants was organized or has been maintained for the purpose of achieving a "national monopoly," nor that the five majors through their present theatre holdings "alone" do not and cannot collectively or individually have a monopoly of exhibition. For when the starting point is a conspiracy to effect a monopoly through restraints of trade, it is relevant to determine what the results of the conspiracy were even if they fell short of monopoly.

An example will illustrate the problem. In the popular sense there is a monopoly if one person owns the only theatre in town. That usually does not, however, constitute a violation of the Sherman Act. But as we noted in United States *v.* Griffith, 334 U.S. 100 . . . , and see Schine Chain Theatres, Inc., *v.* U.S., 334 U.S. 110 . . . , even such an ownership is vulnerable in a suit by the United States under the Sherman Act if the property was acquired, or its strategic position maintained, as a result of practices which constitute unreasonable restraints of trade. Otherwise, there would be reward from the conspiracy through retention of its fruits. Hence the problem of the District Court does not end with enjoining continuance of the unlawful restraints nor with dissolving the combination which launched the conspiracy. Its function includes undoing what the conspiracy achieved. As we have discussed in Schine Chain Theatres, Inc., *v.* United States . . . , the requirement that the defendants restore what they unlawfully obtained is no more punishment than the familiar remedy of restitution. . . .

Moreover, the problem under the Sherman Act is not solved merely by measuring monopoly in terms of size or extent of holding or by concluding that single ownerships were not obtained "for the purpose of achieving a national monopoly." It is the relationship of the unreasonable restraints of trade to the position of the defendants in the exhibition field . . . that is of first importance on the divestiture phase of these cases. . . .

The findings of the District Court are deficient on that score and obscure on another. The District Court in its findings speaks of the absence of a "purpose" on the part of any of the five majors to achieve a "national monopoly" in the exhibition of motion pictures. First, there is no finding as to the presence or absence of monopoly on the part of the five majors in the *first-run* field. . . . Yet the *first-run* field, which constitutes the cream of the exhibition business, is the core of the present cases. Section 1 of the Sherman Act outlaws unreasonable restraints irrespective of the amount of trade or commerce involved (United States *v.* Socony Vacuum Oil Co. . . . .), and Section 2 condemns monopoly of "any part" of trade or commerce. "Any part" is construed to mean an appreciable part of interstate or foreign trade or commerce. United States *v.* Yellow Cab Co., 332 U.S. 218, 225. . . . Second, we pointed out in United States *v.* Griffith . . . that "specific intent" is not necessary to establish a "purpose or intent" to create a monopoly but that the requisite "purpose or intent" is present if monopoly results as a necessary consequence of what was done. The findings of the District Court on this phase of the cases are not clear . . . and must be recast on remand of the cases. Third, monopoly power, whether lawfully or unlawfully acquired, may violate Section 2 of the Sherman Act though it remains unexercised . . . , for as we stated in American Tobacco Co. *v.* United States, 328 U.S. 781, 809, 811 . . . , the existence of power "to exclude competition when it is desired to do so" is itself a violation of Section 2, provided it is coupled with the purpose or intent to exercise that power. The District Court . . . did not address itself to this phase of the monopoly problem. . . .

Exploration of these phases of the cases would not be necessary if, as the Department of Justice argues, vertical integration of producing, distributing and exhibiting motion pictures is illegal *per se*. But the majority of the Court does not take that view. In the opinion of the majority the legality of vertical integration under the Sherman Act turns on (1) the purpose or intent with which it was conceived, or (2) the power it creates and the attendant purpose or intent. First, it runs afoul of the Sherman Act if it was a calculated scheme to gain control over an appreciable segment of the market and to restrain or suppress competition, rather than an expansion to meet legitimate business needs. . . . Second, a vertically integrated enterprise, like other aggregations of business units (United States *v.* Aluminum Co. of America, 2 Cir., 148 F.2d 416), will constitute monopoly which, though unexercised, violates the Sherman Act provided a power to exclude competition is coupled with a purpose or intent to do so. As we pointed out in United States *v.* Griffith . . . , size is itself an earmark of monopoly power. For size carries with it an opportunity for abuse. And the fact that the power created by size was utilized in the past to crush or prevent competition is potent evidence that the requisite purpose or intent attends the presence of monopoly power. . . . Likewise bearing on the question whether monopoly power is created by the vertical integration, is the nature of the market to be served . . . , and the leverage on the market which the particular vertical integration creates or makes possible.

These matters were not considered by the District Court. For that reason, as well as the others we have mentioned, the findings on monopoly and divestiture which we have discussed in this part of the opinion will be set aside. . . .

The judgment in these cases is affirmed in part and reversed in part, and the cases are remanded to the District Court for proceedings in conformity with this opinion.

So ordered. . . .

Mr. Justice Jackson took no part in the consideration or decision of these cases.

Mr. Justice Frankfurter dissented in part. . . .

United States v. Yellow Cab Company, et al.

338 U.S. 338 (1949)

Mr. Justice Jackson delivered the opinion of the Court.

This suit in equity, under Sections 1 and 2 of the Sherman Act . . . originally included three charges of violation: (1) conspiracy to restrain and monopolize transportation of interstate travelers by taxicab between Chicago railroad stations and their homes, offices and hotels; (2) conspiracy to eliminate competition for the business of transporting passengers between different Chicago railroad stations; and (3) conspiracy to restrain and monopolize the sale of taxicabs by control of the principal companies operating them in Chicago, New York, Pittsburgh and Minneapolis. On a previous appeal this Court held the first of the charges not to state a case within the statute, and that charge no longer concerns us. United States v. Yellow Cab Co., 332 U.S. 218. . . . The court below found that the Government failed to prove the second charge and no appeal is taken from that part of the judgment, so that charge has been eliminated. We have held that the residue of the complaint, embodying the third charge, alleges a cause of action within the statute, but only on the expressed assumption that the facts alleged are true, United States v. Yellow Cab Co., supra, 332 U.S. at page 224 . . . ; but the trial court has found that the Government, at the trial, has failed on all the evidence to prove its case. D.C., 80 F.Supp. 936. The cause is before us by a direct appeal under the Expediting Act . . . , and not by any exercise of our discretionary jurisdiction.

The first question proposed by the Government is whether the evidence sustains the findings of fact by the District Court. This is the basic issue, and the Government raises no question of law that has an existence independent of it. This issue of fact does not arise upon the trial court's disregard or misunderstanding of some definite and well-established fact. It extends to almost every detail of the decision, the Government saying that the trial court "ignored . . . substantially all of the facts which the Government deemed significant."

What the Government asks, in effect, is that we try the case de novo on the record, reject nearly all of the findings of the trial court, and substitute contrary findings of our own. Specifications of error which are fundamental to its case ask us to reweigh the evidence and review findings that are almost entirely concerned with imponderables, such as the intent of parties to certain 1929 business transactions, whether corporate officers were then acting in personal or official capacities, what was the design and purpose and intent of those who carried out twenty-year-old transactions, and whether they had legitimate business motives or were intending to restrain trade of their competitors in car manufacture, such as General Motors, Ford, Chrysler and Packard.

These were the chief fact issues in a trial of three weeks' duration. The Government relied in large part on inferences from its 485 exhibits, introduced by nine witnesses. The defendants relied heavily on oral testimony to contradict those inferences. The record is before us in 1,674 closely-printed pages.

The Government suggests that the opinion of the trial court "seems to reflect uncritical acceptance of the defendants' evidence and of defendants' views as to the facts to be given consideration in passing upon the legal issues before the Court." We see that it did indeed accept defendants' evidence and sustained defendants' view of the facts. But we are unable to discover the slightest justification for the accusation that it did so "uncritically." Also, it rejected the inferences the Government drew from its documents, but we find no justification for the statement that it "ignored" them. The judgment below is supported by an opinion, prepared with obvious care, which analyzes the evidence and shows the reasons for the findings. To us it appears to represent the considered judgment of an able trial judge, after patient hearing, that the Government's evidence fell short of its allegations—a not uncommon form of litigation casualty, from which the Government is no more immune than others.

Only last term we accepted the view then advanced by the Government that for triers of fact totally to reject an opposed view impeaches neither their impartiality nor the propriety of their conclusions. . . . Rule 52, Federal Rules of Civil Procedure, 28 U.S.C.A., provides among other things: "Findings of fact shall not be set aside unless clearly erroneous, and due regard shall be given to the opportunity of the trial court to judge the credibility of the witnesses."

Findings as to the design, motive and intent with which men act depend peculiarly upon the credit given to witnesses by those who see and hear them. If defendants' witnesses spoke the truth, the findings are admittedly justified. The trial court listened to and observed the officers who had made the records from which the Government would draw an inference of guilt and concluded that they bear a different meaning from that for which the Government contends.

It ought to be unnecessary to say that Rule 52 applies to appeals by the Government as well as to those by other litigants. There is no exception which permits it, even in an antitrust case to come to this Court for what virtually amounts to a trial *de novo* on the record of such findings as intent, motive and design. While, of course, it would be our duty to correct clear error, even in findings of fact, the Government has failed to establish any greater grievance here than it might have in any case where the evidence would support a conclusion either way but where the trial court has decided it to weigh more heavily for the defendants. Such a choice between two permissible views of the weight of evidence is not "clearly erroneous."

Judgment affirmed.

Mr. Justice Douglas and Mr. Justice Clark took no part in the consideration or decision of this case.

Mr. Justice Black, with whom Mr. Justice Reed, concurs, dissenting.

The evidence showed here without dispute that a manufacturer of taxicabs through a series of stock purchases obtained 62% of the stock of a corporation which itself had large stock interests in local companies operating taxicabs. The man who was president, general manager, director, and dominant stockholder in the taxicab manufacturing company also held an important managerial position in the corporate network that carried on the business of the local taxicab operating companies. The findings of the District Court were that affiliated ownership, management and control were not the result of any deliberate or calculated purpose of the manufacturing company to control the operating companies' purchases of taxicabs, and that no compulsion has been exercised to control such purchases. Consequently the trial court held that despite the integration of corporate management there was no violation of the Sherman Act. I think that the trial court erred in holding that a formed intent to suppress competition is an indispensable element of violations of the Sherman Act.

In United States *v.* Griffith, 334 U.S. 100, 105, 106 . . . we said: "It is, however, not always necessary to find a specific intent to restrain trade or to build a monopoly in order to find that the antitrust laws have been violated. It is sufficient that a restraint of trade or monopoly results as the consequence of a defendant's conduct or business arrangements. . . . To require a greater showing would cripple the Act. . . . Even if we accept the District Court's findings that appellees had no intent or purpose unreasonably to restrain trade or to monopolize, we are left with the question whether a necessary and direct result of the master agreements was the restraining or monopolizing of trade within the meaning of the Sherman Act."

Measured by this test the findings of the trial court here fail to support its legal conclusions that no violation of the Sherman Act has been proven. Since the trial court went on the assumption that subjective intent to suppress competition is an essential ingredient of Sherman law violations, it did not make specific findings as to whether the freedom of the taxicab companies to buy taxicabs from other manufacturers had been hobbled by the defendants' business arrangements, regardless of compulsion, or intent to destroy competition. There was much evidence tending to show this hobbling of competition. I think that the allegations of the complaint were sufficiently broad to present this issue for adjudication by the court. Moreover, presentation of the issue was emphasized by the fact that a large amount of evidence to prove successful accomplishment of monopoly or restraints of trade were admitted without any objection by the defendants based on variance from the pleadings. . . .

There is evidence in the record to the effect that as a result of the corporate arrangements here the manufacturing company obtained sufficient power to dictate the terms of purchases by the local companies; there is also evidence that those companies did thereafter limit their purchases of taxicabs almost exclusively to those sold by the manufacturing defendant. Moreover, the evidence shows that such taxicabs were in some instances bought by the local company at prices above those paid by other taxicab companies wholly free to buy taxicabs in a competitive market. This evidence, if accepted, would support a finding of illegal restraint of trade or monopoly under the Griffith rule. I think the case should be remanded for the trial court to consider the evidence and make findings on this aspect of the case.

United States v. United Shoe Machinery Corp.

110 F.Supp. 295 (1953)

Wyzanski, District Judge. . . .

December 15, 1947 the Government filed a complaint against United Shoe Machinery Corporation under Section 4 of the Sherman Act . . . , in order to restrain alleged violations of Sections 1 and 2 of that Act. . . .

Stripped to its essentials, the 52 page complaint charged, *first*, that since 1912 United had been "monopolizing interstate trade and commerce in the shoe machinery industry of the United States.". . . The *second* principal charge laid by the complaint was that United had been (*a*) "monopolizing the distribution in interstate commerce of numerous . . . shoe factory supplies" and (*b*) "attempting to monopolize the distribution in interstate commerce of . . . other supplies.". . . *Third*, the complaint alleged United was "attempting to monopolize and monopolizing the manufacture and distribution in interstate commerce of tanning machinery used in the manufacture of shoe leather.". . .

In support of this three-pronged attack, directed to shoe machinery, shoe factory supplies, and tanning machinery, the Government set forth detailed allegations with respect to acquisitions, leases, patents, and a host of other aspects of United's business. . . .

After stating its charges, the Government prayed for an adjudication of United's violations of both Section 1 and Section 2 of the Sherman Act; an injunction against future violations; a cancellation of United's shoe machinery leases; a requirement that United offer for sale all machine types "manufactured and commercialized by it and be enjoined from leasing shoe machinery except upon terms . . . approved by the Court"; a requirement that, on such terms as the court may deem appropriate, United make available to all applicants all patents and inventions relating to shoe machinery; an injunction against United manufacturing or distributing shoe factory supplies; a cancellation of exclusive contracts governing shoe factory supplies; and a divestiture of United's ownership of virtually all branches and subsidiaries concerned with shoe factory supplies or tanning machinery.

Defendant answered seasonably, denying all the significant allegations. . . .

A trial of prodigious length followed. . . .

In an antitrust case a trial court's task is to reduce, as far as fairness permits, a complex record to its essentials, so that the parties, the Supreme Court, other courts, the bar, and the general public may understand the decree, and may recognize the premises on which that judgment rests. It is not the Court's duty to make a precise finding on every detail of four decades of an industry. It is not its duty to approach the issues as an historian, an archaeologist, . . . an economist, or even a master appointed to settle every factual dispute. A trial judge who undertakes such tasks will unnecessarily sacrifice the rights of litigants in other cases clamoring for attention. Moreover, he will encourage just that type of extravagant presentation which has come to plague the field of antitrust law. Hence this opinion is to be construed as denying on the ground of immateriality every request not granted. . . .

OPINION ON ALLEGED VIOLATIONS. . . .

There are 18 major processes for the manufacturing of shoes by machine. Some machine types are used only in one process, but others are used in several; and the relationship of machine types to one another may be competitive or sequential. The approximately 1460 shoe manufacturers themselves are highly competitive in many respects, including their choice of processes and other technological aspects of production. Their total demand for machine services, apart from those rendered by dry thread sewing machines in the upper-fitting room, constitutes an identifiable market which is a "part of the trade or commerce among the several States." Section 2 of the Sherman Act. . . .

United, the largest source of supply, is a corporation lineally descended from a combination of constituent companies, adjudged lawful by the Supreme Court of the United States in 1918. . . . It now has assets rising slightly over 100 million dollars and employment rolls around 6,000. In recent years it has earned before Federal taxes 9 to 13.5 million dollars annually.

Supplying different aspects of that market are at least 10 other American manufacturers and some foreign manufacturers, whose products are admitted to the United States free of tariff duty. Almost all the operations performed in the 18 processes can be carried out without the use of any of United's machines, and (at least in foreign areas, where patents are no obstacle), a complete shoe factory can be efficiently organized without a United machine.

Nonetheless, United at the present time is supplying over 75%, and probably 85% of the current demand in the American shoe machinery market, as heretofore defined. This is somewhat less than the share it was supplying in 1915. In the meantime, one important competitor, Compo Shoe Machinery Corporation, became the American innovator of the cement process of manufacture. In that sub-market Compo roughly equals United. . . .

United is the only machinery enterprise that produces a long line of machine types, and covers every major process. It is the only concern that has a research laboratory covering all aspects of the needs of shoe manufacturing; though Compo has a laboratory concentrating on the needs of those in the cement process. . . . Through its own research, United has developed inventions many of which are now patented.

Roughly 95% of its 3915 patents are attributable to the ideas of its own employees.

Although at the turn of the century, United's patents covered the fundamentals of shoe machinery manufacture, those fundamental patents have expired. Current patents cover for the most part only minor developments, so that it is possible to "invent around" them, to use the words of United's chief competitor. However, the aggregation of patents does to some extent block potential competition. It furnishes a trading advantage. It leads inventors to offer their ideas to United, on the general principle that new complicated machines embody numerous patents. And it serves as a hedge or insurance for United against unforseen competitive developments.

In the last decade and a half, United has not acquired any significant patents, inventions, machines, or businesses from any outside source, and has rejected many offers made to it. Before then, while it acquired no going businesses, in a period of two decades it spent roughly $3,500,000 to purchase inventions and machines. Most of these were from moribund companies, though this was not true of the acquisitions underlying the significant Littleway process and the less significant heel seat fitting machines and patents, each of which was from an active enterprise and might have served as a nucleus of important, though, at least initially, not extensive competition.

In supplying its complicated machines to shoe manufacturers, United, like its more important American competitors, has followed the practice of never selling, but only leasing. Leasing has been traditional in the shoe machinery field since the Civil War. So far as this record indicates, there is virtually no expressed dissatisfaction from consumers respecting that system; and Compo, United's principal competitor, endorses and uses it. Under the system, entry into shoe manufacture has been easy. The rates charged for all customers have been uniform. The machines supplied have performed excellently. United has, without separate charge, promptly and efficiently supplied repair service and many kinds of other service useful to shoe manufacturers. These services have been particularly important, because in the shoe manufacturing industry a whole line of production can be adversely affected, and valuable time lost, if some of the important machines go out of function, and because machine breakdowns have serious labor and consumer repercussions. The cost to the average shoe manufacturer of its machines and services supplied to him has been less than 2% of the wholesale price of his shoes.

However, United's leases, in the context of the present shoe machinery market, have created barriers to the entry by competitors into the shoe machinery field.

First, the complex of obligations and rights accruing under United's leasing system in operation deter a shoe manufacturer from disposing of a United machine and acquiring a competitor's machine. . . . The lessee is now held closely to United by the combined effect of the 10-year term, the requirement that if he has work available he must use the machine to full capacity, and by the return charge which can in practice, through the right deduction fund, be reduced to insignificance if he keeps this and other United machines to the end of the periods for which he leased them.

Second, when a lessee desires to replace a United machine, United gives him more favorable terms if the replacement is by another United machine than if it is by a competitive machine.

Third, United's practice of offering to repair, without separate charges, its leased machines, has had the effect that there are no independent service organizations to repair complicated machines. In turn, this has had the effect that the manufacturer of a complicated machine must either offer repair service with his machine, or must face the obstacle of marketing his machine to customers who know that repair service will be difficult to provide. . . .

Although maintaining the same nominal terms for each customer, United has followed, as between machine types, a discriminatory pricing policy. . . . [T]hese sharp and relatively durable differentials are traceable, at least in large part, to United's policy of fixing a higher rate of return where competition is of minor significance, and a lower rate of return where competition is of major significance. . . .

On the foregoing facts, the issue of law is whether defendant in its shoe machinery business has violated that provision of Section 2 of the Sherman Act. . . .

Yet, in these recent authorities[9] there are discernible at least three different, but cognate approaches.

The approach which has the least sweeping implications really antedates the decision in Aluminum. But it deserves restatement. An enterprise has monopolized in violation of Section 2 of the Sherman Act if it has acquired or maintained a power to exclude others as a result of using an unreasonable "restraint of trade" in violation of Section 1 of the Sherman Act. . . .

A more inclusive approach was adopted by Mr. Justice Douglas in United States v. Griffith. . . . He stated that to prove a violation of Section 2 it was not always necessary to show a violation of Section 1. . . . And he concluded that an enterprise has monopolized in violation of Section 2 if it (*a*) has the power to exclude competition, and (*b*) has exercised it, or has the purpose to exercise it. . . . The least that this conclusion means is that it is a violation of Section 2 for one having effective control of the market to use, or plan to use, any exclusionary practice, even though it is not a technical restraint of trade. But the conclusion may go further.

[9] U.S. v. Aluminum Co. of America, 148 F.2d 416 (1945); American Tobacco Co. v. U.S., 328 U.S. 781 (1946); U.S. v. Griffith, 334 U.S. 100 (1948); Schine Chain Theatres v. U.S. 334 U.S. 110 (1948); U.S. v. Paramount Theatres, 334 U.S. 131, (1948); U.S. v. Columbia Steel Co., 334 U.S. 495 (1948). IMS.

Indeed the way in which Mr. Justice Douglas used the terms "monopoly power" and "effective market control," and cited Aluminum suggests that he endorses a third and broader approach, which originated with Judge Hand. It will be recalled that Judge Hand said that one who has acquired an overwhelming share of the market "monopolizes" whenever he does business, . . . apparently even if there is no showing that his business involves any exclusionary practice. But, it will also be recalled that this doctrine is softened by Judge Hand's suggestion that the defendant may escape statutory liability if it bears the burden of proving that it owes its monopoly solely to superior skill. . . .

This Court finds it unnecessary to choose between the second and third approaches. For, taken as a whole, the evidence satisfies the tests laid down in both Griffith and Aluminum. The facts show that (1) defendant has, and exercises, such overwhelming strength in the shoe machinery market that it controls that market, (2) this strength excludes some potential, and limits some actual, competition, and (3) this strength is not attributable solely to defendant's ability, economies of scale, research, natural advantages, and adaptation to inevitable economic laws. . . .

To combat United's market control, a competitor must be prepared with knowledge of shoemaking, engineering skill, capacity to invent around patents, and financial resources sufficient to bear the expense of long developmental and experimental processes. The competitor must be prepared for consumers' resistance founded on their long-term, satisfactory relations with United, and on the cost to them of surrendering United's lease. Also, the competitor must be prepared to give, or point to the source of, repair and other services, and to the source of supplies for machine parts, expendable parts, and the like. Indeed, perhaps a competitor who aims at any large scale success must also be prepared to lease his machines. These considerations would all affect *potential* competition, and have not been without their effect on *actual* competition.

Not only does the evidence show United has control of the market, but also the evidence does not show that the control is due entirely to excusable causes. The three principal sources of United's power have been the original constitution of the company, the superiority of United's products and services, and the leasing system. The first two of these are plainly beyond reproach. . . .

But United's control does not rest solely on its original constitution, its ability, its research, or its economies of scale. There are other barriers to competition, and these barriers were erected by United's own business policies. Much of United's market power is traceable to the magnetic ties inherent in its system of leasing, and not selling, its more important machines. The lease-only system of distributing complicated machines has many "partnership" aspects, and it has exclusionary features such as the 10-year term, the full capacity clause, the return charges, and the failure to segregate service charges from machine charges. Moreover, the leasing system has aided United in maintaining a pricing system which discriminates between machine types.

In addition to the foregoing three principal sources of United's power, brief reference may be made to the fact that United has been somewhat aided in retaining control of the shoe machinery industry by its purchases in the secondhand market, by its acquisitions of patents, and, to a lesser extent by its activities in selling to shoe factories supplies which United and others manufacture. . . .

[T]hey are not practices which can be properly described as the inevitable consequences of ability, natural forces, or law. They represent something more than the use of accessible resources, the process of invention and innovation, and the employment of those techniques of employment, financing, production, and distribution, which a competitive society must foster. They are contracts, arrangements, and policies which, instead of encouraging competition based on pure merit, further the dominance of a particular firm. In this sense, they are unnatural barriers; they unnecessarily exclude actual and potential competition; they restrict a free market. While the law allows many enterprises to use such practices, the Sherman Act is now construed by superior courts to forbid the continuance of effective market control based in part upon such practices. Those courts hold that market control is inherently evil and constitutes a violation of Section 2 unless economically inevitable, or specifically authorized and regulated by law.

It is only fair to add that . . . United's power does not rest on predatory practices. Probably few monopolies could produce a record so free from any taint of that kind of wrongdoing. The violation with which United is now charged depends not on moral considerations, but on solely economic considerations. United is denied the right to exercise effective control of the market by business policies that are not the inevitable consequences of its capacities or its natural advantages. That those policies are not immoral is irrelevant. . . .

Moreover, . . . United has not proved that monopoly is economically compelled by the thinness of the shoe machinery market. It has not shown that no company could undertake to develop, manufacture, and distribute certain types of machines, unless it alone met the total demand for those types of machines.

Nor has United affirmatively proved that it has achieved spectacular results and comparable economies of production, distribution, and service could not be achieved as well by, say, three important shoe machinery firms, as by one. Compo with a much smaller organization indicates how much research can be done on a smaller scale. Yet since Compo is limited to the simpler cement process machines, too much reliance should not be placed on this comparison. Nonetheless, one point is worth recalling. Compo's inventors first found practical ways to introduce the cement process which United had considered and rejected. This experience illustrates the familiar truth that one of the dangers of extraordinary experience is that those who have it may fall into grooves created by their own expertness. They refuse to believe that hurdles which they have learned from experience are insurmountable, can in fact be overcome by fresh, independent minds.

So far, nothing in this opinion has been said of defendant's *intent* in regard to its power and practices in the shoe machinery market. This point can be readily disposed of by reference once more to Aluminum. . . . Defendant intended to engage in the leasing practices and pricing policies which maintained its market power. That is all the intent which the law requires when both the complaint and the judgment rest on a charge of "monopolizing," not merely "attempting to monopolize." Defendant having willed the means, has willed the end.

Next, come those issues relating to supplies. . . .

In certain of those supply fields . . . United has control of the market . . . [which] comes principally from United's power over the shoe machinery market. And for that reason the exercise of dominant power in those supply fields is unlawful. An enterprise that by monopolizing one field, secures dominant market power in another field, has monopolized the second field, in violation of Section 2 of the Sherman Act. . . .

OPINION ON REMEDY. . . .

The Government's proposal that the Court dissolve United into three separate manufacturing companies is unrealistic. United conducts all machine manufacture at one plant in Beverly, with one set of jigs and tools, one foundry, one laboratory for machinery problems, one managerial staff, and one labor force. It takes no Solomon to see that this organism cannot be cut into three equal and viable parts. . . .

A petition for dissolution should reflect greater attention to practical problems and should involve supporting economic data and prophesies such as are presented in corporate reorganization and public utility dissolution cases. Moreover, the petition should involve a more formal commitment by the Attorney General, than is involved in the divergent proposals that his assistants have made in briefs and in oral arguments addressed to the Court. On the whole, therefore, the suggested remedy of dissolution is rejected.

From the opinion on defendant's violations it follows that some form of relief regarding defendant's leases and leasing practices is proper and necessary. . . .

Although leasing should not now be abolished by judicial decree, the Court agrees with the Government that the leases should be purged of their restrictive features. In the decree filed herewith, the term of the lease is shortened, the full capacity clause is eliminated, the discriminatory commutative charges are removed, and United is required to segregate its charges for machines from its charges for repair service. . . .

The Court also agrees with the Government that if United chooses to continue to lease any machine type, it must offer that type of machine also for sale. . . . Insofar as United's machines are sold rather than leased, they will ultimately, in many cases, reach a second-hand market. From that market, United will face a type of substitute competition which will gradually weaken the prohibited market power which it now exercises. Moreover, from that market, or from United itself, a competitor of United can acquire a United machine in order to study it, to copy its unpatented features, and to experiment with improvements in, or alterations of, the machine. Thus, in another and more direct way, United's market power will be diminished. . . .

One other phase of the decree to which this opinion should expressly advert is the method of handling those subsidiaries and branches which produce supplies in fields which United has monopolized. The clearest examples are nails and tacks, and eyelets for the shoe machinery market. These are large scale monopolizations attributable to the machinery monopoly. And United should be divested of its business of manufacturing and distributing these particular supplies, because this is the kind of dissolution which can be carried out practically, and which will also reduce monopoly power in each of the affected supply fields. . . .

United States v. E. I. duPont de Nemours and Company

118 F.Supp. 41 (1953)

Leahy, Chief Judge.

This is a civil suit by the United States of America under Section 4 of the Sherman Act, charging defendant with monopolizing, attempting to monopolize and combining and conspiring to monopolize trade and commerce among the several states of the United States in cellophane and caps and bands. . . .

Defendant, E. I. duPont de Nemours and Company, is a Delaware corporation. It is successor to duPont Cellophane Company, Inc. Throughout the period covered by the complaint, it or its predecessors manufactured and sold, in interstate and foreign commerce, regenerated cellulose in the form of film (cellophane) and in the form of bands. Prior to the filing of the complaint in this case, it also manufactured and sold cellulosic caps.

DuPont entered the cellophane business in 1923. It collaborated, under written agreements with La Cellophane (a subsidiary of the Comptoir which is the largest French rayon producer), in establishing the first duPont cellophane company. In 1929 duPont Cellophane Company, Inc., was reincorporated as a wholly owned subsidiary of duPont. In 1936, duPont took over the operation of this business and dissolved duPont Cellophane Company, Inc. . . .

Certain issues of fact and law must control the decision in this case. When these controlling issues are isolated, it will be apparent there are fatal deficiencies in the Government's proof, and the record fails to establish those facts which are essential to support the charges in the complaint.

The history of duPont's cellophane business is a record of competitive achievement. DuPont was the first American company to manufacture this new wrapping material. To pioneer the cellophane business required foresight, and a willingness to take risks. DuPont had little technical experience in this line of chemistry. The product had not been proven as a packaging material. It had had little acceptance in this country.

DuPont entered the business in the only manner that was practicable. It acquired the commercial process from the French. This process was obtained on the best terms duPont could negotiate. The two groups, American and French, had already been successful partners in rayon. No desire to limit competition was involved, for neither partner to the venture was engaged in business in competition with the other, and there is no indication anyone was interested.

DuPont saw the chance for profit and utility for cellophane if it could be introduced into the mass production packaging markets of the United States. It decided to bring a new competing material into the flexible packaging market, an established field of competitive business activity.

Cellophane was not at first acceptable in the trades to which it was offered. Manufacturing techniques were crude; quality unsatisfactory, and costs made price of cellophane prohibitive for many uses. There were distribution and merchandising problems to be met. Only by effective competition could duPont hope to gain recognition for its product in markets where other materials were entrenched. The business had to be built up by creative research.

DuPont's technological achievements were of high order. Through research it improved manufacturing efficiency, reduced costs, improved quality, developed new types of materials and lowered prices to obtain acceptance for its product, all in the face of competition. Research results were continuously put to use in its plants.

The product obtained from the French did not meet the needs of the American market. DuPont invented a new product, moistureproof cellophane, which proved to be the product upon which the cellophane business has been built. It obtained a product patent under which all its moistureproof cellophane was produced during the period of the monopoly charged in the complaint. It then exploited that patent, well within the purposes and intentions of the patent grant. Its production expanded; it made many types of moistureproof cellophane; it gave increasing service to its customers; it neither curtailed its initiative nor restricted the capital which it was willing to devote to the enterprise. DuPont achieved through business method an increasing success in its competition with other packaging materials.

As cellophane got recognition in the trade, others entered various phases of the business as converters, users, suppliers of raw materials, manufacturers of equipment, and the like. Cellophane creates competition. Throughout the flexible packaging markets this competition is felt. It stimulates efforts of other producers to manufacture more efficiently. It stimulates research. The consumption of flexible packaging materials including cellophane has grown at a rapid rate. Within these markets the competition is intense. New producers have entered. No one material or one supplier controls—certainly not duPont, which has neither the power to raise prices nor to exclude competitors.

After reviewing the development of this business, plaintiff has been unable to bring a single person who says he was injured or who claims to have been denied an opportunity to participate. Prices have consistently been lowered and reflect competitive pressures. Production has expanded. Benefits from research have been passed on to consumers. DuPont has not conducted its cellophane business in a restrictive way. There are no artificial controls which it can exercise in the markets where its product is sold. . . .

The charge here is duPont monopolizes cellophane. The charge involves two questions: 1. does duPont possess monopoly powers; and 2., if so, has it achieved such powers by "monopolizing" within the meaning of the Act and under United States *v.* Aluminum Company of America. Unless the first is decided against defendant, the second is not reached. First, then, to the question of existence of monopoly power. . . .

Cellophane is not a unique flexible packaging material in any functional or economic sense. In terms of uses for which cellophane is sold, and the qualities it brings to each use as a wrapping material, cellophane is interchangeable and *in fact* continually interchanged with many flexible packaging materials. . . .

When duPont commenced sale of cellophane, it was not of a quality which would enable it to compete for flexible packaging business. Cellophane was brittle, not available in the roll form essential for machine packaging operations, non-moistureproof. It was necessary for duPont to engage in research to overcome these deficiencies, and, as they were overcome to continue research looking toward a quality improvement so cellophane would remain competitive with other flexible packaging materials in meeting the requirements of buyers of flexible packaging materials. . . .

DuPont did not engage in cellophane research with the intent of monopolizing the manufacture of cellophane. . . .

The purpose of duPont's research has been to enable it to improve profits and to compete with other manufacturers of flexible packaging materials, including other makers of cellophane, by reducing cost, improving quality and developing types of moistureproof cellophane designed to meet specific packaging needs. This research has involved developments at all stages of the manufacturing processes, and improvement in every phase of cellophane quality. . . .

The objective of duPont was to reduce price to a level where cellophane could compete with other flexible packaging materials. Price of cellophane in relation to prices of other flexible packaging materials was such that only luxury items would use it as a wrap. It was necessary to develop volume, lower cost and improve quality and bring the price of cellophane down to a point where it would receive acceptance in the packaging markets. DuPont sought a low profit per unit of sale in effort to achieve lower prices which would develop volume sales and increase profits. . . .

DuPont's proportion of the United States production of flexible packaging materials has increased in almost direct relation to the steady decrease of the ratio of cellophane prices to glassine and waxed paper prices. . . .

The price of cellophane was reduced to expand the market for cellophane. DuPont did not reduce prices for cellophane with intent of monopolizing manufacture or with intent of suppressing competitors. . . .

DuPont never lowered cellophane prices below cost, and never dropped cellophane prices temporarily to gain a competitive advantage. . . .

Cellophane is forced to meet competition of other flexible packaging materials. The competition between the materials is intense and duPont cannot exercise market control or monopoly powers. . . .

During the period duPont entered the flexible packaging business, and since its introduction of moistureproof cellophane, sales of cellophane have increased. Total volume of flexible packaging materials used in the United States has also increased. DuPont's relative percentage of the packaging business has grown as a result of its research, price, sales and capacity policies, but duPont cellophane even in uses where it has competed has not attained the bulk of the business, due to competition of other flexible packaging materials.

[Further,] Competition existed between duPont and Sylvania, and later Olin, for the sale of cellophane. Many customers have shifted back and forth between the producers, or divided their purchases between producers in changing proportions. . . .

Moistureproof cellophane was a duPont invention. No other party made any contribution to its development.

DuPont got five basic patents upon its inventions of the product moistureproof cellophane and methods for its manufacture. . . .

Principal growth in the cellophane industry occurred after duPont's invention of moistureproof cellophane, which by 1940 accounted for over 80% of all cellophane sales in the United States. . . .

DuPont expanded cellophane capacity to meet reasonably foreseeable demand. In most cases sales achieved were in excess of the amount forecast at the time of plant expansion.

Capacity was not expanded with the purpose of stifling competition, creating excess capacity to overhang the market, or forestalling potential competitors. . . .

Most of the increase in duPont's capacity to produce cellophane has resulted from improved efficiency of manufacturing with existing equipment rather than installation of new plant. Better efficiency resulted in increased output per unit of existing plant.

Plaintiff conceded duPont's expansion of productive capacity was not illegal.

DuPont has never sought to create a shortage of cellophane and has not closed down plant nor taken any other action with the intention of creating a shortage. . . .

No proof was presented any person failed to manufacture cellophane as the result of any act done by duPont.

There is no proof there has been any potential competitor who desired to manufacture cellophane and did not do so.

There is no proof duPont possesses power to exclude potential competitors who may desire to manufacture cellophane.

DuPont employed lawful business methods in attempting to keep apprised of competitive developments and did not attempt to stifle competitors.

No evidence was offered any potential competitor was excluded from manufacture of cellophane as a result of duPont's size or prestige in the chemical industry. . . .

Sylvania began manufacture of moistureproof cellophane after issuance to duPont of its basic product patent. . . .

When duPont made a price reduction on its cellophane during the period 1930–1947, Sylvania would obtain from its customers a copy of the new duPont price list, and thereafter, in order to remain competitive, would issue its own price list back dated to an effective date the same as on the duPont list. Although effective date of the two lists was the same, the lists were not issued to the trade at the same time. . . .

DuPont established prices for its cellophane independently of Sylvania. There were no agreements as to what prices should be charged, one company would follow the prices of the other, or published prices would be observed. Proof does not support an inference of agreement between duPont and Sylvania as to prices. . . .

DuPont acted in good faith in development of its cellophane business. It sought to act in ways that would not violate United States law.

DuPont's purpose in the cellophane business was to make money by enlarging its activities in industry, and it was offered a means by acquiring a secret process for a new product.

In the development of its cellophane business, duPont sought to enlarge the market from a narrow one to a broad one. At outset, demand was narrow and price high. By research directed to quality of product and efficiency of manufacture, cost was reduced and quality improved. By this means duPont wanted to get volume sales in the wrapping industry. As costs went down, prices were reduced, markets expanded, so duPont's return on investment was satisfactory. DuPont's motive in taking these steps was to make money and to compete.

DuPont did not seek to attain success in the cellophane business with intent of suppressing or excluding competition. . . .

DuPont devoted manpower and expense to development of packaging machinery and did not attempt to assert any control over the use or sale of machinery to which its efforts had contributed, although the same machines handle competing cellophane and other flexible wrapping materials. DuPont encouraged end users to employ such machinery for packaging with unprinted cellophane, rather than protecting sales of duPont's converters. DuPont did not vertically integrate, either forward by engaging in conversion of cellophane, or backward by engaging in manufacture of wood pulp, the principal raw material. These actions are inconsistent with a monopolistic intent, but are consistent with a purpose to stimulate use of cellophane for volume packaging purposes. . . .

Waxed paper, glassine, and sulphite paper were dominant flexible packaging materials in 1924 and are today. . . .

DuPont has been unable to achieve as much as 20% of production of flexible packaging materials. . . .

The record establishes domestic buyers of cellophane do not lack alternative sources of supply, and duPont does not have power to restrain free competition at the distribution level of the industry. . . .

DuPont does not have power to fix and maintain arbitrary and noncompetitive terms of sale. Terms at which duPont cellophane is sold must meet customs and requirements of the flexible packaging trade. . . .

The record establishes duPont does not have power to exclude others who would engage in the manufacture and sale of cellophane.

No evidence was shown anyone desired to manufacture cellophane and was unable because of any act done by duPont.

No proof was shown duPont has economic power to prevent others from manufacturing cellophane.

No proof was shown duPont sought to exclude others from manufacturing cellophane.

No proof was shown duPont has power to subvert the use and to engross cellophane patents, trademarks, trade secrets, or "know-how.". . .

I recognized through trial the principal issue is whether duPont's position gives it market control, and hence monopoly power arbitrarily to raise prices and to exclude competitors. The complaint charges duPont "has had for many years past virtually absolute control of the markets in the United States for cellophane" and such market control has resulted in monopoly powers that have "become self-sustaining and self-perpetuating.". . .

1. Does duPont have power, without regard to competitive forces, to raise price of cellophane either directly or by limiting production, deteriorating quality, or by any other means?

2. Does duPont have power alone to exclude competition in the production and sale of cellophane? . . .

Monopoly power can be distinguished from the normal freedom of business only in degree. Nothing except death is an absolute. Plaintiff cannot rest on a showing duPont makes cellophane and has some degree of control over its sales, production and prices. Cf. United States *v.* Columbia Steel Co. . . . ; United States *v.* Aluminum Co. of America. . . .

Many sellers have some freedom over their price, production and general business conduct. Each must make his best guess of his future requirements; he must set price at which he will attempt to sell; and he may raise price if costs or other factors dictate. Such business decisions do not represent degree of control over prices or production which constitutes monopoly power. Prohibited degree of control is that which permits disregard for competitive factors. . . .

"Market control" or lack of "market control" are ultimate facts. They are determined by fact-finding processes, and on the basis of knowledge and analysis of all competitive factors which bear on a seller's power to raise prices, or to exclude competition. Existence of monopoly powers is not made on the basis of assumptions as to competitive markets. If the price, quantity of production and sale, and the quality of a seller's product are determined by pressures exerted on him by buyers and sellers of another's product, the products and the sellers must, for purposes of any realistic analysis, be in the same "market" and must be in competition with each other. . . .

Facts, in large part uncontested, demonstrate duPont cellophane is sold under such intense competitive conditions acquisition of market control or monopoly power is a practical impossibility. . . .

Shifts of business have been proved. It has been proved in every major end use; duPont cellophane has lost and gained actual paying customers, as a result of cost and quality judgments by these customers. It has been proved these gains and losses are substantial. . . .

Power arbitrarily to raise prices is principal indicium of monopoly power and market control. This is the test to be applied in adjudicating monopolization. Under market conditions which have prevailed, duPont does not possess power to raise cellophane prices without regard for competitive pressures. The market would penalize any attempt to do so with lower sales and smaller profits. . . .

DuPont could not have developed volume of cellophane business without lowering its prices. It was only as duPont lowered price and narrowed relative spread between cellophane prices and the prices of these other materials that it was accepted for end uses where wax paper and glassine were established. Only by reduction of price has cellophane been able to achieve an appreciable volume of sales in competition with other packaging materials.

Evidence shows a degree of price sensitivity in the flexible packaging markets. This is reflected both statistically and in terms of concrete experience with specific accounts. . . .

The Government argues duPont's power to control prices is evidenced by its profits, and duPont was able to achieve predetermined rates of return. Plaintiff's own proposed findings, however, disclose rates of return varied substantially from year to year. There is no evidence as to rate of return earned by any other manufacturer of flexible packaging materials, such as waxed paper or glassine. Evidence did show duPont's rates of return were somewhat higher than Sylvania's, but this resulted from duPont's superior efficiency. Years of profit do not establish monopoly power over prices. They establish this: duPont was an efficient business company. . . .

After an examination of raw materials, technology and plant capacity to distribution, there is no evidence of power to exclude competition. . . .

Thus, there are not present in the cellophane business any of the orthodox indicia of monopoly which appear in monopoly cases. . . .

For years courts have tussled with the task of reconciling the Sherman Act with lawful monopolies by patent grant. Many cases under the Act have drawn the line according to the larger aims of public policy—a vigorously competitive economy. Courts have recognized new processes and patents are perhaps the most desirable form of competition. The holder of a patent is, in accordance with the patent laws, permitted to exert monopoly control over what he has created.

Evidence does not disclose combining of competing or independent process patents or efforts to control unpatented products. We have here a case involving the grant to duPont on its own invention of a broad product patent, the validity of which is conceded by plaintiff, and a patent which evidence discloses was of such scope that no one without a grant of a license under it could have manufactured lawfully the product claimed. No case of this kind has ever been brought before. To declare, as plaintiff seeks, the award of this patent, with the rights implicit in its ownership, is to be ignored in applying the Sherman Act, is to ask the court to declare the Sherman Act repealed statutory provisions under which patents are granted. This I will not do. . . .

Defendant contends the offense of monopolization requires, in addition to proof of monopoly power or market control, proof such power or control was achieved in a manner prohibited by the statute. Plaintiff contends mere possession of the power, no matter how acquired, in itself establishes a violation. Once power has been obtained, plaintiff argues, it does not even have to be exercised. Mere possession of power, it is argued, is sufficient to constitute offense of monopolization.

It has been recognized under the Sherman Act "monopoly in the concrete" is not prohibited under the section. Standard Oil Co. of New Jersey *v.* United States, 221 U.S. 1, 62. The Act, using the verb "monopolize," prohibits conduct rather than status. It is directed against activities rather than results. This is not a matter of semantics. It is a matter of facts. That this is so is obvious from fact the statute carried criminal as well as civil sanctions. Thus decisions recognized the manner in which a monopoly position was obtained was a crucial consideration in determining whether or not a defendant has monopolized within the meaning of the Act.

The decisions state a defendant may lawfully obtain a monopoly position if that position is "thrust upon it." Thus the right to normal growth and to enjoy the results of technical achievement and successful competition has been preserved. . . .

The decisions . . . demonstrate, if the challenged position is acquired, as it has been in this case, by superior technical skill and effective competitive activity, the resulting power from that position does not establish monopolization within the meaning of the statute. . . .

I am able, after critical examination of the record, to determine duPont's position is the result of research, business skill and competitive activity. Much of duPont's evidence was designed to show research, price and sales policies of that Company are responsible for its success and these policies were conceived and carried forward in a coordinated fashion with skill, gaining for duPont substantial recognition in the packaging industry.

DuPont was a pioneer. . . .

This record discloses from the outset duPont set on an intensive research program to improve the quality and characteristics of cellophane and to lower its cost. . . .

The facts destroy the charges here made. There has been no monopolization or conspiracy or combination or attempt to monopolize shown. The record reflects not the dead hand of monopoly but rapidly declining prices, expanding production, intense competition stimulated by creative research, the development of new products and uses and other benefits of a free economy. DuPont nor any other American company similarly situated should be punished for its success. Nothing warrants intervention of this court of equity. The complaint should be dismissed.

INTERCORPORATE STOCK-
HOLDING AND MERGERS

The cases presented in this chapter provide a brief history of legislative and court attitudes towards mergers. In the Thatcher case (which marked what most observers considered the judicial emasculation of the original Section 7 of the Clayton Act) the Court decided that the Federal Trade Commission's power to prevent mergers which might substantially lessen competition extended only to acquisitions of stock. This opened the way to merger via *asset* acquisition and, for all practical purposes, eliminated the Clayton Act as an effective antimerger weapon. The Columbia Steel case then indicates the difficulty of effectively applying Sherman Act standards to the merger problem. Finally, the Pillsbury Mills decision represents the latest turn in public policy on this important issue. Armed with an amended Clayton Act—one which contains no asset loophole—the Commission began the difficult task of establishing criteria for testing the competitive effects, and therefore the legality, of corporate acquisitions. Notable in the decision is the Commission's refusal to adopt either the standards of reasonableness laid down in Section 3 Clayton Act cases, or those previously employed in Sherman Act suits.

Thatcher Manufacturing Company v. *Federal Trade Commission*

272 U.S. 554 (1926)

Mr. Justice McReynolds delivered the opinion of the Court.

The Commission entered complaint against the petitioner, March 1, 1921, and charged that the latter contrary to Section 7 of the Clayton Act, first acquired the stock of four competing corporations—Lockport Glass Company, Essex Glass Company, Travis Glass Company and Woodbury Glass Company—and thereafter took transfers of all the business and assets of the first three and caused their dissolution. . . . [T]he Commission ruled that the acquisitions of all these stocks were unlawful and ordered the petitioner to cease and desist from ownership, operation, management and control of the assets, properties, rights, etc., of the Lockport, Essex and Travis Glass Companies secured through such stock ownership, and to divest itself of the assets, properties, rights, etc., formerly held by them. Also, that it should divest itself of the stock of the Woodbury Glass Company.

The court below held that the last-named company was not in competition with petitioner within the meaning of the statute and modified the order accordingly. Therein we agree and to that extent affirm its decree.

The court further ruled, in effect, that as the stocks of the remaining three companies were unlawfully obtained and ownership of the assets came through them, the Commission properly ordered the holder so to dispossess itself of the properties as to restore prior lawful conditions. With this we cannot agree. When the Commission institutes a proceeding based upon the holding of stock contrary to Section 7 of the Clayton Act, its power is limited by Section 11 to an order requiring the guilty person to cease and desist from such violation, effectually to divest itself of the stock, and to make no further use of it. The Act has no application to ownership of a competitor's property and business obtained prior to any action by the Commission, even though this was brought about through stock unlawfully held. The purpose of the Act was to prevent continued holding of stock and the peculiar evils incident thereto. If purchase of property has produced an unlawful status a remedy is provided through the courts. . . . The Commission is without authority under such circumstances. Affirmed in part; reversed in part.

Mr. Justice Brandeis, with whom the Chief Justice, Mr. Justice Holmes and Mr. Justice Stone joined, dissented in part. . . .

United States v. Columbia Steel Company, et al.

334 U.S. 495 (1948)

Mr. Justice Reed delivered the opinion of the Court.

The United States brings this suit under Section 4 of the Sherman Act to enjoin United States Steel Corporation and its subsidiaries from purchasing the assets of the largest independent steel fabricator on the West Coast on the ground that such acquisition would violate Sections 1 and 2 of the Sherman Act. The complaint . . . charged that if the contract sale between United States Steel and Consolidated Steel Corporation were carried out, competition in the sale of rolled steel products and in fabricated steel products would be restrained, and that the contract indicated an effort on the part of United States Steel to attempt to monopolize the market in fabricated steel products. After a trial before a single judge in the district court, judgment was entered in favor of the defendants, and the government brought the case here by direct appeal. . . .

The steel production involved in this case may be spoken of as being divided into two stages; the production of rolled steel products and their fabrication into finished steel products. . . . The steel fabrication involved herein may also be divided into structural fabrication and plate fabrication. . . . Both plate and structural fabricated products are made to specifications for a particular purpose. . . . The facilities required for structural fabrication are quite different from those required for plate fabrication. . . .

United States Steel and its subsidiaries engage in the business of producing rolled steel products and in structural fabrication, but do no plate fabrication work. Consolidated Steel, the sale of whose assets the government seeks to enjoin, is engaged only in structural fabrication and plate fabrication. United States Steel with its subsidiaries is the largest producer of rolled steel products in the United States, with a total investment of more than a billion and a half dollars. During the ten year period 1937–1946 United States Steel produced almost exactly a third of all rolled steel products produced in the United States, and average sales for that period were nearly a billion and a half dollars. Consolidated, by contrast, had plants whose depreciated value was less than ten million dollars. During the five year period 1937–1941, Consolidated had average sales of only twenty million dollars, and the United States Steel committee which negotiated the terms of the purchase of Consolidated estimated that Consolidated's sales in the future would run to twenty-two million dollars annually and agreed with Consolidated on a purchase price of slightly in excess of eight million dollars. . . .

Columbia Steel, a wholly-owned subsidiary of United States Steel, has been the largest rolled steel producer in the Pacific Coast area since 1930, . . . and has also served as a selling agent for rolled steel subsidiaries of United States Steel, and for two subsidiaries of that company engaged in structural fabrication . . . , though neither it nor any other subsidiary of United States Steel in the Consolidated area was a fabricator of any kind. . . . Consolidated has sold its products during the past ten years in eleven states. . . . It is that market which the government views as significant in determining the extent of competition between United States Steel and Consolidated. It is not the usual Pacific and Mountain States groups employed by the Census. . . .

Rolled steel products have traditionally been sold on a basing point system. Prior to World War II rolled steel was sold on the West Coast at a price computed on the basis of eastern basing points, even though both United States Steel and Bethlehem Steel produced rolled steel products in California. Fabricators such as Consolidated thus did not get the full benefit of their proximity to the western market. The competitive disadvantages under which western fabricators worked is illustrated by the fact that United States Steel has been the largest seller of fabricated structural steel in the Consolidated market, even though it has no fabricating plants in the area. . . . This use of eastern basing points makes past figures on rolled steel products sales from producers in the Consolidated market unreliable in determining effective competition for the future sales of rolled steel in that market. United States Steel now uses Geneva as a basing point.

The urgent wartime demand for steel prompted the government to construct new rolled steel plants in the West. The largest of these plants was erected at Geneva, Utah, at a cost of nearly $200,000,000, and was designed, constructed, and operated by United States Steel for the account of the government. . . . On May 1, 1946, United States Steel submitted a bid for the Geneva plant of $47,500,000. . . . The bid stipulated that Geneva products would be sold with Geneva as a basing point. This would offer possibilities for a reduction in the price of rolled steel products to West Coast purchasers and their customers. . . . [T]he bid was silent as to the acquisition of fabricating facilities by United States Steel to provide a market for Geneva products.

On May 23, 1946, the War Assets Administration announced that the bid of United States Steel was accepted. . . .

On June 17, 1946, the Attorney General advised the War Assets Administration that the proposed sale did not in his opinion constitute a violation of the antitrust laws, and the sale was consummated two days thereafter. . . . The Attorney General noted that the ingot capacity of United States Steel had declined from 35.3% of the total national capacity in 1939 to 31.4% in 1946, and that if the Geneva plant were acquired, the percentage would be increased to 32.7%. Considering only the Pacific Coast and Mountain States, the acquisition of Geneva, the Attorney General said, would increase United States Steel's percentage of capacity in that area from 17.3% to 39%. United States Steel, however, estimated that on acquisition of Geneva it would have 51% of ingot capacity in the Pacific Coast area. . . .

Prior to the sale of the Geneva plant, Alden G. Roach, President of Consolidated, approached Fairless of United States Steel and indicated that he would like to sell the business of Consolidated. . . . Fairless replied that United States Steel . . . did not want to discuss the purchase of Consolidated until after the Geneva issue was decided. After the sale of Geneva was affected in June, Fairless spoke again with Roach and arranged to have a committee from United States Steel make an investigation of the Consolidated plants. . . . After further negotiations . . . a purchase agreement was executed on December 14 according to which Columbia agreed to buy the physical assets of Consolidated and four subsidiaries. Fairless testified on the witness stand that United States Steel's purpose in purchasing Consolidated was to assure a market for plates and shapes produced at Geneva, and Roach testified that Consolidated's purpose was to withdraw the stockholders' equity from the fabrication business with its cyclical fluctuations at a time when a favorable price could be realized.

. . . We turn first to the charge that the proposed purchase will lessen competition by excluding producers of rolled steel products other than United States Steel from supplying the requirements of Consolidated. Over the ten-year period from 1937 to 1946 Consolidated purchased over two million tons of rolled steel products, including the abnormally high wartime requirements. Whatever amount of rolled steel products Consolidated uses in the future will be supplied insofar as possible from other subsidiaries of United States Steel, and other producers of rolled steel products will lose Consolidated as a prospective customer.

The parties are in sharp dispute as to the size and nature of the market for rolled steel products with which Consolidated's consumption is to be compared. The appellees argue that rolled steel products are sold on a national scale, and that for the major producers the entire United States should be regarded as the market. Viewed from this standpoint, Consolidated's requirements are an insignificant fraction of the total market, less than $\frac{1}{2}$ of 1%. The government argues that the market must be more narrowly drawn. . . . If all sales of rolled steel products in the Consolidated market are considered, Consolidated's purchases of two million tons represent a little more than 3% of the total of 60 million tons. . . . If the comparable market is construed even more narrowly, and is restricted to the consumption of plates and shapes in the Consolidated market, figures for 1937 indicate that Consolidated's consumption of plates and shapes was 13% of the total. . . .

We read the record as showing that the trial court did not accept the theory that the comparable market was restricted to the demand for plates and shapes in the Consolidated area, but did accept the government's theory that the market was to be restricted to the total demand for rolled steel products in the eleven-state area. On that basis the trial court found that the steel requirements of Consolidated represented "a small part" of the consumption in the Consolidated area, that Consolidated was not a "substantial market" for rolled steel producers selling in competition with United States Steel, and that the acquisition of Consolidated would not injure any competitor of United States Steel engaged in the production and sale of rolled steel products in the Consolidated market or elsewhere. We recognize the difficulty of laying down a rule as to what areas or products are competitive, one with another. In this case and on this record we have circumstances that strongly indicate to us that rolled steel production and consumption in the Consolidated marketing area is the competitive area and product for consideration.

In analyzing the injury to competition resulting from the withdrawal of Consolidated as a purchaser of rolled steel products, we have been considering the acquisition of Consolidated as a step in the vertical integration of United States Steel. Regarded as a seller of fabricated steel products rather than as a purchaser of rolled steel products, however, the acquisition of Consolidated may be regarded as a step in horizontal integration as well, since United States Steel will broaden its facilities for steel fabrication through the purchase of Consolidated. . . . The parties agree that United States Steel does no plate fabrication, and that competition is restricted to fabricating structural steel products and iron. . . .

We turn first to the field of fabricated structural steel plates. As in the case of rolled steel, the appellee's claim that structural fabricators sell on a national scale, and that . . . for the period 1937–1942 . . . total bookings in the entire country were nearly 10,000,000 tons, of which Consolidated's share was only 84,533 tons. The government argues that competition is to be measured with reference to the eleven-state area in which Consolidated sells its products. Viewed on this basis, total bookings for the limited area for the six-year period were 1,665,698, of which United States Steel's share was 17% and Consolidated's 5%. The Government claims that Consolidated has become a more important factor since that period, and alleges that bookings for 1946 in the Consolidated market were divided among 90 fabricators, of which United States Steel had 13% and Consolidated and Bethlehem each had 11%. The next largest structural fabricators had 9%, 6% and 3% of the total. . . . The figures on which the government relies demonstrate that at least in the past competition in structural steel products has been conducted on a national scale. Five of the ten structural fabricators having the largest sales in the Consolidated market perform their fabrication operations outside the area, including United States Steel and Bethlehem Steel. Purchasers of fabricated structural products have been able to secure bids from fabricators throughout the country, and therefore statistics showing the share of United States Steel and Consolidated in the total consumption of fabricated structural products in any prescribed area are of little probative value in ascertaining the extent to which consumers of these products would be injured through elimination of competition between the two companies.

As in the case of rolled steel products, however, wartime developments have made prewar statistics of little relevance. The appellees urge three reasons why eastern fabricators will be at a competitive disadvantage with western fabricators for the western market: the availability of rolled steel products from the Geneva plant and other West Coast plants at a lower price, the increase in commercial freight rates on fabricated products, and the abolition of land grant rates.[1] . . . Whatever competition may have existed in the past between Consolidated and the two bridge subsidiaries of United States Steel, the appellees urge, will exist to a much lesser extent in the future. Consequently, even though the government may be correct in claiming that the eleven-state area is the proper market for measuring competition with Consolidated, the government may not at the same time claim that prewar statistics as to United States Steel's share of that market are of major significance.

[1] Land grant rates are special rates received by the government from certain railroads for shipments of government property on government bills of lading. IMS.

Apart from the question of the geographical size of the market, the appellees urge that the bookings for fabricated structural steel products are of little significance because Consolidated and United States Steel make different types of structural steel products. . . . The appellees support their argument with an elaborate statistical analysis of bids by the two companies. Those figures show that Consolidated and United States Steel submitted bids for the same project in a very small number of instances. . . . The government has introduced very little evidence . . . to show that in fact the types of structural steel products sold by Consolidated are similar to those sold by United States Steel.

The Government also argues that competition will be eliminated between Consolidated and National Tube in the sale of pipe. . . . [T]he government claims that Consolidated and National Tube compete on a nationwide scale in the field of large diameter pipe for oil and gas pipelines. Other types of pipe made by the two concerns are apparently not competitive as the government does not contest this assertion of the appellees. Consolidated in the past has specialized in comparatively light walled pipe for low pressure purposes such as irrigation and water transmission, whereas National Tube has made a heavy walled pipe for high pressure purposes which is used chiefly in the oil and gas industry. National Tube pipe is substantially cheaper to produce. The record does show, however, that in the last few years Consolidated has supplied large diameter pipe for oil and gas pipelines on at least four occasions in three of which National Tube also supplied part of the pipe requirements. Although the record does not show the extent of Consolidated's business in this field, one of the witnesses estimated that Consolidated's contract to furnish 90% of the pipe for the Trans-Arabian pipeline would run to almost $30,000,000. The appellees seek to minimize the importance of competition in this field by pointing out that the pipe to be used for the Trans-Arabian pipeline is 30 and 31 inches in diameter which is too large a size to be made by the seamless process employed by National Tube. . . . The appellees further claim that under normal circumstances Consolidated and National Tube would not compete in this field because Consolidated pipe sells for $30 a ton more than National pipe, and that Consolidated is able to sell its pipe only because of the inability of National Tube and other concerns to take on additional orders. . . .

. . . [T]he trial court . . . concluded that there was no substantial competition between National Tube and Consolidated in the sale of pipe. . . .

The trial court also concluded that the government had failed to prove that United States Steel had attempted to monopolize the business of fabricating steel products in the Consolidated market in violation of Section 2. The trial judge apparently was of the opinion that since the purchase of Consolidated did not constitute a violation of Section 1, it could not constitute a violation of Section 2, since every attempt to monopolize must also constitute an illegal restraint. In his findings the trial judge concluded that the purchase agreement was entered into "for sound business reasons" and with no intent to monopolize the production and sale of fabricated steel products.

In support of its position that the proposed contract violates Section 1 of the Sherman Act, the government urges that . . . the acquisition . . . excludes other producers of rolled steel products from the Consolidated market and constitutes an illegal restraint *per se* to which the rule of reason is inapplicable. Or, phrasing the argument differently, the government's contention seems to be that the acquisition of facilities which provide a controlled market for the output of the Geneva plant is a process of vertical integration and invalid *per se* under the Sherman Act. . . .

The government relies heavily on United States *v.* Yellow Cab Co. . . . and . . . concluded that the case stands for the proposition that it is illegal *per se* for a manufacturer to preempt any market for his goods through vertical integration provided that an "appreciable" amount of interstate commerce is involved.

We do not construe our holding in the Yellow Cab Case to make illegal the acquisition by United States Steel of this outlet for its rolled steel without consideration of its effect on the opportunities of other competitor producers to market their rolled steel. In discussing the charge in the Yellow Cab Case, we said that the fact that the conspirators were integrated did not insulate them from the act, not that corporate integraion violated the act. . . . Nothing in the Yellow Cab Case supports the theory that all exclusive dealing arrangements are illegal *per se*.

A subsidiary will in all probability deal only with its parent for goods the parent can furnish. That fact, however, does not make the acquisition invalid. When other elements of Sherman Act violations are present, the fact of corporate relationship is material and can be considered in the determination of whether restraint or attempt to restrain exists. . . .

The legality of the acquisition by United States Steel of a market outlet for its rolled steel through the purchase of the manufacturing facilities of Consolidated depends not merely upon the fact of that acquired control but also upon many other factors. Exclusive dealings for rolled steel between Consolidated and United States Steel, brought about by vertical integration or otherwise, are not illegal, at any rate until the effect of such control is to unreasonably restrict the opportunities of competitors to market their product. . . .

It seems clear to us that vertical integration, as such without more, cannot be held violative of the Sherman Act. It is an indefinite term without explicit meaning. Even in the iron industry where could a line be drawn—at the end of mining the ore, the production of the pig-iron or steel ingots, when the rolling mill operation is completed, fabrication on order, or some stage of manufacture into standard merchandise? No answer would be possible and therefore the extent of permissible integration must be governed, as other factors of Sherman Act violations, by the other circumstances of individual cases. Technological advances may easily require a basic industry plant to expand its processes into semi-finished or finished goods so as to produce desired articles in greater volume and with less expense.

It is not for courts to determine the course of the Nation's economic development. . . . If businesses are to be forbidden from entering into different stages of production that order must come from Congress, not the courts.

Applying the standards laid down in the Paramount case, we conclude that the so-called vertical integration resulting from the acquisition of Consolidated does not unreasonably restrict the opportunities of the competitor producers of rolled steel to market their product. We accept as the relevant competitive market the total demand for rolled steel products in the eleven-state area; over the past ten years Consolidated has accounted for only 3% of that demand, and if expectations as to the development of the western steel industry are realized, Consolidated's proportion may be expected to be lower than that figure in the future. Nor can we find a specific intent in the present case to accomplish an unreasonable restraint. . . .

. . . In determining what constitutes unreasonable restraint, we do not think the dollar volume is in itself of compelling significance; we look rather to the percentage of business controlled, the strength of the remaining competition, whether the action springs from business requirements or purpose to monopolize, the probable development of the industry, consumer demands, and other characteristics of the market. . . . The relative effect of percentage command of a market varies with the setting in which the factor is placed. . . .

We conclude that in this case the government has failed to prove that the elimination of competition between Consolidated and the structural fabricating subsidiaries of United States Steel constitutes an unreasonable restraint. If we make the doubtful assumption that the United States Steel could be expected in the future to sell 13% of the total of structural steel products in the Consolidated trade area and that Consolidated could be expected to sell 11%, we conclude that where we have the present unusual conditions of the western steel industry and in view of the facts of this case . . . it cannot be said that there would be an unreasonable restraint of trade. To hold this does not imply that additional acquisitions of fabricating facilities for structural steel would not become monopolistic. Notwithstanding, some differences as to the business of Consolidated and United States Steel in respect to the character of structural steel products fabricated by each, there is competition between the two for both light and heavy work. The western steel industry is developing. . . . [I]n view of the number of West Coast fabricators . . . and the ability of out-of-the-area fabricators to compete . . . , this acquisition is permissible.

We likewise conclude that the elimination of competition between Consolidated and National Tube (a United States Steel subsidiary) does not constitute an unreasonable restraint. Competition at the time of the contract was restricted to sale of large diameter pipe for oil and gas pipelines. . . . The record does show that in three instances Consolidated and National Tube each supplied pipe for a new pipeline. It is clear that these line pipe contracts were obtained by Consolidated in a seller's market. . . .

We turn last to the allegation of the government that United States Steel has attempted to monopolize the production and sale of fabricated steel products in the Consolidated market. We think that the trial court applied too narrow a test of this charge; even though the restraint effected may be reasonable under Section 1, it may constitute an attempt to monopolize forbidden by Section 2 if a specific intent to monopolize may be shown. To show that specific intent the government recites the long history of acquisitions of United States Steel, and argues that the present acquisition when viewed in the light of that history demonstrates the existence of a specific intent to monopolize. Although this Court held in 1920 that United States Steel had not violated Section 2 through the acquisition of 180 formerly independent concerns, we may look to those acquisitions as well as to the eight acquisitions from 1924 to 1943 to determine the intent of United States Steel in acquiring Consolidated.

We look not only to those acquisitions, however, but also to the latest acquisition—the government-owned plant at Geneva. We think that last acquisition is of significance in ascertaining the intent of United States Steel in acquiring Consolidated. The bid of United States Steel for the Geneva plant emphasized the importance of erecting finishing facilities to assure a market for Geneva's production . . . , and it is doubtful whether objections could be raised if United States Steel proposed to build instead of to buy from a competitor fabricating facilities similar to those possessed by Consolidated. The reasons given by Consolidated and United States Steel for the purchase and sale of the assets here involved seem not to involve any action condemned by the Sherman Act. Granting that the sale will to some extent affect competition, the acquisition of a firm outlet to absorb a portion of Geneva's rolled steel production seems to reflect a normal business purpose rather than a scheme to circumvent the law. United States Steel, despite its large sales, many acquisitions and leading position in the industry, has declined in the proportion of rolled steel products it manufactures in comparison with its early days. In 1901 it produced 50.1%; in 1911, 45.7%; in 1946, 30.4%. For the period 1937–1946, it produced 33.2%. Its size is impressive. Size has significance also in an appraisal of alleged violations of the Sherman Act. But the steel industry is also of impressive size and the welcome westward extension of that industry requires that the existing companies go into production there or abandon that market to other organizations. . . .

. . . [T]he government has not persuaded us that the proposed contract violates our public policy as stated in the Sherman Act.

The judgment of the District Court is affirmed.

Mr. Justice Douglas, with whom Mr. Justice Black, Mr. Justice Murphy, and Mr. Justice Rutledge, concurred, dissented. . . .

United States of America before Federal Trade Commission in the Matter of Pillsbury Mills, Inc.

Docket No. 6000 (1953)

Chairman Howrey delivered the opinion of the Commission.

The complaint in this case charges that respondent Pillsbury Mills, Inc. has violated Section 7 of the Clayton Act, as amended, by acquiring the assets of two of its competitors, namely, Ballard and Ballard Company and Duff's Baking Mix Division of American Home Products Corporation. It alleges that Pillsbury and Duff were, prior to the acquisitions, leaders throughout the United States (including the southeast) in the sale of flour-base mixes, and that Pillsbury and Ballard were leaders in the southeastern part of the United States in the sale of family flour, bakery flour, and mixes. . . .

Respondent Pillsbury is the second largest flour miller in the United States. Prior to the acquisition it was the 2nd largest seller of family flour, the 2nd largest seller of flour-base mixes, the 3rd largest seller of bakery flour, and among the 15 largest sellers of formula feed in the United States. . . .

On June 12, 1951, respondent acquired all the assets of Ballard for approximately $5,172,000. On March 7, 1952, it acquired Duff for about $2,238,000.

By these acquisitions respondent increased its capacity for milling flour approximately 6 percent, for manufacturing mixes about 40 percent, and for manufacturing commercial feed by almost 57 percent; its total sales of bakery flour increased 2.8 percent, family flour 23.8 percent, feeds 34.4 percent, and mixes 40.9 . . . percent; its feed position improved from "among the first fifteen" to tenth place. . . .

Attorneys supporting the complaint contend that the foregoing shows a "substantiality" of acquisitions sufficient to bring the mergers within the "substantiality doctrine" of the *Standard Stations* and *International Salt* cases.

The record, however, contains much more in the way of economic and business facts—facts about Pillsbury, Ballard and Duff, about their respective shares of the market and about the structure, behavior and characteristics of the flour market in general.

During the 11-year period ending in 1951 Pillsbury's net sales grew from approximately $47,000,000 to $224,500,000; its total assets increased from $30,000,000 to $95,500,000; and its net worth grew from $23,000,000 to $42,000,000. Its history during this period was marked by a number of acquisitions. . . .

Duff, in 1950, was the 5th largest seller of mixes in the United States and the 5th largest seller of mixes in the southeast. . . .

By the acquisitions respondent was promoted in the southeastern area from 5th to 2nd place in family flour, from 3rd to 1st place in bakery flour, and increased its 1st place position in the mix market in the southeast from 22.7 percent to almost 45 percent. . . .

In 1945 the ten largest firms in the United States, measured by milling capacity, controlled about 34 percent of the industry's capacity. In 1951 the ten largest companies—the same firms as in 1945—had 40 percent of the capacity. Between 1945 and 1951, while the industry was losing about 67,000 cwt. in daily capacity, the ten largest companies increased their daily capacity by 57,000 cwt. Of this total increase, over 39,000 cwt. or 68 percent resulted from acquisitions. If the acquisition of Ballard by Pillsbury is included, the daily capacity gain is 62,000 cwt. with acquisitions accounting for over 71 percent of the increase. . . .

For many years Ballard had offered effective competition to Pillsbury in the southeast. In 1945 the Ballard flour mill had the largest capacity of any mill in this area. In 1951 it shared this distinction with the General Mills plant in Louisville. At the time it was acquired by Pillsbury it owned and operated one of the largest and most modern formula feed plants in the southeast. The Ballard brands of flour, formula feeds and prepared mixes enjoyed widespread consumer acceptance. Ballard had shown a profit for many years prior to its acquisition. It had sizable net earnings for the eleven month period just before its acquisition. It was an important factor in the competitive market. . . .

Respondent's and Ballard's prices differed in different locations prior to the acquisition. Afterwards the prices of the two brands became identical. . . .

Three questions are presented by brief and argument on appeal:

1. Do recent cases decided under Section 3 of the Clayton Act[2] apply to Section 7 cases; that is, where "substantiality" of the acquisition has been established, is it necessary to examine economic consequences or determine the probable effects of the acquisition?

2. If Section 3 cases are not applicable, what tests do apply under Section 7; do Sherman Act tests apply or does Section 7 have tests of its own?

[2] The cases referred to are: Standard Oil Co. of California *v.* United States; International Salt Co. *v.* United States; United States *v.* Richfield Oil Corp.; Automatic Canteen Co. of America *v.* Federal Trade Commission. IMS.

3. Does the record show *prima facie*, by reliable evidence, that the effect of the acquisitions may be substantially to lessen competition or tend to create a monopoly in certain market areas?

I

The attorneys supporting the complaint rely, in the first place, on the "substantiality" doctrine of International Salt, Standard Stations and other Section 3 cases. To be on the safe side, however, they also introduced proof of market structure and characteristics which they claim are sufficient, even if the Commission rejects the substantiality theory, to show that respondent's acquisitions will substantially lessen competition.

Section 3 of the Clayton Act prohibits the use of tying and exclusive dealing contracts the effect of which "may be to substantially lessen competition or tend to create a monopoly." The International Salt case . . . held that the test of potential injury to competition was satisfied by proof that in one year the company had sold for use in its machines 119,000 tons of industrial salt valued at $500,000. Such a market, the Court said, was not "insignificant or insubstantial" and it is "unreasonable, *per se*, to foreclose competitors from any substantial market."

In the Standard Stations case . . . the Court appeared to read out of the qualifying clause any real consideration of the effect upon competition and declared that the requirement was satisfied by proof that a substantial share of the market was affected by the practice. . . . $57,646,233 worth of gasoline, amounting to 6.7 percent of the total, was held to be a "substantial share."

Although there is a considerable difference between the two cases, it may be assumed for present purposes that in each case the Court held that the qualifying clause of Section 3 is satisfied by proof that competition has been foreclosed in a substantial share of the line of commerce affected.

It does not follow, however, that because the qualifying clauses of Sections 3 and 7 are expressed in the same language they prescribe the same tests. . . .

Accordingly, the respective tests prescribed by Sections 3 and 7 are to be determined in the light of the purpose of each section.

The primary purpose of Section 3 is the protection of buyers and sellers in the marketing process—to guarantee to buyers the right to handle any goods they see fit, and to sellers the opportunity to obtain the business of any buyer whose trade they wish to seek.

Section 7, on the other hand, is directed toward adverse changes in competitive patterns that may result from mergers. It is concerned with the effects of acquisitions on the character of competition, with the maintenance of competition in every market to the end that business rivalry may produce better products at lower costs.

While both sections are designed to protect the competitive process, they reach this goal by different routes—one by protecting the seller and buyer segment of our economy, the other by protecting competition on an over-all basis.

The impact of a tying contract or a requirements contract is different from that of an acquisition. The force of the former falls principally upon buyers or upon competitors of the company which imposes the contract, the effect of such contracts is thus to cut off these competitors from what would otherwise be part of their natural market. In contrast, an acquisition seldom has such an immediate impact upon competitors. The reason that acquisitions are, under certain circumstances, to be regarded as illegal is not because of their effect on buying and selling practices but because of their probable effect on competition.

Moreover, a further distinction can be drawn from the fact that tying and exclusive dealing contracts are frequently coercive, while acquisitions are usually voluntary in nature.

Competition cannot be directly measured; no single set of standards can be applied to the whole range of American industries. No single characteristic of an acquisition would of itself be sufficient to determine its effect on competition. For this reason it would not be sufficient to show that an acquiring and an acquired company together control a substantial amount of sales, or that a substantial portion of commerce is affected.[3]

Much as the simplified test laid down in Standard Stations and International Salt may aid in the presentation of proof in cases under Section 3, it is not in itself a reliable guide for the Commission in carrying out its long-run responsibility to prevent reductions in competition through acquisitions of assets or stock.

Furthermore, neither case can be construed as depriving the Federal Trade Commission, as an administrative agency, of the right to examine relevant economic factors and competitive effects (even in Section 3 cases) in the event it desires to do so. . . .

As we understand it, the Federal Trade Commission has a great . . . task . . . in administering the broad provisions of Section 7 of the Clayton Act. There must be a case-by-case examination of all relevant factors in order to ascertain the probable economic consequences. . . .

II

This does not mean that we are thrown back on Sherman Act tests. In fact, one of the purposes of amended Section 7 was to re-establish the difference between Sherman Act and Clayton Act violations and to restate the legislative view, largely repudiated by the case law, that the tests of the Sherman Act have no proper place in the application of Section 7.

[3] The attorneys supporting the complaint suggest the following test for Section 7 cases: "Where a leading factor in the relevant market having a substantial share of that market, acquires another factor in that market also having a substantial share of that market, the inference arises that competition may be substantially lessened in the lines of commerce involved."

. . . Market control, restraint of trade, injury to competition, tendency toward monopoly are the subjects of both the Sherman and Clayton Acts. But the standard of illegality is different; otherwise Congress would have been wasting its time by enacting duplicating legislation. The difference is usually said to be that under Section 7 the undesired condition may not yet be in existence; there is only a reasonable probability that it will come to pass if nothing is done to stop it. This, of course, was the underlying purpose of the original Clayton Act. It was designed to "supplement" the Sherman Act, to prohibit practices which singly and in themselves were not covered by that act, to arrest potential violations of the Sherman Act in their incipiency and before consummation. . . .

Putting aside the broad concepts of competition and monopoly, the essential difference seems to be that the Clayton Act requires a lower standard of proof of the same kind of facts—"evidence which is quantitatively or qualitatively less impressive than where the Sherman Act is invoked." More specifically, the merger in United States *v.* Columbia Steel Co., 334 U.S. 495 (1948), which was examined under the Sherman Act, would probably not have been approved had new Section 7 been in existence and invoked against it.

Section 7, before it was amended, prohibited corporate acquisitions of stock which might have any one of the following effects: (1) substantial lessening of competition between the merging companies, (2) restraint of commerce in any section or community, or (3) tendency to create a monopoly. This language, if taken literally, would have precluded almost every merger where competition existed between the two merging companies. As we have indicated, the courts shied away from this drastic interpretation and invoked the rule of reason of the Sherman Act.

Section 7, as amended, prohibits the acquisition of assets as well as stock, thus closing the long-standing loophole on this point. The acquisition is prohibited "where in any line of commerce in any section of the country, the effect of such acquisition may be substantially to lessen competition, or to tend to create a monopoly."

The earlier test as to competition between the acquiring and acquired companies is eliminated and so is the earlier alternative test of "to restrain such commerce in any section or community." The elimination of the first test eliminates the possibility of a strict and literal interpretation which would strike down local and unimportant acquisitions; the elimination of the second test removes any likelihood that broad Sherman Act tests will again be applied. . . .

As we see it, amended Section 7 sought to reach the mergers embraced within its sphere in their incipiency, and to determine their legality by tests of its own. These are not the rule of reason of the Sherman Act, that is, unreasonable restraint of trade, nor are Section 7 prohibitions to be added to the list of *per se* violations. Somewhere in between is Section 7, which prohibits acts that "may" happen in a particular market, that looks to "a reasonable probability," to "substantial" economic consequences, to acts that "tend" to a result. Over all is the broad purpose to supplement the Sherman Act and to reach incipient restraints.

While these are far from specific standards—specificity would in any event be inconsistent with the "convenient vagueness" of antitrust prohibitions—they can, we believe, be applied on a case-by-case basis. We think the present case is the type Congress had in mind—one that presents a set of facts which would be insufficient under the Sherman Act but nonetheless establishes, *prima facie*, a violation of Section 7 of the Clayton Act.

III

. . . A few words should be said about the problem of proof in antitrust cases. Competition is a complex and constantly changing phenomenon. It has never been sharply defined. Injury to competition, as distinguished from injury to a competitor, is seldom capable of proof by direct testimony and may therefore be inferred from all the surrounding circumstances. "An antitrust charge may . . . be proved by circumstantial evidence, and the circumstances may include actions affecting any of the broad issues of fact posed in the complaint."

Analysis of the competitive effects of an acquisition should begin, we believe, with the relevant facts concerning the competitive pattern of the industry as a whole and its markets, particularly in the period preceding the acquisition. From such facts, and from information about the specific merger, it should be possible to determine what changes the acquisition can be expected to make in the character of competition in the markets concerned.

Counsel supporting the complaint say they have made such an analysis; that the evidence was not limited to the application of Section 3 cases to Section 7, but included in addition "an extensive showing of the character of the markets and the market setting in which the acquisitions took place.". . .

This evidence establishes, it seems to us, a *prima facie* case. The pattern of competition in the southeast, particularly in the cities, has undergone a considerable change as a result of the mergers. Unless explained, contradicted or rebutted, and respondent will have every opportunity to do this when it puts in its case, it is a change which constitutes a move away from healthy competitive conditions.

There is nothing in the record to indicate that the mergers will at present convert the industry in the southeast from a competitive to a noncompetitive pattern. The inference, in fact, must be to the contrary inasmuch as large national distributors, such as, General Mills and Quaker Oats, and large regional distributors remain to furnish effective competition to Pillsbury Mills. However, in the urban markets at least, the mergers lead in the direction of what is sometimes called oligopolistic or "monopolistic" competition, that is, to a situation where the remaining competition in the particular market is between big companies.

If, for example, respondent should continue to acquire competitors at the rate it has since 1940, and other large companies should do the same, the urban markets in the southeast may come to be dominated by a few large milling companies. This, of course, has been the trend in other industries. In some of them, under the policy of the Sherman Act, competition between the big companies continues to protect the consumer interest. But, as we understand it, it was this sort of trend that Congress condemned and desired to halt when it adopted the new Clayton Act anti-merger provision.

This matter, therefore, should be remanded to the hearing examiner for further consideration in conformity with this opinion.

Mr. Mead, while concurring in the result, will file a separate concurring opinion.

PART II

Loose-Knit Confederations

Chapter 3 — DIRECT PRICE-FIXING AGREEMENTS

Cases instituted under Section 1 of the Sherman Act do, in a sense, fall into a simpler and far more consistent pattern than those brought under Section 2. With the exception of the Appalachian Coals decision, the Court has steadily refused to consider the "reasonableness" of direct price fixing agreements, holding instead that these agreements among individual competitors were *per se* violations of the law. This, combined with the adoption of a Section 2 rule of reason in the Standard Oil of New Jersey decision presented above, introduced into the law what has come to be called the "double standard." In other words, while agreements among individual competitors concerning matters such as price policy have been held to be illegal in and of themselves, consolidations which yielded equal or greater market power have been tested for their "reasonableness." Feeling among economists on the double standard is divided. Two otherwise widely divergent groups agree that it is inconsistent to permit a firm to accomplish by consolidation what it is not permitted to do by contract. They part company, however, on the method of eliminating this "inconsistency." Some feel that the double standard can best be eliminated by abolishing the rule of reason used in Section 2 cases and thereby expanding the area of *per se* violation. Others propose to subject Section 1 as well as Section 2 cases to a test of reasonableness, a proposal which would—if adopted—allow defendants to justify conspiratorial activities by showing that favorable economic results were produced. A third group of economists and lawyers, who might be called "traditionalists," contend that the double standard is necessary if we are to maintain a dynamic, progressive and noncartelized economy. To accomplish this they feel nothing must be done to penalize business size which may result from successful and fair competition only, while at the same time we must continue to hold any and all attempts to mitigate the force of competition through collusion and conspiracy to be violations of the law.

The cases presented below are intended to show court attitudes towards price-fixing agreements. Although with the exception of Appalachian Coals, price-fixing conspiracies were uniformly condemned, the force of the opinions varies. Thus, where the Trenton Potteries' condemnation hinged at least in part on the market power of the conspirators, the later and controlling Socony-Vacuum decision held any attempt to influence prices, regardless of the market power of the group, to be illegal. Only in the Appalachian Coals case did the Court explicitly attempt to consider the "reasonableness" of price-fixing agreements, and even here one might contend that it was the lack of market power, not the "reasonableness" of the agreement, which prevented condemnation. In any event, the Socony-Vacuum decision marked the revival of the double standard, which was eventually attacked from another direction in the Alcoa case (see Chapter 1).

Addyston Pipe and Steel Company v. *United States*

175 U.S. 211 (1899)

Note: This case involved an agreement among the six leading manufacturers of iron pipe to divide the market into several regional monopolies, and to fix prices.

Mr. Justice Peckham . . . delivered the opinion of the Court. . . .

We are thus brought to the question whether the contract or combination proved in this case is one which is either a direct restraint or a regulation of commerce among the several States or with foreign nations contrary to the act of Congress [the Sherman Act]. It is objected on the part of the appellants that even if it affected interstate commerce the contract or combination was only a reasonable restraint upon a ruinous competition among themselves, and was formed only for the purpose of protecting the parties thereto in securing prices for their product that was fair and reasonable to themselves and the public. . . .

. . . [W]e are of the opinion that the agreement or combination was not one which simply secured for its members fair and reasonable prices for the article dealt in by them. Even if the objection thus set up would, if well founded in fact, constitute a defense, we agree with the Circuit Court of Appeals in its statement of the special facts upon this branch of the case and with its opinion thereon as set forth by Circuit Judge Taft, as follows:

The defendants being manufacturers and vendors of cast-iron pipe entered into a combination to raise the price for pipe . . . [in] considerably more than three-quarters of the territory of the United States, . . . significantly called by the associates 'pay' territory. . . . Within the margin of the freight per ton which Eastern manufacturers would have to pay to deliver pipe in 'pay' territory, the defendants, by controlling two-thirds of the output in 'pay' territory, were practically able to fix prices. . . . The most cogent evidence that they had this power is the fact everywhere apparent in the record that they exercised it. . . .

The defendants were by their combination therefore able to deprive the public in a large territory of the advantage otherwise accruing to them from the proximity of defendants' pipe factories and, by keeping prices just low enough to prevent competition by Eastern manufacturers, to compel the public to pay an increase over what the price would have been if fixed by competition between defendants, nearly equal to the advantage in freight rates enjoyed by defendants over Eastern competitors. The defendants acquired this power by voluntarily agreeing to sell only at prices fixed by their committee and by allowing the highest bidder at the secret 'auction pool' to become the lowest bidder of them at the public letting. Now, the restraint thus imposed on themselves was only partial. It did not cover the United States. There was not a complete monopoly. It was tempered by the fear of competition and it affected only a part of the price. But this certainly does not take the contract of association out of the annulling effect of the rule against monopolies. . . .

It has been earnestly pressed upon us that the prices at which the cast-iron pipe was sold in 'pay' territory were reasonable. . . . We do not think the issue an important one, because . . . we do not think that at common law there is any question of reasonableness open to the courts with reference to such a contract. Its tendency was certainly to give defendants the power to charge unreasonable prices, had they chosen to do so. But if it were important we should unhesitatingly find that the prices charged in the instances which were in evidence were unreasonable. . . .

The facts thus set forth show conclusively that the effect of the combination was to enhance prices beyond a sum which was reasonable. . . .

The views above expressed lead generally to an affirmance of the judgment of the Court of Appeals [but to] the extent that the present decree includes in its scope the enjoining of defendants thus situated from combining in regard to contracts for selling pipe in their own State, it is modified and limited to that portion of the combination or agreement which is interstate in character. As thus modified the decree is affirmed.

United States v. *Trenton Potteries Co. et al.*

273 U.S. 392 (1927)

Mr. Justice Stone delivered the opinion of the Court.

Respondents, 20 individuals and 23 corporations, were convicted in the District Court of violating the Sherman Antitrust Law. . . . The indictment was in two counts. The first charged a combination to fix and maintain uniform prices for the sale of sanitary pottery, in restraint of interstate commerce; the second, a combination to restrain interstate commerce by limiting sales of pottery to a special group known to respondents as "legitimate jobbers." On appeal, the Circuit Court of Appeals reversed the conviction on both counts on the ground that there were errors in the conduct of the trial. . . . This court granted certiorari. . . .

Respondents, engaged in the manufacture or distribution of 82% of the vitreous pottery fixtures produced in the United States for use in bathrooms and lavatories, were members of a trade organization known as the Sanitary Potters' Association. . . .

There is no contention here that the verdict was not supported by sufficient evidence that respondents, controlling some 82% of the business of manufacturing and distributing in the United States vitreous pottery, combined to fix prices and to limit sales in interstate commerce to jobbers.

The issues raised here by the Government's specification of errors relate only to the decision of the Circuit Court of Appeals upon its review of certain rulings of the District Court made in the course of its trial. It is urged that the court below erred in holding in effect that the trial court should have submitted to the jury the question whether the price agreement complained of constituted an unreasonable restraint of trade. . . .

The trial court charged, in submitting the case to the jury that, if it found the agreements or combination complained of, it might return a verdict of guilty without regard to the reasonableness of the prices fixed, or the good intentions of the combining units, whether prices were actually lowered or raised or whether sales were restricted to the special jobbers, since both agreements of themselves were unreasonable restraints. . . . The court below held specifically that the trial court erred and held in effect that the charge as given on this branch of the case was erroneous. . . . The question therefore to be considered here is whether the trial judge correctly withdrew from the jury the consideration of the reasonableness of the particular restraints charged.

That only restraints upon interstate commerce which are unreasonable are prohibited by the Sherman Law was the rule laid down by the opinions of this Court in the Standard Oil and Tobacco Cases. But it does not follow that agreements to fix or maintain prices are reasonable restraints and therefore permitted by the statute, merely because the prices themselves are reasonable. Reasonableness is not a concept of definite and unchanging content. Its meaning necessarily varies in the different fields of the law, because it is used as a convenient summary of the dominant considerations which control in the application of legal doctrines. Our view of what is a reasonable restraint of commerce is controlled by the recognized purpose of the Sherman Law itself. Whether this type of restraint is reasonable or not must be judged in part at least, in the light of its effect on competition, for whatever difference of opinion there may be among economists as to the social and economic desirability of an unrestrained competitive system, it cannot be doubted that the Sherman Law and the judicial decisions interpreting it are based upon the assumption that the public interest is best protected from the evils of monopoly and price control by the maintenance of competition. . . .

The aim and result of every price-fixing agreement, if effective, is the elimination of one form of competition. The power to fix prices, whether reasonably exercised or not, involves power to control the market and to fix arbitrary and unreasonable prices. The reasonable price fixed today may through economic and business changes become the unreasonable price of tomorrow. Once established, it may be maintained unchanged because of the absence of competition secured by the agreement for a price reasonable when fixed. Agreements which create such potential power may well be held to be in themselves unreasonable or unlawful restraints, without the necessity of minute inquiry whether a particular price is reasonable or unreasonable as fixed and without placing on the Government in enforcing the Sherman Law the burden of ascertaining from day to day whether it has become unreasonable through the mere variation of economic conditions. Moreover, in the absence of express legislation requiring it, we should hesitate to adopt a construction making the difference between legal and illegal conduct in the field of business relations depend upon so uncertain a test as whether prices are reasonable —a determination which can be satisfactorily made only after a complete survey of our economic organization and a choice between rival philosophies. . . .

The charge of the trial court, viewed as a whole, fairly submitted to the jury the question whether a price-fixing agreement as described in the first count was entered into by the respondents. Whether the prices actually agreed upon were reasonable or unreasonable was immaterial in the circumstances charged in the indictment and necessarily found by the verdict. The requested charge[1] . . . [was] inapplicable to the case in hand and rightly refused. . . .

Mr. Justice Van Devanter, Mr. Justice Sutherland and Mr. Justice Butler dissented.

Mr. Justice Brandeis took no part in the consideration or decision of this case.

Appalachian Coals, Inc. v. *United States*

288 U.S. 344 (1933)

Mr. Chief Justice Hughes delivered the opinion of the Court.

This suit was brought to enjoin a combination alleged to be in restraint of interstate commerce in bituminous coal and in attempted monopolization of part of that commerce, in violation of Sections 1 and 2 of the Sherman Antitrust Act. . . . The District Court, composed of three Circuit Judges, made detailed findings of fact and entered final decree granting the injunction. . . .

Defendants, other than Appalachian Coals, Inc., are 137 producers of

---

[1] Defendants had requested that the court charge the following: "The essence of the law is injury to the public. It is not every restraint of competition and not every restraint of trade that works an injury to the public; it is only an undue and unreasonable restraint of trade that has such an effect and is deemed unlawful." IMS.

bituminous coal in eight districts (called for convenience Appalachian territory). . . . In 1929 (the last year for which complete statistics were available) the total production of bituminous coal east of the Mississippi River was 484,786,000 tons, of which defendants mined 58,011,367 tons, or 11.96 percent. In the so-called Appalachian territory and the immediately surrounding area, the total production was 107,008,209 tons, of which defendants' production was 54.21 percent, or 64 percent if the output of "captive" mines (16,455,001 tons) be deducted. With a further deduction of 12,000,000 tons of coal produced in the immediately surrounding territory, which however, is not essentially different from the particular area described in these proceedings as Appalachian territory, defendants' production in the latter region was found to amount to 74.4 percent.

The challenged combination lies in the creation by the defendant producers of an exclusive selling agency. This agency is the defendant Appalachian Coals, Inc., which may be designated as the Company. Defendant producers own all its capital stock, their holdings being in proportion to their production. The majority of the common stock, which has exclusive voting right, is held by seventeen defendants. By uniform contracts, separately made, each defendant producer constitutes the Company an exclusive agent for the sale of all coal (with certain exceptions) which the producer mines in Appalachian territory. The Company agrees to establish standard classifications, to sell all the coal of all its principals at the best prices obtainable and, if all cannot be sold, to apportion orders upon a stated basis. . . .

The Government's contention, which the District Court sustained, is that the plan violates the Sherman Antitrust Act—in the view that it eliminates competition among the defendants themselves and also gives the selling agency power substantially to affect and control the price of bituminous coal in many interstate markets. . . .

Defendants insist that the primary purpose of the formation of the selling agency was to increase the sale, and thus the production, of Appalachian coal through better methods of distribution, intensive advertising and research; to achieve economies in marketing, and to eliminate abnormal, deceptive and destructive trade practices. . . . Defendants contend that the evidence establishes that the selling agency will not have the power to dominate or fix the price of coal in any consuming market; that the price of coal will continue to be set in an open competitive market; and that their plan by increasing the sale of bituminous coal from Appalachian territory will promote, rather than restrain, interstate commerce.

First. There is no question as to the test to be applied in determining the legality of the defendants' conduct. The purpose of the Sherman Antitrust Act is to prevent undue restraints of interstate commerce, to maintain its appropriate freedom in the public interest, to afford protection from the subversive or coercive influences of monopolistic endeavor. . . . Its general phrases, interpreted to attain its fundamental objects, set up the essential standard of reasonableness. They call for vigilance in the detection and frustration of all efforts unduly to restrain the free course of interstate commerce, but they do not seek to establish a mere delusive liberty either by making impossible the normal and fair expansion of that commerce or the adoption of reasonable measures to protect it from injurious and destructive practices and to promote competition upon a sound basis. . . .

In applying this test, a close and objective scrutiny of particular conditions and purposes is necessary in each case. Realities must dominate the judgment. The mere fact that the parties to an agreement eliminate competition between themselves is not enough to condemn it. . . . The question of the application of the statute is one of intent and effect, and is not to be determined by arbitrary assumptions. It is therefore necessary in this instance to consider the economic conditions peculiar to the coal industry, the practices which have obtained, the nature of defendants' plan of making sales, the reasons which led to its adoption, and the probable consequences of the carrying out of that plan in relation to market prices and other matters affecting the public interest in interstate commerce in bituminous coal.

Second. The findings of the District Court, upon abundant evidence, leave no room for doubt as to the economic condition of the coal industry. That condition, as the District Court states, "for many years has been indeed deplorable.". . . And in a graphic summary of the economic situation, the court found that "numerous producing companies have gone into bankruptcy or into the hands of receivers, many mines have been shut down, the number of days of operation per week have been greatly curtailed, wages to labor have been substantially lessened, and the States in which coal producing companies are located have found it increasingly difficult to collect taxes."

Third. The findings also fully disclose the proceedings of the defendants in formulating their plan and the reasons for its adoption. . . . The District Court found that "the evidence tended to show that other selling agencies with a control of at least 70 percent of the production in their respective districts will be organized if the petition in this case is dismissed"; that in that event "there will result an organization in most of the districts whose coal is or may be competitive with Appalachian coal; but the testimony tends to show that there will still be substantial, active competition in the sale of coal in all markets in which Appalachian coal is sold."

Defendants refer to the statement of purposes in their published plan of organization—that it was intended to bring about "a better and more orderly marketing of the coals from the region to be served by this company. . . ."

No attempt was made to limit production. The producers decided that it could not legally be limited and, in any event, it could not be limited practically. . . .

Fourth. Voluminous evidence was received with respect to the effect of defendants' plan upon market prices. As the plan has not gone into operation, there are no actual results upon which to base conclusions. The question is necessarily one of prediction. The court below found that, as between defendants themselves, competition would be eliminated. . . .

The more serious question relates to the effect of the plan upon competition between defendants and other producers. As already noted, the District Court found that "the great bulk" of the coal produced in Appalachian territory is sold "in the highly competitive region east of the Mississippi river and north of the Ohio river under an adverse freight rate." Elaborate statistics were introduced. . . . It would be impossible to make even a condensed statement of this evidence, . . . but an examination of it fails to disclose an adequate basis for the conclusion that the operation of the defendants' plan would produce an injurious effect upon competitive conditions, in view of the vast volume of coal available, the conditions of production, and the network of transportation facilities at immediate command. . . .

Fifth. We think that the evidence requires the following conclusions:

(1) With respect to defendant's purposes, we find no warrant for determining that they were other than those they declared. Good intentions will not save a plan otherwise objectionable, but knowledge of actual intent is an aid in the interpretation of facts and prediction of consequences. . . .

The unfortunate state of the industry would not justify any attempt unduly to restrain competition or to monopolize, but the existing situation prompted defendants to make, and the statute did not preclude them from making, an honest effort to remove abuses, to make competition fairer, and thus to promote the essential interests of commerce. The interests of producers and consumers are interlinked. When industry is grievously hurt, when producing concerns fail, when unemployment mounts and communities dependent upon profitable production are prostrated, the wells of commerce go dry. So far as actual purposes are concerned, the conclusion of the court below was amply supported that defendants were engaged in a fair and open endeavor to aid the industry in a measurable recovery from its plight. The inquiry then, must be whether despite this objective the inherent nature of their plan was such as to create an undue restraint upon interstate commerce.

(2) The question thus presented chiefly concerns the effect upon prices. The evidence as to the conditions of the production and distribution of bituminous coal, the available facilities for its transportation, the extent of developed mining capacity, makes it impossible to conclude that defendants through the operation of their plan will be able to fix

the price of coal in the consuming markets. . . . Defendants' coal will continue to be subject to active competition. In addition to the coal actually produced and seeking markets in competition with defendants' coal, enormous additional quantities will be within reach and can readily be turned into the channels of trade if an advance of price invites that course. . . .

The contention is, and the court below found, that while defendants could not fix market prices, the concerted action would "affect" them, that is, that it would have a tendency to stabilize market prices and to raise them to a higher level than would otherwise obtain. But the facts found do not establish, and the evidence fails to show, that any effect will be produced which in the circumstances of this industry will be detrimental to fair competition. . . .

The fact that the correction of abuses may tend to stabilize a business, or to produce fairer price levels, does not mean that the abuses should go uncorrected or that cooperative endeavor to correct them necessarily constitutes an unreasonable restraint of trade. The intelligent conduct of commerce through the acquisition of full information of all relevant facts may properly be sought by the cooperation of those engaged in trade, although stabilization of trade and more reasonable prices may be the result. . . .

Decisions cited in support of a contrary view were addressed to very different circumstances from those presented here. They dealt with combinations which on the particular facts were found to impose unreasonable restraints through the suppression of competition, and in actual operation had that effect. . . .

(3) The question remains whether, despite the foregoing conclusions, the fact that the defendants' plan eliminates competition between themselves is alone sufficient to condemn it. Emphasis is placed upon defendants' control of about 73 percent of the commercial production in Appalachian territory. But only a small percentage of that production is sold in that territory. . . . Defendants insist that . . . no valid objection could have been interposed under the Sherman Act if the defendants had eliminated competition between themselves by a complete integration of their mining properties in a single ownership. . . . We agree that there is no ground for holding defendants' plan illegal merely because they have not integrated their properties and have chosen to maintain their independent plants, seeking not to limit but rather to facilitate production. We know of no public policy, and none is suggested by the terms of the Sherman Act, that, in order to comply with the law, those engaged in industry should be driven to unify their properties and businesses, in order to correct abuses which may be corrected by less drastic measures. Public policy might indeed be deemed to point in a different direction. . . . The argument that integration may be considered a normal expansion of business, while a combination of independent producers in

selling agency should be treated as abnormal—that one is a
enterprise and the other is not—makes but an artificial distinc-
Antitrust Act aims at substance. Nothing in theory or experi-
ates that the selection of a common selling agency to represent
of producers should be deemed to be more abnormal than the
formation of a huge corporation bringing various independent units into
one ownership. Either may be prompted by business exigencies, and the
statute gives to neither a special privilege. The question in either case is
whether there is an unreasonable restraint of trade or an attempt to monopolize. If there is, the combination cannot escape because it has chosen
corporate form; and, if there is not, it is not to be condemned because
of the absence of corporate integration. . . .

We recognize . . . that the case has been tried in advance of the operation of defendants' plan. . . . If in actual operation it should prove to
be an undue restraint upon interstate commerce, . . . the decision upon
the present record should not preclude the Government from seeking the
remedy which would be suited to such a state of facts. . . .

The decree will be reversed and . . . the court shall retain jurisdiction of the cause. . . . Reversed and remanded.

Mr. Justice McReynolds thinks that the court below reached the
proper conclusion and that its decree should be affirmed.

United States v. Socony-Vacuum Oil Company

310 U.S. 150 (1940)

Mr. Justice Douglas delivered the opinion of the Court.

Respondents were convicted by a jury . . . under an indictment
charging violations of Section 1 of the Sherman Antitrust Act. . . . The
Circuit Court of Appeals reversed and remanded for a new trial. . . .
The case is here on a petition and cross-petition for certiorari, both of
which we granted because of the public importance of the issues
raised. . . .

The indictment was returned in December 1936 in the United States
District Court for the Western District of Wisconsin. It charges that certain major oil companies, selling gasoline in the Mid-Western area . . . ,
(1) "combined and conspired together for the purpose of artificially raising and fixing the tank car prices of gasoline" in the "spot markets" in
East Texas and Mid-Continent fields; (2) "have artificially raised and
fixed said spot market tank car prices of gasoline and have maintained said
prices at artificially high and non-competitive levels, and at levels agreed
upon among them and have thereby intentionally increased and fixed the
tank car prices of gasoline contracted to be sold and sold in interstate
commerce as aforesaid in the Mid-Western area"; (3) "have arbitrarily,"
by reason of the provisions of the prevailing form of jobber contracts

which made the price to the jobber dependent on the average spot market price, "exacted large sums of money from thousands of jobbers with whom they have had such contracts in said Mid-Western area"; and (4) "in turn have intentionally raised the general level of retail prices prevailing in said Mid-Western area."

The *manner* and *means* of effectuating such conspiracy are alleged in substance as follows: Defendants, from February 1935 to December 1936 "have knowingly and unlawfully engaged and participated in two concerted gasoline buying programs" for the purchase "from independant refiners in spot transactions of large quantities of gasoline in the East Texas and Mid-Continent fields at uniform, high, and at times progressively increased prices." The East Texas buying program is alleged to have embraced purchases of gasoline in spot transactions from most of the independent refiners in the East Texas field, who were members of the East Texas Refiners' Marketing Association, formed in February 1935 with the knowledge and approval of some of the defendants "for the purpose of selling and facilitating the sale of gasoline to defendant major oil companies." It is alleged that arrangements were made and carried out for allotting orders for gasoline received from defendants among the members of that association; and that such purchases amounted to more than 50% of all gasoline produced by those independent refiners. The mid-Continent buying program is alleged to have included "large and increased purchases of gasoline" by defendants from independent refiners located in the Mid-Continent fields pursuant to allotments among themselves. Those purchases, it is charged, were made from independent refiners who were assigned to certain of the defendants at monthly meetings of a group representing defendants. It is alleged that the purchases in this buying program amounted to nearly 50% of all gasoline sold by those independents. As respects both the East Texas and the Mid-Continent buying programs, it is alleged that the purchases of gasoline were in excess of the amounts which defendants would have purchased but for those programs; that at the instance of certain defendants these independent refiners curtailed their production of gasoline. . . .

The methods of marketing and selling gasoline in the Mid-Western area are set forth in the indictment in some detail. Since we hereafter develop the facts concerning them, it will suffice at this point to summarize them briefly. Each defendant major oil company owns, operates or leases retail service stations in this area. It supplies those stations, as well as independent retail stations, with gasoline from its bulk storage plants. All but one sell large quantities of gasoline to jobbers in tank car lots under term contracts. In this area these jobbers exceed 4,000 in number and distribute about 50% of all gasoline distributed to retail service stations therein, the bulk of the jobbers' purchases being made from the defendant companies. The price to the jobbers under those contracts with defendant companies is made dependent on the spot market price, pursuant to a formula hereinafter discussed. And the spot market tank car prices of gasoline directly and substantially influence the retail prices in the area. In sum, it is alleged that defendants by raising and fixing the tank car prices of gasoline in these spot markets could and did increase the tank car prices and the retail prices of gasoline sold in the Mid-Western area. The vulnerability of these spot markets to that type of manipulation or stabilization is emphasized by the allegation that spot market prices published in the journals were the result of spot sales made chiefly by independent refiners of a relatively small amount of the gasoline sold in that area—virtually all gasoline sold in tank car quantities in spot market transactions in the Mid-Western area being sold by independent refiners, such sales amounting to less than 5% of all gasoline marketed therein.

So much for the indictment. . . .

The first meeting of the Tank Car Committee[2] was held February 5, 1935, and the second on February 11, 1935. At these meetings the alleged conspiracy was formed, the substance of which, so far as it pertained to the Mid-Continent phase, was as follows:

It was estimated that there would be between 600 and 700 tank cars of distress gasoline produced in the Mid-Continent oil field every month by about 17 independent refiners. These refiners, not having regular outlets for the gasoline, would be unable to dispose of it except at distress prices. Accordingly, it was proposed and decided that certain major companies (including the corporate respondents) would purchase gasoline from these refiners. The Committee would assemble each month information as to the quantity and location of this distress gasoline. Each of the major companies was to select one (or more) of the independent refiners having distress gasoline as its "dancing partner," and would assume responsibility for purchasing its distress supply. In this manner buying power would be coordinated, purchases would be effectively placed, and the results would be much superior to the previous haphazard purchasing. There were to be no formal contractual commitments to purchase this gasoline, either between the major companies or between the majors and the independents. Rather it was an informal gentlemen's agreement or understanding whereby each undertook to perform his share of the joint undertaking. Purchases were to be made at the "fair going market price.". . .

Before the month was out all companies alleged to have participated in the program (except one or two) made purchases; 757 tank cars were bought from all but three of the independent refiners who were named in the indictment as sellers. . . .

On May 27, 1935, this Court held . . . that the code-making authority conferred by the National Industrial Recovery Act was an unconstitutional delegation of legislative power. Shortly thereafter the Tank Car

[2] A division of the N.R.A.—sanctioned Petroleum Administrative Board. IMS.

Stabilization Committee held a meeting to discuss their future action. It was decided that the buying program should continue. . . .

In the meetings when the Mid-Continent buying program was being formulated it was recognized that it would be necessary or desirable to take the East Texas surplus gasoline off the market so that it would not be a "disturbing influence in the Standard of Indiana territory." The reason was that weakness in East Texas spot market prices might make East Texas gasoline competitive with Mid-Continent gasoline in the Mid-Western area and thus affect Mid-Continent spot market prices. . . .

Early in 1935 the East Texas Refiners' Marketing Association was formed to dispose of the surplus gasoline manufactured by the East Texas refiners. . . .

And it is clear that this East Texas buying program was, as we have said, supplementary or auxiliary to the Mid-Continent program. . . .

As a result of these buying programs it was hoped and intended that both the tank car and the retail markets would improve. The conclusion is irresistible that defendants' purpose was not merely to raise the price of gasoline in their sales to jobbers and consumers in the Mid-Western area. Their agreement or plan embraced not only buying on the spot markets but also, at least by clear implication, an understanding to maintain such improvements in Mid-Western prices as would result from those purchases of distress gasoline. The latter obviously would be achieved by selling at the increased prices, not by price cutting. Any other understanding would have been wholly inconsistent with and contrary to the philosophy of the broad stabilization efforts which were under way. In essence the raising and maintenance of the spot market prices were but the means adopted for raising and maintaining prices to jobbers and consumers. . . . Certainly there was enough evidence to support a finding by the jury that such were the scope and purpose of the plan. . . .

Respondents do not contend that the buying programs were not a factor in the price rise and in the stabilization of the spot markets during 1935 and 1936. But they do contend that they were relatively minor ones, because of the presence of other economic forces. . . .

In *United States* v. *Trenton Potteries Co.* . . . , this Court sustained a conviction under the Sherman Act where the jury was charged that an agreement on the part of the members of a combination, controlling a substantial part of an industry, upon the prices which the members are to charge for their commodity is in itself an unreasonable restraint of trade without regard to the reasonableness of the prices or the good intentions of the combining units. . . . This Court pointed out that the so-called "rule of reason" announced in *Standard Oil Co.* v. *United States*, 221 U.S. 1, and in *United States* v. *American Tobacco Co.*, 221 U.S. 106, had not affected this view of the illegality of price-fixing agreements. . . .

But respondents claim that other decisions of this Court afford them adequate defenses to the indictment. Among those on which they place reliance are *Appalachian Coals, Inc.* v. *United States*, 288 U.S. 344. . . .

[I]n reality the only essential thing in common between the instant case and the Appalachian Coals case is the presence in each of so-called demoralizing or injurious practices. The methods of dealing with them were quite divergent. In the instant case there were buying programs of distress gasoline which had as their direct purpose and aim the raising and maintenance of spot market prices and of prices to jobbers and consumers in the Mid-Western area, by the elimination of distress gasoline as a market factor. The increase in the spot market prices was to be accomplished by a well organized buying program on that market: regular ascertainment of the amounts of surplus gasoline; assignment of sellers among the buyers; regular purchases at prices which would place and keep a floor under the market. Unlike the plan in the instant case, the plan in the *Appalachian Coals* case was not designed to operate *vis-a-vis* the general consuming market and to fix the prices on that market. Furthermore, the effect, if any, of that plan on prices was not only wholly incidental but also highly conjectural. For the plan had not then been put into operation. Hence this Court expressly reserved jurisdiction in the District Court to take further proceedings if, *inter alia*, in "actual operation" the plan proved to be "an undue restraint upon interstate commerce." And as we have seen it would *per se* constitute such a restraint if price-fixing were involved. . . .

Thus for over forty years this Court has consistently and without deviation adhered to the principle that price-fixing agreements are unlawful *per se* under the Sherman Act and that no showing of so-called competitive abuses or evils which those agreements were designed to eliminate or alleviate may be interposed as a defense. . . .

Therefore the sole remaining question on this phase of the case is the applicability of the rule of the *Trenton Potteries* case to these facts.

Respondents seek to distinguish the *Trenton Potteries* case from the instant one. . . .

But we do not deem those distinctions material.

In the first place, there was abundant evidence that the combination had the purpose to raise prices. And likewise, there was ample evidence that the buying programs at least contributed to the price rise and the stability of the spot markets, and to increases in the price of gasoline sold in the Mid-Western area during the indictment period. That other factors also may have contributed to that rise and stability of the markets is immaterial. . . . Proof that there was a conspiracy, that its purpose was to raise prices, and that it caused or contributed to a price rise is proof of the actual consummation or execution of a conspiracy under Section 1 of the Sherman Act.

Secondly, the fact that sales on the spot markets were still governed by some competition is of no consequence. For it is indisputable that

that competition was restricted through the removal by respondents of a part of the supply which but for the buying programs would have been a factor in determining the going prices on those markets. . . . Competition was not eliminated from the markets; but it was clearly curtailed, since restriction of the supply of gasoline, the timing and placement of the purchases under the buying programs and the placing of a floor under the spot markets obviously reduced the play of the forces of supply and demand.

The elimination of so-called competitive evils is no legal justification for such buying programs. . . . If the so-called competitive abuses were to be appraised here, the reasonableness of prices would necessarily become an issue in every price-fixing case. In that event the Sherman Act would soon be emasculated; its philosophy would be supplanted by one which is wholly alien to a system of free competition; it would not be the charter of freedom which its framers intended.

. . . Those who controlled the prices . . . would have it in their power to destroy or drastically impair the competitive system. But the thrust of the rule is deeper and reaches more than monopoly power. Any combination which tampers with price structures is engaged in an unlawful activity. Even though the members of the price-fixing group were in no position to control the market, to the extent that they raised, lowered, or stabilized prices they would be directly interfering with the free play of market forces. The Act places all such schemes beyond the pale and protects that vital part of our economy against any degree of interference. Congress . . . has not permitted the age-old cry of ruinous competition and competitive evils to be a defense to price-fixing conspiracies. It has no more allowed genuine or fancied competitive abuses as a legal justification for such schemes than it has the good intentions of the members of the combination. If such a shift is to be made, it must be done by the Congress. Certainly Congress has not left us with any such choice. . . .

Nor is it important that the prices paid by the combination were not fixed in the sense that they were uniform and inflexible. Price-fixing as used in the *Trenton Potteries* case has no such limited meaning. . . . Hence, prices are fixed within the meaning of the *Trenton Potteries* case . . . because they are agreed upon. And the fact that, as here, they are fixed at the fair going market price is immaterial. . . .

Under the Sherman Act a combination formed for the purpose and with the effect of raising, depressing, fixing, pegging, or stabilizing the price of a commodity in interstate or foreign commerce is illegal *per se*. . . . Price-fixing agreements may have utility to members of the group though the power possessed or exerted falls far short of domination and control. Monopoly power . . . is not the only power which the Act strikes down, as we have said. Proof that a combination was formed for the purpose of fixing prices and that it caused them to be fixed or contributed to that result is proof of the completion of a price-fixing conspiracy under Section 1 of the Act. The indictment in this case charged that this combination had that purpose and effect. And there was abundant evidence to support it. Hence the existence of power on the part of members of the combination to fix prices was but a conclusion from the finding that the buying programs caused or contributed to the rise and stability of prices. . . .

The judgment of the Circuit Court of Appeals is reversed and that of the District Court affirmed.

The Chief Justice and Mr. Justice Murphy did not participate in the consideration or decision of this case.

Mr. Justice Roberts with whom Mr. Justice McReynolds concurred, dissented. . . .

Chapter 4

TRADE ASSOCIATION ACTIVITIES

The problem of distinguishing between those trade association activities which serve to improve businessmen's knowledge of market conditions and thereby make competition more perfect, and those which have as their purpose the elimination of competition is often a difficult one. The dissemination of trade statistics, for example, may result in greater price uniformity either by providing entrepreneurs with a greater grasp of business conditions and thereby enabling them to more intelligently perform their economic function, or by discouraging competition through methods such as insuring that price reductions become immediately known and met. Although difficult, the problem is not insoluble. The following cases indicate that it is possible to distinguish the legal from the illegal, the socially desirable from the socially undesirable. In the first case reported below, it was held that minute disclosure of the operations of individual members provided the lumber manufacturers' trade organization with information which was used to convince firms in the industry of the necessity of maintaining a spirit of harmony. This substitution of co-operation for competition was found to have gone so far that the Sherman Act had been violated. In the Sugar Institute case the Court, both in its decision and in framing an appropriate decree, attempted to trace the fine line that separates those activities which restrain competition from those which raise the plane of competition. Finally, in the Tag Manufacturers case the various criteria which have evolved over the years for determining the permissible sphere of trade association activities were applied to exonerate an association whose members accounted for some 95 per cent of the industry's capacity. A comparison of the Tag case with those preceding it provides a good indication of the extent to which the earlier rulings have led to a modification and refinement of trade association methods, and throws light on what may be a new, broader interpretation of the legality of exchange of certain types of trade information. It is also interesting to compare the Tag decision to those portions of the Cement case (see Chapter 5) dealing with trade association activities.

American Column and Lumber Co. et al. v. United States

257 U.S. 377 (1921)

Mr. Justice Clarke delivered the opinion of the Court.

The unincorporated "American Hardwood Manufacturers' Association" was formed in December, 1918, by the consolidation of two similar associations, from one of which it took over a department of activity designated the "Open Competition Plan," and hereinafter referred to as the "Plan."

Participation in the Plan was optional with the members of the Association, but, at the time this suit was commenced, of its 400 members, 365, operating 465 mills, were members of the Plan. The importance and strength of the Association is shown by the admission in the joint answer that, while the defendants operated only 5 percent of the number of mills engaged in hardwood manufacture in the country, they produced one-third of the total production of the United States. . . . The defendants are the members of the Plan, their personal representatives, and F. R. Gadd, its "Manager of Statistics."

The bill alleged, in substance, that the Plan constituted a combination and conspiracy to restrain interstate commerce in hardwood lumber by restricting competition and maintaining and increasing prices, in violation of the Antitrust Act of 1890. . . .

The answer denied that the Plan had any such purpose and effect as charged, and averred that it promoted competition, especially among its own members.

A temporary injunction, granted by the District Court, restricting the activities of the Plan in specified respects, by consent of the parties, was made permanent and a direct appeal brings the case here for review.

The activities which we shall see were comprehended within the "Open Competition Plan" (which is sometimes called the "New Competition") have come to be widely adopted in our country, and, as this is the first time their legality has been before this court for decision, some detail of statement with respect to them is necessary.

There is very little dispute as to the facts. . . .

[T]he Plan proposed a system of cooperation among the members, of the interchange of reports of sales, prices, production, and practices, and in meetings of the members for discussion, for the avowed purpose of substituting "cooperative competition" for "cutthroat competition," of keeping "prices at reasonably stable and normal levels," and of improving the "human relations" among the members. But the purpose to agree upon prices or production was always disclaimed.

Coming, now, to the fully worked out paper plan as adopted:

It required each member to make six reports to the secretary, viz.:
  1. A *daily* report of all sales actually made. . . .

2. A *daily* shipping report, with exact copies of the invoices.
3. A *monthly* production report. . . .
4. A *monthly* stock report by each member. . . .
5. Price-lists. . . .
6. Inspection reports. . . .

All of these reports by members are subject to complete audit by representatives of the association. Any member who fails to report *shall not receive the reports* of the secretary, and failure to report for twelve days in six months shall cause the member failing to be dropped from membership.

Plainly it would be very difficult to devise a more minute disclosure of everything connected with one's business than is here provided for by this Plan, and very certainly only the most attractive prospect could induce any man to make it to his rivals and competitors.

But, since such voluminous disclosures to the secretary would be valueless, unless communicated to the members in a condensed and interpreted form, provision is made for this. . . .

This extensive interchange of reports, supplemented as it was by monthly meetings at which an opportunity was afforded for discussion "of all subjects of interest to the members," very certainly constituted an organization through which agreements, actual or implied, could readily be arrived at and maintained, if the members desired to make them.

Such, in outline, was the paper plan adopted by the association, but, elaborate though it was, in practice . . . important additions were made to it. . . .

. . . The Plan provided for a monthly "market report letter" to go to all members of the association. . . .

This elaborate plan for the interchange of reports does not simply supply to each member . . . the data for judging the market. . . . It goes much farther. It not only furnishes such information . . . but also reports . . . significant suggestions as to both future prices and production. . . . It is plain that the only element lacking in this scheme to make it a familiar type of the competition suppressing organization is a definite agreement as to production and prices. But this is supplied: By the disposition of men "to follow their most intelligent competitors," especially when powerful; by the inherent disposition to make all the money possible, joined with the steady cultivation of the value of "harmony" of action; and by the system of reports, which makes the discovery of price reductions inevitable and immediate. The sanctions of the plan obviously are financial interest, intimate personal contact, and business honor, all operating under the restraint of exposure of what would be deemed bad faith and of trade punishment by powerful rivals. . . .

It has been repeatedly held by this court that the purpose of the statute is to maintain free competition in interstate commerce and that any concerted action by any combination of men or corporations to cause, or which in fact does cause, direct and undue restraint of competition in such commerce, falls within the condemnation of the act and is unlawful. . . .

With this rule of law and the details of the Plan in mind, we come to consider what the record shows as to the purpose of this combination and as to its effect upon interstate commerce. . . .

It is plain that as the Plan was the "clearing house" of the members, "for information on prices, trade statistics, and practices," so Gadd was the "clearing house" of the Plan, and that what he said and did, acquiesced in by the members, as it was, must be accepted as the authoritative expression of the combination.

The record shows that the lumber market was inactive in the months of January and February and the first part of March of 1919. It grew better late in March, and progressively stronger until in July, when it became very active, with prices high and so continued until the end of the year we are considering.

In the first quarter of the year the problem was to maintain the war prices then prevailing rather than to advance them, and . . . the members of the Plan began actively to cooperate through the meetings, to suppress competition by restricting production. This is very clearly shown by the excerpts following from the minutes of meetings and from the market letters and sales reports distributed at them.

Thus, at the meeting held at Cincinnati, on January 21, 1919, in the discussion of business conditions, the chairman said:

"If there is *no increase in production*, particularly in oak, there is going to be good business. . . . *No man is safe in increasing production.* If he does, he will be in bad shape, as the demand won't come.". . .

Much more of like purport appears in the minutes of the meetings throughout the year, but this is sufficient to convincingly show that one of the prime purposes of the meetings, held in every part of the lumber district, and of the various reports, was to induce members to cooperate in restricting production, thereby keeping the supply low and the prices high, and that whenever there was any suggestion of running the mills to an extent which would bring up the supply to a point which might affect prices, the advice against operations which might lead to such result was put in the strongest possible terms. The cooperation is palpable and avowed, its purpose is clear, and we shall see that it was completely realized.

Next, the record shows clearly that the members of the combination were not satisfied to secure, each for himself, the price which might be obtainable even as the result of cooperative restriction of production but that throughout the year they assiduously cultivated, through the letters of Gadd, speaking for them all, and through the discussions at the meetings, the general conviction that higher and higher prices were obtainable and a disposition on the part of all to demand them. The intention to create such a common purpose is too clear to be doubted. . . .

To this we must add that constantly throughout the minutes of the various meetings there is shown discussion of the stock and production reports in which the shortage of supply was continually emphasized, with the implication, not disguised, that higher prices must result. Men in general are so easily persuaded to do that which will obviously prove profitable that this reiterated opinion from the analyst of their association, with all obtainable data before him, that higher prices were justified and could easily be obtained, must, inevitably have resulted, as it did result, in concert of action in demanding them.

But not only does the record thus show a persistent purpose to encourage members to unite in pressing for higher and higher prices, without regard to cost, but there are many admissions by members, not only that this was the purpose of the Plan, but that it was fully realized. . . .

[T]he purpose of the organization, and especially of the frequent meetings, was to bring about a concerted effort to raise prices regardless of cost or merit, and so was unlawful, and . . . the members were soon entirely satisfied that the Plan was "carrying out the purpose for which it was intended."

As to the price conditions during the year: Without going into detail, the record shows that the prices of the grades of hardwood in most general use were increased to an unprecedented extent during the year. . . . While it is true that 1919 was a year of high and increasing prices generally, and that wet weather may have restricted production to some extent, we cannot but agree with the members of the Plan themselves, as we have quoted them, and with the District Court, in the conclusion that the united action of this large and influential membership of dealers contributed greatly to this extraordinary price increase. . . .

To call the activities of the defendants, as they are proved in this record, an "Open Competition Plan" of action is plainly a misleading misnomer.

Genuine competitors do not make daily, weekly, and monthly reports of the minutest details of their business to their rivals, as the defendants did; they do not contract, as was done here to submit their books to the discretionary audit, and their stocks to the discretionary inspection, of their rivals, for the purpose of successfully competing with them; and they do not submit the details of their business to the analysis of an expert, jointly employed, and obtain from him a "harmonized" estimate of the market as it is, and as, in his specially and confidentially informed judgment, it promises to be. This is not the conduct of competitors, but is so clearly that of men united in an agreement, express or implied, to act together and pursue a common purpose under a common guide that, if it did not stand confessed a combination to restrict production and increase prices in interstate commerce, and as, therefore, a direct restraint upon that commerce, as we have seen that it is, that conclusion must inevitably have been inferred from the facts which were proved. To pronounce such abnormal conduct on the part of 365 natural competitors, controlling one-third of the trade of the country in an article of prime necessity, a "new form of competition," and not an old form of combination in restraint of trade, as it so plainly is, would be for this court to confess itself blinded by words and forms to realities which men in general very plainly see, and understand and condemn, as an old evil in a new dress and with a new name.

The Plan is, essentially, simply an expansion of the gentlemen's agreement of former days, skillfully devised to evade the law. To call it open competition, . . . cannot conceal the fact that the fundamental purpose of the Plan was to procure "harmonious" individual action among a large number of naturally competing dealers with respect to the volume of production and prices, without having any specific agreement with respect to them, and to rely for maintenance of concerted action in both respects, not upon fines and forfeitures as in earlier days, but upon what experience has shown to be the more potent and dependable restraints, of business honor and social penalties—cautiously reinforced by many and elaborate reports, which would promptly expose to his associates any disposition in any member to deviate from the tacit understanding that all were to act together under the subtle direction of a single interpreter of their common purposes, as evidenced in the minute reports of what they had done and in their expressed purposes as to what they intended to do.

In the presence of this record it is futile to argue that the purpose of the Plan was simply to furnish those engaged in this industry, with widely scattered units, the equivalent of such information as is contained in the newspaper and government publications with respect to the market for commodities sold on Boards of Trade or Stock Exchanges. One distinguishing and sufficient difference is that the published reports go to both buyer and seller, but these reports go to the seller only; and another is that there is no skilled interpreter of the published reports, such as we have in this case, to insistently recommend harmony of action likely to prove profitable in proportion as it is unitedly pursued.

Convinced, as we are, that the purpose and effect of the activities of the Open Competition Plan, here under discussion, were to restrict competition, and thereby restrain interstate commerce in the manufacture and sale of hardwood lumber, by concerted action in curtailing production and in increasing prices, we agree with the District Court that it constituted a combination and conspiracy in restraint of interstate commerce within the meaning of the Antitrust Act of 1890 . . . and the decree of that court must be

Affirmed.

Mr. Justice Holmes, dissented. Mr. Justice Brandeis, with whom Mr. Justice McKenna concurred separately dissented emphasizing that small businessmen "frustrated in their efforts to rationalize competition [might] be led to enter the inviting field of consolidation."

Sugar Institute v. *United States*

297 U.S. 553 (1936)

Mr. Chief Justice Hughes delivered the opinion of the Court.

This suit was brought to dissolve the Sugar Institute, Inc., a trade association, and to restrain the sugar refining companies which composed it, and the individual defendants, from engaging in an alleged conspiracy in restraint of interstate and foreign commerce in violation of the Sherman Antitrust Act . . . Section 1. . . .

The record is unusually voluminous. . . . We shall attempt to deal only with the salient and controlling points of the controversy. These involve (1) the special characteristics of the sugar industry and the practices which obtained before the organization of the Sugar Institute, (2) the purposes for which the Institute was founded, (3) the agreement and practices of the members of the Institute, and (4) the application of the Antitrust Act and the provisions of the decree.

First. The sugar industry and practices prior to the formation of the Sugar Institute. The fifteen defendant companies, members of the Institute, refine practically all of the imported raw sugar processed in this country. Their product is known as "domestic refined." Prior to the organization of the Institute in 1927, they provided more than 80 percent of the sugar consumed in the United States, and they have since supplied from 70 to 80 percent. . . . Both beet sugar and off-shore sugar[1] are sold at a small differential below defendants' sugar. The trial court found that there was no agreement between defendants and the beet sugar manufacturers, or with the off-shore interests, to maintain any differential. . . .

The court . . . found that the "basis prices,"[2] quoted by the several refiners in any particular trade area, "were generally uniform both before and after the Institute, because economically the defendants' sugar, save for exceptional instances was and is a thoroughly standardized product."

It is a fundamental and earnest contention of defendants that . . . a proper appraisal of [their] motives and transactions . . . cannot be made without full appreciation of the sorry condition into which the industry had fallen. . . .

The court found that . . . the practice developed on the part of some, but not all, refiners of giving secret concessions. . . . The court also found that various causes contributed to the development of those selling methods on the part of the unethical refiners, chief among which was an

---

[1] Off-shore sugar is the trade term applied to sugar which has been refined in insular possessions. IMS.

[2] The "basis price" is the price per pound per 100-pound bag of fine-granulated or granulated sugar. Prices of other grades and packages are in terms of stipulated differentials from the basis price. IMS.

overcapacity since the war of at least 50 percent. Other probable causes were the lack of statistical information . . . , uncertainties prevailing in the market for raw sugar . . . , the fact that . . . most sugar has been sold through brokers, and the standardization of defendants' products. . . .

[T]he evidence and findings leave no doubt that the industry was in a demoralized state which called for remedial measures. . . .

Second. The purposes for which the Institute was founded. . . . Defendants urge that the abolition of the vicious and discriminatory system of secret concessions, through the adoption of the principle of open prices publicly announced, without discrimination, was their dominant purpose in forming the Institute, and that other purposes were the supplying of accurate trade statistics, the elimination of wasteful practices, the creation of a credit bureau, and the institution of an advertising campaign. The court recognized the existence of these purposes in its findings . . . [but the] "dominant purposes" were found to be as follows: ". . . to create and maintain a uniform price structure, thereby eliminating and suppressing price competition among themselves and other competitors; to maintain relatively high prices for refined, as compared with contemporary prices of raw sugar; to improve their own financial position by limiting and suppressing numerous contract terms and conditions; and to make as certain as possible that no secret concessions should be granted. In their efforts to accomplish these purposes, defendants have ignored the interests of distributors and consumers of sugar."

. . . We think that it is manifest that the finding as to dominant purposes was not based upon any assumption *a priori*, but was an inference of fact which the court drew from the facts it deemed to be established with respect to the scope of the agreement between the members of the Institute and the actual nature and effect of their concerted action. . . .

We turn to the transactions from which the inference of purpose is drawn.

Third. The agreement and practices of members of the Institute. . . . [T]he findings of restraint of trade rest upon the basic agreement of the refiners to sell only upon prices and terms openly announced, and upon certain supplementary restrictions.

1. *The "basic agreement."* . . . The distinctive feature of the "basic agreement" was not the advance announcement of prices, or a concert to maintain any particular basis price for any period, but a requirement of adherence, without deviation, to the prices and terms publicly announced. Prior to the Institute, the list prices which many of the "unethical" refiners announced, "were merely nominal quotations and bore no relation to the actual 'selling basis' at which their sugar was sold. . . . The selling price was the price at which they purported to sell; the secret concessions were from this basis." And, in the case of some of the "unethical" refiners, changes in selling bases were made from time to time without formal pub-

lic announcement in advance. The Institute sought to prevent such departures. . . . The court found:

Under the Institute, defendants agreed to sell, and in general did sell sugar only upon open prices, terms and conditions publicly announced in advance of sales, and they agreed to adhere and in general did adhere without deviation, to such prices, terms and conditions until they publicly announced changes.

It was because of the range and effect of this restriction, and the consequent deprivation of opportunity to make special arrangements, that the court found that the agreement and the course of action under it constituted an unreasonable restraint of trade. . . .

The court found that "the number of price changes for refined as compared to raw sugar" has been relatively less since the Institute than before. . . . There was "a marked increase in margin and a substantial increase in profits despite a concededly large excess capacity.". . . Factors "largely responsible" for this relative stability of prices . . . were the dissemination among the refiners of statistical information, "while withholding it in large part from the buyers," and the steps taken by defendants "to eliminate the possibilities of price variations to distributors or ultimate purchasers at any given time and thereby deprive them of the opportunity, by underselling, to disturb the price structure." Other factors were "the friendly cooperative spirit which the Institute brought to the Industry" and the assurance to each refiner that he need meet only the prices, terms, and conditions announced by his competitors in advance of sales.

. . . [T]he question, as we have seen, is not really with respect to the practice of making price announcements in advance of sales, but as to defendants' requirement of adherence to such announcements without the deviations which open and fair competition might require or justify. The court did not condemn mere open price announcements in advance of sales. The court was careful to say in its opinion that it found it "unnecessary to pass upon the legality of the use of the Institute" for relaying such announcements, "if each refiner entirely independent of the others voluntarily made his own announcements without obligation to adhere thereto."

2. *Supplementary restrictions.* The requirements and practices designed to support the basic agreement, and which the trial court condemned, relate to the employment of brokers and warehousemen, transportation, consignment points, long-term contracts, quantity discounts, and other contract terms and conditions, and to the withholding of statistical information.

. . . Some statistical information collected by the Institute was supplied only to its members; some was supplied as well to representatives of off-shore refiners [and some] . . . were widely distributed through news agencies, banks and brokers. . . .

The trial court found that [many] . . . statistics supplied to members or off-shore refiners were [not] available except through the Institute and none were supplied or available to the trade. What the court considered to be "vital data". . . were withheld from purchasers. The court concluded that, by collecting and circulating only among themselves that information, defendants obtained an unfair advantage with respect to purchasers and effected an unreasonable restraint.

. . . We cannot say . . . that the finding of the trial court, in connection with its exhaustive examination of conditions in the trade, is without adequate support. . . .

Fourth. The application of the Antitrust Act and the provisions of the decree. The restrictions imposed by the Sherman Antitrust Act . . . are not mechanical or artificial. We have repeatedly said that they set up the essential standard of reasonableness. . . . Designed to frustrate unreasonable restraints, they do not prevent the adoption of reasonable means to protect interstate commerce from destructive or injurious practices and to promote competition upon a sound basis. . . . Nor does the fact that the correction of abuses may tend to stabilize a business, or to produce fairer price levels, require that abuses should go uncorrected or that an effort to correct them should for that reason alone be stamped an unreasonable restraint of trade. . . . Further, the dissemination of information is normally an aid to commerce. As free competition means a free and open market among both buyers and sellers, competition does not become less free merely because of the distribution of knowledge of the essential factors entering into commercial transactions. The natural effect of the acquisition of the wider and more scientific knowledge of business conditions on the minds of those engaged in commerce, and the consequent stabilizing of production and price, cannot be said to be an unreasonable restraint or in any respect unlawful. . . .

The freedom of concerted action to improve conditions has an obvious limitation. The end does not justify illegal means. The endeavor to put a stop to illicit practices must not itself become illicit. As the statute draws the line at unreasonable restraints, a cooperative endeavor which trangresses that line cannot justify itself by pointing to evils afflicting the industry or to a laudable purpose to remove them. . . .

In the instant case, a fact of outstanding importance is the relative position of defendants in the sugar industry. We have noted that the fifteen refiners, represented in the Institute, . . . supply from 70 to 80 percent of the sugar consumed. . . . Another outstanding fact is that defendants' product is a thoroughly standardized commodity. In their competition, price, rather than brand, is generally the vital consideration. . . . The fact that, because sugar is a standardized commodity, there is a strong tendency to uniformity of price, makes it the more important that such opportunities as may exist for fair competition should not be impaired. . . .

In determining the relief to be afforded, appropriate regard should be had to the special and historic practice of the sugar industry. The restraints, found to be unreasonable, were the offspring of the basic agreement. The vice in that agreement was not in the mere open announcement of prices and terms in accordance with the customs of the trade. That practice which had grown out of the special character of the industry did not restrain trade. The trial court did not hold that practice to be illegal and we see no reason for condemning it. The unreasonable restraints which the defendants imposed lay not in advance announcements, but in the steps taken to secure adherence, without deviation, to prices and terms thus announced. . . . But, in ending that restraint, the beneficial and curative agency of publicity should not be unnecessarily hampered. . . . [S]uch provision for publicity may be helpful in promoting fair competition. If the requirement that there must be adherence to prices and terms openly announced in advance is abrogated and the restraints which followed that requirement are removed, the just interests of competition will be safeguarded and the trade will still be left with whatever advantage may be incidental to its established practice.

The decree. The court below did not dissolve the Institute. The practices which had been found to constitute unreasonable restraints were comprehensively enjoined. . . .

Paragraphs 1 and 2 of the specifications enjoin the carrying out of the open price plan so far as it seeks to compel uniform terms, regardless of circumstances, and an adherence to prices, terms, etc., announced in advance. . . .

In view of those provisions, and of the other forty specified restrictions, we think that paragraphs 3, 4, and 5 with respect to the reporting or relaying of information as to current or future prices should be eliminated. These paragraphs are as follows:

"3. . . . [S]ystematically reporting . . . information as to current or future prices, terms, conditions, or freight applications. . . .

"4. Relaying by or through . . . any . . . common agency, information as to current or future prices, terms, conditions or freight applications. . . .

"5. Giving any prior notice of any change . . . in prices, terms, conditions or freight applications. . . ."

Such reporting . . . does not appear to involve any unreasonable restraint of competition.

[Paragraph 7 was then modified to permit the Institute to withhold from buyers information of a confidential character.]

The decree is modified in the particulars above stated and, as thus modified, is affirmed.

It is so ordered.

Mr. Justice Sutherland and Mr. Justice Stone took no part in the consideration and decision of this case.

Tag Manufacturing Institute et al. v. *Federal Trade Commission*
174 F.2d 452 (]949)

Before Magruder, Chief Judge, Woodbury, Circuit Judge, and Peters, District Judge.

Magruder, Chief Judge. Petitioners in this case ask us . . . to review and set aside or modify a cease and desist order of the Federal Trade Commission. . . .

On May 2, 1941, the Commission issued its complaint. . . . The complaint alleged that . . . petitioners "have entered into and carried out an understanding, agreement, combination, and conspiracy to restrict, restrain, suppress and eliminate price competition in the sale and distribution of said tag products" in interstate commerce; that pursuant to said agreement, petitioners "have fixed and maintained, and still fix and maintain, uniform prices, terms and conditions of sale for said tag products"; that the acts and practices of petitioners "have a dangerous tendency to and have actually hindered and prevented price competition" in the sale of tags in interstate commerce, have placed in petitioners the power to control and enhance prices on said products, have unreasonably restrained such commerce "and constitute unfair methods of competition in commerce within the intent and meaning of the Federal Trade Commission Act.". . .

The manufacturing petitioners sell and distribute approximately 95 percent of the tag products purchased and used in the United States, with 55 percent of the business of the industry shared by the four largest manufacturers.

Certain standardized tags are made in advance of sale and sold out of stock, such as plain unprinted stock shipping tags. However, over 80 percent of the business is in made-to-order tags, the varieties of which are almost unlimited, representing as they do selective combinations of materials and processes, or component elements, in various sizes and shapes. The much greater part of the products of the industry, particularly of made-to-order tags, is sold direct to consumers, but there is a considerable volume of sales to distributors and others for resale. To some extent, tag manufacturers buy from other manufacturers, for resale, types of tags which they do not themselves manufacture. Orders for tags are generally small in dollar value, averaging between $20 and $40, and a thousand or more orders for tags are placed with manufacturers each business day.

In such an industry, it would evidently not be practicable for a manufacturer to give a price on each order, based upon an individual cost estimate of that order. Hence, early in the history of the industry, manufacturers began to issue price lists to their salesmen, distributors, and customers. The simple stock tags were customarily listed at stated prices for the finished product. With respect to the more elaborate, and infinitely various made-to-order tags, the price lists would enumerate the prices of the various basic components, such as tag stock, strings, wires, punches, eyelets, stapling, gumming, printing, etc.—from which the price for any particular tag, made up from the desired combination of components, might be computed.

. . . The price list does serve to indicate to the trade the scale of prices which the seller hopes and expects to maintain in the generality of future transactions until further notice. . . . In other words, from the nature of things it is reasonably to be expected that off-list sales would be the exception rather than the rule, and that the greater portion of sales would be at the prices stated in the seller's current price list. This is particularly true in an industry such as the tag industry, with its wide variety of products and tremendous number of sales transactions each of small dollar volume on the average.

The issuance of price lists by tag manufacturers had become established as a general practice in the industry prior to the formation of the Institute and prior to the execution of the various Tag Industry Agreements, later to be described, which formed the principal basis of the Commission's complaint against petitioners.

The Institute was organized in 1933, and has operated continuously since that time. All the manufacturing petitioners have become members of the Institute. At all times since its organization, the active management of the Institute has been in the hands of petitioner Frank H. Baxter, its secretary-treasurer and executive director. The Institute has concerned itself with typical trade association activities, and among other things has fostered efforts at more refined standardization of tag products and components thereof.

While the National Industrial Recovery Act . . . was in effect, a Code of Fair Competition for the Tag Industry was promulgated. . . . Under the Code, a so-called "open-price plan of selling" was prescribed, under which each member of the industry was required to file a schedule of his prices and terms of sale. . . . Further, it was provided that no member of the industry "shall sell such product for less than such price or upon terms or conditions more favorable" than stated in his filed price schedule. . . .

After the National Industrial Recovery Act was invalidated . . . members of the industry adopted a succession of four Tag Industry Agreements, so-called, in 1935, 1936, 1937 and 1940. The 1940 agreement was in effect when the Commission's complaint was filed, and was still in effect at the time of the final hearing before the Commission. . . .

[T]he agreements were concerned chiefly with the reporting and dissemination of industry statistics. . . .

Article II of the 1940 agreement requires the Subscribers to report to the Associates (Baxter) the prices, terms and conditions of each sale of or contract to sell any tag products covered by the agreement. . . .

A further important provision of Article II is as follows:

. . . Nothing herein shall be construed as a limitation or restriction upon the right of each Subscriber independently to establish such prices, or such terms and conditions of sale, or policies of whatever nature affecting prices or sales, as he may deem expedient. Nothing in any report made to the Associates by any Subscriber hereunder shall be construed as a representation or pledge as to prices, terms, conditions of sale, or policies in current or future transactions.

With reference to the use by Baxter of the foregoing information, it is provided . . . :

All information relating to prices, terms and conditions of sale disseminated to the Subscribers pursuant hereto shall be freely and fully available to public agencies, distributors and consumers of the products, and to any other properly interested persons; and shall be disseminated in the same manner as to Subscribers, to such of them as may apply therefore and arrange for payment of the reasonable cost of such service.

Each subscriber agrees that he will notify purchasers from him of the availability of this information.

Article III of the 1940 agreement requires each Subscriber throughout the life of the agreement to mail to Baxter "duplicates of every invoice or other memorandum of shipment or delivery of the products and of all credit memoranda applicable thereto. . . ." It is provided that the Associates (Baxter) "shall compile the information submitted to them pursuant to this Article in such a way as not to disclose the information of any one Subscriber or the names of any purchasers. . . ."

Article IV of the 1940 agreement relates to the enforcement of the aforesaid reporting undertakings. It is recited that a breach of Article II or Article III by any Subscriber . . . [shall cause to be imposed on him fines ranging from $5–$25 per day; and for] failure to transmit copies of invoices or memoranda as described in Article III "within ten (10) days after the date of mailing of the original of each such invoice or memorandum," the "liquidated damages" [fines] are stated to be an amount equivalent to 10 percent of the aggregate value of all the Subscriber's transactions proved to be affected by such failure, up to a maximum of $100 applicable to a single day's billing by one Subscriber. . . .

The final Article in the 1940 agreement, Article V, provides for termination of the entire agreement "by written agreement of a majority of the parties.". . . It is further provided that any manufacturer of tag products "may become a subscriber to this Agreement at any time by signing the same and making the payments provided in Article I hereof.". . .

We think the evidence does warrant a finding that during the life of the Tag Industry Agreements there has from time to time been considerable list price uniformity with respect to types of tags constituting a large portion of the industry's business. Such a finding, in conjunction with the unchallenged finding that on the average 75 percent of the industry's business is done at list, would warrant the inference that during the years in which the Tag Industry Agreements have been in effect there has been a considerable uniformity of actual selling prices. The evidence does not, however, warrant the Commission's finding that the effect of the operation of the Tag Industry Agreements "has resulted in a substantial uniformity of prices for tags and tag products among the respondent members." In the first place, this implies that the instances of departure from uniformity are insignificant and unsubstantial—which certainly cannot be said. In the second place, there is no evidence that such uniformity as has existed is a result of the operation of the Tag Industry Agreements, for it does not appear whether there has been an increase or decrease of uniformity either in list prices or in actual selling prices since the agreements have been in operation. . . .

In support of its conclusion, the Commission refers to the provisions in the Tag Industry Agreements designed to insure compliance with the reporting commitments of the Subscribers. . . . The evidence is uncontradicted that Baxter's only concern with off-list transactions was to find out if they had been reported, after the event, as the agreement required. If the investigation indicated a violation of any reporting obligation of a Subscriber, Baxter would institute proceedings for assessment of "liquidated damages" as specified in the agreement. Total assessments for acts of non-compliance amounted to less than $10,000 for the period 1935–1941. The record contains not a single instance of an assessment for failure to adhere to a list price. . . .

Whether they are "liquidated damages," as they purport to be, or "penalties," as the Commission calls them, is hardly decisive. If the reporting commitments they are designed to buttress are otherwise lawful, the agreement does not become a violation of the antitrust laws or the Federal Trade Commission Act merely because the reporting plan is accompanied by a penalty provision which would not be legally enforceable. . . .

There has been some tendency to look askance at reporting agreements between competitors, where the information exchanged is reserved exclusively to themselves and withheld from buyers or the public generally. Presumably this is because such secrecy more readily suggests the inference that the agreement is inspired by some unlawful purpose and precludes the argument that the information thus secretly exchanged serves a function similar to that of market information made available through the activities of commodity exchanges, trade journals, etc. . . .

It is noteworthy that the Commission has failed to produce a single tag buyer to testify that he was unaware of the existence of this information service, or that he sought information from Baxter and could not get it, or that he sought to subscribe to the service and was refused. . . .

We have come to the conclusion that the reporting agreements herein, and the practices of petitioners thereunder, are lawful under the controlling authorities. . . . Once a price list has been issued to the trade it necessarily becomes pretty much public property. There is certainly nothing secret about it. It would be no great feat for a manufacturer to obtain copies of his competitors' price lists. The Tag Industry Agreement merely facilitates the assembling of such data. As to the obligation of Subscribers to report off-list sales and to furnish copies of all invoices, that is no more than the reporting of past transactions. The Commission has endeavored to show that the agreement was something more than this, that it was a price-fixing agreement having the purpose and actual effect of restraining and preventing price competition. We believe that such findings are unsupported by the evidence or by any reasonable inferences to be drawn therefrom. We say this with full recognition of our limited scope of review of findings of fact by the Commission. . . .

Since, in our view of the case, the cease and desist order will have to be set aside, it becomes unnecessary for us to consider certain seriously pressed objections by petitioners to the breadth of the order.

A judgment will be entered setting aside the order of the Commission.

Chapter 5

DELIVERED PRICE SYSTEMS

The legality of various delivered price systems has, in the past ten years, come in for more attention than perhaps any other single business method. Beginning with the Corn Products and Staley cases in 1945, the Federal Trade Commission won a series of cases which—taken together—gave rise to more criticism of that administrative body than it had ever before met.

The Corn Products and Staley cases, decided on the same day, represent an important phase in the Commission's battle against price discrimination (see also Chapter 8, below). The first case applies the prohibitions contained in Section 2(a) of the Robinson-Patman amendment to the Clayton Act to a single basing point system of delivered prices, and represents the only delivered price case which did not involve conspiracy. The second case is of importance for its refusal to allow the use of the good faith defense in an industry in which unlawful delivered prices had been systematically matched in order to eliminate all vestiges of price competition. The Cement case, which attracted more attention than the others, set forth the doctrine that collusive adoption of a delivered price system was an unfair method of competition within the meaning of the Federal Trade Commission Act. Despite the furor created by the decision, its novelty stems largely from the fact that it was brought under Section 5 of the Federal Trade Commission Act rather than Section 1 of the Sherman Act. Finally, the Rigid Steel Conduit opinion extended the conspiracy doctrine of the Cement case to include conscious parallelism. In assessing the novelty of this latter doctrine, however, it is well to read the Interstate Circuit decision, presented in another connection in Chapter 10 below.[1]

---

[1] Students interested in more thorough discussions of delivered pricing than those presented in the cases might see J. M. Clark, "The Law and Economics of Basing Points: Appraisal and Proposals," *American Economic Review*, Vol. XXXIX, No. 2 (March, 1949); George W. Stocking, "The Economics of Basing Point Pricing," *Law and Contemporary Problems*, Vol. 15, No. 2 (Spring, 1950); Clair Wilcox, *Public Policies Toward Business* (Homewood, Ill.: Richard D. Irwin, 1955), Chapter 8; Fritz Machlup, *The Basing Point System* (Philadelphia: Blakiston, 1949).

Corn Products Refining Company v. *Federal Trade Commission*

324 U.S. 726 (1945)

Mr. Chief Justice Stone delivered the opinion of the Court.

Petitioners, a parent corporation and its sales subsidiary, use a basing point system of pricing in their sales of glucose. They sell only at delivered prices, computed by adding to a base price at Chicago the published freight tariff from Chicago to the several points of delivery, even though deliveries are in fact made from their factory at Kansas City as well as from their Chicago factory. Consequently there is included in the delivered price on shipments from Kansas City an amount of "freight" which usually does not correspond to freight actually paid by petitioners.

The Federal Trade Commission instituted this proceeding under Section 11 of the Clayton Act . . . , charging that petitioners' use of this single basing point system resulted in discriminations in price between different purchasers of the glucose, and violated Section 2(*a*) of the Act, as amended by Section 1 of the Robinson-Patman Act. . . . The complaint also charged petitioners with other discriminations in prices, or in services rendered to favored customers, . . . all in violation of Section 2(*a*) or Section 2(*e*) of the Clayton Act, as amended. . . .

After hearings, at which much of the evidence was stipulated, the Commission made its findings of fact. It concluded that petitioners had violated Section 2 of the Clayton Act, as amended, and ordered them to cease and desist from such violations. On petition to review the Commission's order, the Circuit Court of Appeals for the Seventh Circuit sustained the order, except in particulars not material here. 144 F.2d 211.

We granted certiorari . . . because the questions involved are of importance in the administration of the Clayton Act in view of the widespread use of basing point price systems. The principal questions for decision are whether, when shipments are made from Kansas City, petitioners basing point system results in discriminations in price between different purchasers of glucose, within the meaning of Section 2(*a*); and, if so, whether there is support in the evidence for the finding of the Commission that these discriminations have the effect on competition defined by that section. Further questions are raised as to whether the other discriminations charged violate Section 2(*a*) and Section 2(*e*).

I. BASING POINT PRACTICES

The evidence as to petitioners' basing point system for the sale of glucose was stipulated. The Commission found from the evidence that petitioners have two plants for the manufacture of glucose or corn syrup, one at Argo, Illinois, within the Chicago switching district, and the other at Kansas City, Missouri. The Chicago plant has been in operation since

1910, and that at Kansas City since 1922. Petitioners' bulk sales of glucose are at delivered prices, which are computed, whether the shipments are from Chicago or Kansas City, at petitioners' Chicago prices, plus the freight rate from Chicago to the place of delivery. Thus purchasers in all places other than Chicago pay a higher price than do Chicago purchasers. And in the case of all shipments from Kansas City to purchasers in cities having a lower freight rate from Kansas City than from Chicago, the delivered price includes unearned or "phantom" freight, to the extent of the difference in freight rates. Conversely, when the freight from Kansas City to the point of delivery is more than that from Chicago, petitioners must "absorb" freight upon shipments from Kansas City, to the extent of the difference in freight.

The Commission illustrated the operation of the system by petitioners' delivered prices for glucose in bulk in twelve western and southwestern cities, to which shipments were usually made from Kansas City. On August 1, 1939, the freight rates to these points of delivery from Chicago were found to exceed those from Kansas City by from 4 to 40 cents per hundred pounds, and to that extent the delivered prices included unearned or phantom freight. As petitioners' Chicago price was then $2.09 per hundred pounds, this phantom freight factor with respect to deliveries to these twelve cities represented from 2 to 19% of the Chicago base price. From this it follows, as will presently be seen, that petitioners' net return at their Kansas City factory on sales to these twelve cities, in effect their f.o.b. factory price, varied according to the amount of phantom freight included in the delivered price.

Much of the petitioners' glucose is sold to candy manufacturers, who are in competition with each other in the sale of their candy. Glucose is the principal ingredient in many varieties of low priced candies, which are sold on narrow margins of profit. Customers for such candies may be diverted from one manufacturer to another by a difference in price of a small fraction of a cent per pound. . . .

Manufacturers who pay unearned or phantom freight under petitioners' basing point system necessarily pay relatively higher costs for their raw material than do those manufacturers whose location with relation to the basing point is such that they are able to purchase at the base price plus only the freight actually paid. The Commission found that the payment of these increased prices imposed by the basing point system "may . . . diminish" the manufacturers' ability to compete with those buyers at lower prices.

The Commission concluded from these facts that petitioners' basing point system resulted in discriminations in price among purchasers of glucose, and that the discriminations result in substantial harm to competition among such purchasers. Petitioners challenge each conclusion.

First. . . . Petitioners' pricing system results inevitably in systematic price discriminations, since the prices they receive upon deliveries from

Kansas City bear relation to factors other than actual costs of production or delivery. As in the case of the twelve cities selected by the Commission for illustrative purposes, the freight actually paid by petitioners in making deliveries usually varies from the freight factor from Chicago, used in computing the delivered price. When the actual freight is the lesser of the two, petitioners charge and collect unearned or phantom freight; when it is the greater, petitioners absorb the excess freight, which they pay, but do not include in the computation of their delivered price.

In either event, on shipments from Kansas City, the delivered price to the purchaser depends not only on the base price plus the actual freight from Kansas City, but also upon the difference between the actual freight paid and the freight rate from Chicago which is included in the delivered price. The difference also results in varying net prices to petitioners at their factory at Kansas City, according to the destination of the glucose. The factory net varies according as petitioners collect phantom freight or absorb freight, and in each case in the amount of this freight differential. The price discriminations resulting from this systematic inclusion of the freight differential in computing the delivered price are not specifically permitted by the statute. Hence they are unlawful, unless, as petitioners argue, there is an implicit exception to the statute for such a basing point system.

Petitioners point out that there is no discrimination under this basing point system between buyers at the same points of delivery, and argue that the prohibition of Section 2(a) is directed only at price discriminations between buyers at the same delivery points. There is nothing in the words of the statute to support such a distinction. . . . The purchasers of glucose from petitioners are found to be in competition with each other, even though they are in different localities. The injury to the competition of purchasers in different localities is no less harmful than if they were in the same city.

We find nothing in the legislative history of the Clayton or Robinson-Patman Acts to support the suggested distinction. . . .

Petitioners further contend that basing point systems were well known prior to the enactment of the Robinson-Patman Act and were considered by Congress to be legal. From this petitioners conclude that they remained legal in the absence of a clear command to the contrary. . . . But we think that the premise falls, and with it the conclusion, whatever it might be if the premise were valid.

In support of the legality of basing point systems, petitioners rely on *Maple Flooring Assn.* v. *United States,* 268 U.S. 563, 570, and *Cement Manufacturers Assn.* v. *United States,* 268 U.S. 588, 597. But these were suits to restrain violations of the Sherman Act, and did not involve the prohibition of the Clayton Act upon discriminations in price. The only question for decision in those cases was whether there was a concerted price-fixing scheme among competing sellers, accomplished in part by their adoption of a uniform basing point system; in fact, no prohibited concert of action was found.

In any event, the basing point systems involved in those cases were quite unlike that used by petitioners. In the *Maple Flooring* case, *supra*, the single basing point was so close to most of the points of production as to result in but trivial freight variances; and the defendants in that case were willing to sell on an f.o.b. mill basis, whenever the purchaser so requested. In the *Cement* case, *supra*, the defendants used a multiple basing point system, with a basing point at or near each point of production. Under this system, any manufacturer, in order to compete in the territory closer freightwise to another, would absorb freight, by adjusting his mill price to make his delivered price as low as that of his competitors. Under this system the delivered price for any locality was determined by the nearest basing point. We have no occasion to decide whether a basing point system such as that in the *Cement* case is permissible under the Clayton Act, in view of the provisions of Section 2(*b*), permitting reductions in price in order to meet a competitor's equally low price. Cf. *Federal Trade Commission* v. *A. E. Staley Mfg. Co.*, decided this day. . . .

Finally, petitioners argue that Congress, by the rejection of a provision of the Robinson-Patman Bill, which would have in effect prohibited all basing point systems, has indicated its intention to sanction all such systems. This provision . . . would have defined "price," as used in Section 2 of the Clayton Act, as meaning "the amount received by the vendor after deducting actual freight or cost of other transportation, if any, allowed or defrayed by the vendor."

The practical effect of this provision would have been to require that the price of all commodities sold in interstate commerce be computed on an f.o.b. factory basis, in order to avoid the prohibited discriminations in selling price. It would have prohibited any system of uniform delivered prices, as well as any basing point system of delivered prices. . . .

Such a drastic change in existing price systems as would have been effected by the proposed amendment engendered opposition, which finally led to the withdrawal of the provision by the House Committee on the Judiciary. . . . We think this legislative history indicates only that Congress was unwilling to require f.o.b. factory pricing, and thus to make all uniform delivered price systems and all basing point systems illegal *per se*. On the contrary we think that it left the legality of such systems to be determined accordingly as they might be within the reach of Section 2(*a*), as enacted, and its more restricted prohibitions of discriminations in delivered prices.

We conclude that the discriminations involved in petitioners' pricing system are within the prohibition of the Act. We pass to the question whether these discriminations had the prescribed effect on competition.

Second. Section 2(*a*) of the Clayton Act, as amended, prohibits only discriminations whose "effect . . . may be substantially to lessen competition. . . ." Petitioners insist that the Commission's findings, based upon the facts stipulated, do not support its conclusion that petitioners' discriminations have the prescribed effect.

It is to be observed that Section 2(*a*) does not require a finding that the discriminations in price have in fact had an adverse effect on competition. The statute is designed to reach such discriminations "in their incipiency," before the harm to competition is effected. It is enough that they "may" have the prescribed effect. . . . But as was held in the *Standard Fashion* case . . . , with respect to the like provisions of Section 3 of the Clayton Act, prohibiting tying clause agreements, the effect of which "may be to substantially lessen competition," the use of the word "may" was not to prohibit discriminations having "the mere possibility" of those consequences, but to reach those which would probably have the defined effect on competition.

Since petitioners' basing point system results in a Chicago delivered price which is always lower than any other, including that at Kansas City, a natural effect of the system is the creation of a favored price zone for the purchasers of glucose in Chicago and vicinity, which does not extend to other points of manufacture and shipment of glucose. Since the cost of glucose, a principal ingredient of low-priced candy, is less at Chicago, candy manufacturers there are in a better position to compete for business. . . . The consequence is, as found by the Commission, that several manufacturers of candy, who were formerly located in Kansas City or other cities served from petitioners' Kansas City plant, have moved their factories to Chicago.

Further, . . . the Commission's findings that glucose is a principal ingredient of low priced candy and that differences of small fractions of a cent in sales price of such candy are enough to divert business from one manufacturer to another, readily admit of the Commission's inference that there is a reasonable probability that the effect of the discriminations may be substantially to lessen competition.

The weight to be attributed to the facts proven or stipulated, and the inferences to be drawn from them, are for the Commission to determine, not the courts. . . . We cannot say that the Commission's inference here is not supported by the stipulated facts, or that it does not support the Commission's order.

[Sections II, III and IV of the decision found that petitioners' booking practices, its discounts to purchasers of by-products, and certain of its advertising allowances violated Sections 2(*a*) and 2(*e*) of the Clayton Act.]

The several violations of Sections 2(*a*) and 2(*e*) of the Clayton Act, found by the Commission, sustained by the court below, and brought here for review, fall within the prohibitions of the Act. The Commission's conclusions are amply supported by its findings and the evidence, and the judgment is affirmed.

Mr. Justice Roberts took no part in the consideration or decision of this case.

Mr. Justice Jackson concurred in the result.

Federal Trade Commission v. *A. E. Staley Manufacturing Company and Staley Sales Corporation*

324 U.S. 746 (1945)

Mr. Chief Justice Stone delivered the opinion of the Court.

Respondents, a parent company and its sales subsidiary, are engaged in the manufacture and sale of glucose or corn syrup in competition with others, including the Corn Products Refining Company, whose methods of marketing and pricing its products are described in our opinion in Corn Products Refining Company *v.* Federal Trade Commission. . . . Respondents, in selling their glucose, have adopted a basing point delivered price system comparable to that of the Corn Products Refining Company. Respondents sell their product, manufactured at Decatur, Illinois, at delivered prices based on Chicago, Illinois, the price in each case being the Chicago price plus freight from Chicago to point of delivery.

In this proceeding, brought under Section 11 of the Clayton Act . . . , the Federal Trade Commission charged that respondents' pricing system resulted in price discriminations between different purchasers of glucose in violation of Section 2(*a*) of the Clayton Act, as amended by the Robinson-Patman Act. . . . The case was heard by the Commission on stipulations of facts and exhibits, upon the basis of which the Commission ultimately made its findings. Applying the same principles as in the Corn Products Refining Company case, it concluded that respondents had made discriminations between different purchasers in the price of their product; and that respondents were unable to justify the discriminations, as permitted by Section 2(*b*) of the Clayton Act, by showing that they were made "in good faith" to meet a competitor's equally low price. The Commission accordingly made its order directing respondents to cease and desist from the price discriminations.

On review of the Commission's order, the Court of Appeals for the Seventh Circuit set the Commission's order aside, one judge dissenting. 144 F.2d 221. . . . We grant certiorari. . . .

The principal question for decision is whether respondents, who adopted the discriminatory price system of their competitors, including the Corn Products Refining Company, have sustained the burden of justifying their price system under Section 2(*b*) of the Clayton Act, as amended, by showing that their prices were made "in good faith" to meet the equally low prices of competitors. A further question is whether there was evidence to support the Federal Trade Commission's findings that respondents, in granting to certain favored buyers, discriminatory prices for their product, did not act "in good faith" to meet a competitor's equally low price within the meaning of Section 2(*b*) of the Clayton Act.

The Commission found that at all relevant times respondents have sold glucose, shipped to purchasers from their plant at Decatur, Illinois, on a delivered price basis, the lowest price quoted being for delivery to Chicago purchasers. Respondents' Chicago price is not only a delivered price at that place. It is also a basing point price upon which all other delivered prices, including the price at Decatur, are computed by adding to the base price, freight from Chicago to the point of delivery. The Decatur price, as well as the delivered price at all points at which the freight from Decatur is less than the freight from Chicago, included an item of unearned or "phantom" freight, ranging in amount in instances mentioned by the Commission from 1 cent per hundred pounds at St. Joseph, Missouri, to 18 cents at Decatur. The Chicago price, as well as that at points at which the freight from Decatur exceeds freight from Chicago, required respondents to "absorb" freight, varying in instances cited by the Commission from 4 cents per one hundred pounds at St. Louis, Missouri, to 15½ cents per hundred pounds at Chicago.

The Commission found that this inclusion of unearned freight or absorption of freight in calculating the delivered prices operated to discriminate against purchasers at all points where the freight rate from Decatur was less than that from Chicago and in favor of purchasers at points where the freight rate from Decatur was greater than that from Chicago. It also made findings comparable to those made in the Corn Products Refining Company case that the effect of these discriminations between purchasers, who are candy and syrup manufacturers competing with each other, was to diminish competition between them. . . .

These findings and the conclusion of the Commission that the price discriminations involved are prohibited by Section 2(*a*), are challenged here. But for the reasons we have given in our opinion in the Corn Products Refining Company case the challenge must fail. The sole question we find it necessary to discuss here is whether respondents have succeeded in justifying the discriminations by an adequate showing that the discriminations were made "in good faith" to meet equally low prices of competitors.

We consider first, respondents' asserted justification of the discriminations involved in its basing point pricing system. As we hold in the Corn Products Refining Company case with respect to a like system, price discriminations are necessarily involved where the price basing point is distant from the point of production. This is because, as in respondents' case, the delivered prices upon shipments from Decatur usually include an item of unearned or phantom freight or require the absorption of freight with the consequent variations in the seller's net factory prices. Since such freight differentials bear no relation to the actual cost of delivery, they are systematic discriminations prohibited by Section 2(*a*), whenever they have the defined effect upon competition.

Respondents sought to justify these discriminations before the Commission, by a stipulation detailing the history and use of their present pricing system. From this it appears that in 1920, when respondents began the manufacture of glucose or corn syrup, they found that syrup manufactured by their competitors "was being sold at delivered prices in the various markets of the United States;" that in Chicago two large factories were manufacturing syrup and delivering it in Chicago at prices lower than prices than prevailing in any other market; and that the delivered price in such other markets was generally equal to the Chicago price plus the published freight rate from Chicago to the point of delivery. Respondents thus found in operation a pricing system which, if followed, would produce exact identity in prices of glucose of the several producers when sold in any city of the United States. Respondents, to gain access to the markets thus established, made their sales "by first quoting the same prices as were quoted by competitors and then making whatever reduction in price . . . was necessary to obtain business." When respondents soon found that their product would command the same market price as that of their competitors, they "adopted the practice of selling at the same delivered prices as [their] competitors, whatever they might be." Respondents have followed the same practice since June 19, 1936, the date of enactment of the Robinson-Patman Act. . . .

But respondents argue that they have sustained their burden of proof, as prescribed by Section 2(*b*), by showing that they have adopted and followed the basing point system of their competitors. In the Corn Products Refining Company case we hold that this price system of respondents' competitor in part involves unlawful price discriminations, to the extent that freight differentials enter into the computation of price, as a result of the selection as a basing point of a place distant from the point of production and shipment. Thus it is the contention that a seller may justify a basing point delivered price system, which is otherwise outlawed by Section 2, because other competitors are in part violating the law by maintaining a like system. If respondents' argument is sound, it would seem to follow that even if the competitor's pricing system were wholly in violation of Section 2 of the Clayton Act, respondents could adopt and follow it with impunity.

This startling conclusion is admissible only upon the assumption that the statute permits a seller to maintain an otherwise unlawful system of discriminatory prices, merely because he had adopted it in its entirety, as a means of securing the benefits of a like unlawful system maintained by his competitors. But Section 2(*b*) does not concern itself with pricing systems or even with all the seller's discriminatory prices to buyers. It speaks only of the seller's "lower" price and of that only to the extent that it is made "in good faith to meet an equally low price of a competitor." The Act thus places emphasis on individual competitive situations, rather than upon a general system of competition. Respondents are here seeking to justify delivered prices which discriminate in favor of buyers in Chicago and at points nearer, freightwise, to Chicago than to Decatur, by a pricing system involving phantom freight and freight absorption. We think the conclusion is inadmissible, in view of the clear Congressional purpose not to sanction by Section 2(*b*) the excuse that the person charged with a violation of the law was merely adopting a similarly unlawful practice of another.

The statutory test is whether respondents, by their basing point system, adopted a "lower price . . . in good faith to meet an equally low price of a competitor." This test presupposes that the person charged with violating the Act would, by his normal, non-discriminatory pricing methods, have reached a price so high, that he could reduce it in order to meet the competitor's equally low price. On the contrary, respondents have used their pricing system to adopt the delivery prices of their Chicago competitors, by charging their own customers upon shipments from Decatur the Chicago base price plus their competitors' costs of delivery from Chicago. Even though respondents, at many delivery points, enjoyed freight advantages over their competitors, they did not avail of the opportunity to charge lower delivered prices. Instead they maintained their own prices at the level of their competitors' high prices, based upon the competitors' higher costs of delivery, by including phantom freight in their own delivered prices.

Respondents have never attempted to establish their own nondiscriminatory price system, and then reduced their price when necessary to meet competition.

Instead they have slavishly followed in the first instance a pricing policy which, in their case, resulted in systematic discriminations, by charging their customers upon shipments from Decatur, the Chicago base price plus their competitors' actual costs of delivery from Chicago. Moreover, there is no showing that if respondents had charged non-discriminatory prices, they would be higher in all cases than those now prevailing under their basing point system. Hence, it cannot be said that respondents' price discriminations have resulted in "lower" prices to meet equally low prices of a competitor. . . .

We cannot say that a seller acts in good faith when it chooses to adopt such a clearly discriminatory pricing system, at least where it has never attempted to set up a non-discriminatory system, giving to purchasers, who have the natural advantage of proximity to its plant, the price advantages which they are entitled to expect over purchasers at a distance. And for like reasons, we must reject respondents' argument that the Commission's order could be rendered nugatory, by respondents' establishing such a high factory price as always to admit of reductions in order to meet the prices of competitors who are using a Chicago basing point system. For we think it could not be said that this practical continuation of the present discriminatory basing point system would be in good faith. But it does not follow that respondents may never absorb freight when their factory price plus actual freight is higher than their competitors' price, or that sellers, by so doing, may not maintain a uniform delivered price at all points of delivery, for in that event there is no discrimination in price.

Congress has left to the Commission the determination of fact in each case whether the person, charged with making discriminatory prices, acted in good faith to meet a competitor's equally low prices. The determination of this fact from the evidence is for the Commission. . . . In the present case, the Commission's finding that respondents' price discriminations were not made to meet a "lower" price and consequently were not in good faith, is amply supported by the record, and we think the Court of Appeals erred in setting aside this portion of the Commission's order to cease and desist. . . .

The Commission's order will be sustained. The Judgment below will be reversed, and the cause remanded with instructions to enforce the Commission's order. So ordered.

Mr. Justice Roberts took no part in the consideration or decision of this case.

Mr. Justice Jackson concurred in the result.

Federal Trade Commission v. *Cement Institute, et al.*

333 U.S. 683 (1948)

Mr. Justice Black delivered the opinion of the Court.

We granted certiorari to review the decree of the Circuit Court of Appeals which, with one judge dissenting, vacated and set aside a cease and desist order issued by the Federal Trade Commission against the respondents. . . . Those respondents are: The Cement Institute . . . ; the 74 corporate members of the Institute; and 21 individuals who are associated with the Institute. . . .

The proceedings were begun by a Commission complaint of two counts. The first charged that certain alleged conduct set out at length constituted an unfair method of competition in violation of section 5 of the Federal Trade Commission Act. . . . The core of the charge was that the respondents had restrained and hindered competition in the sale and distribution of cement by means of a combination among themselves made effective through mutual understanding or agreement to employ a multiple basing point system of pricing. It was alleged that this system resulted in the quotation of identical terms of sale and identical prices for cement by the respondents at any given point in the United States. This system had worked so successfully, it was further charged, that for many years prior to the filing of the complaint, all cement buyers throughout the nation, with rare exceptions, had been unable to purchase cement for delivery in any given locality from any one of the respondents at a lower price or on more favorable terms than from any of the other respondents.

The second count of the complaint, resting chiefly on the same allegations of fact set out in Count I, charged that the multiple basing point system of sales resulted in systematic price discriminations between the customers of each respondent. These discriminations were made, it was alleged, with the purpose of destroying competition in price between the various respondents in violation of Paragraph 2 of the Clayton Act, . . . as amended by the Robinson-Patman Act. . . .

Resting upon its findings, the Commission ordered that respondents cease and desist from "carrying out any planned common course of action, understanding, agreement, combination, or conspiracy" to do a number of things . . . , all of which things, the Commission argues, had to be restrained in order effectively to restore individual freedom of action among the separate units in the cement industry. . . .

Jurisdiction. At the very beginning we are met with a challenge to the Commission's jurisdiction. . . . [Respondents'] argument runs this way: Count I in reality charges a combination to restrain trade. Such a combination constitutes an offense under Section 1 of the Sherman Act. . . . Hence, continue respondents, the Commission, whose jurisdiction is limited to "unfair methods of competition," is without power to institute proceedings. . . . Assuming, without deciding, that the conduct charged in each count constitutes a violation of the Sherman Act, we hold that the Commission does have jurisdiction to conclude that such conduct may also be an unfair method of competition and hence constitute a violation of Section 5 of the Federal Trade Commission Act. . . .

The Multiple Basing Point Delivered Price System. Since the multiple basing point delivered price system of fixing prices and terms of cement sales is the nub of this controversy, it will be helpful at this preliminary stage to point out in general what it is and how it works. A brief reference to the distinctive characteristics of "factory" or "mill prices" and "delivered prices" is of importance to an understanding of the basing point delivered price system here involved.

Goods may be sold and delivered to customers at the seller's mill or warehouse door or may be sold free on board (f.o.b.) trucks or railroad cars immediately adjacent to the seller's mill or warehouse. In either event the actual cost of the goods to the purchaser is, broadly speaking, the seller's "mill price" plus the purchaser's cost of transportation. However, if the seller fixes a price at which he undertakes to deliver goods to the purchaser where they are to be used, the cost to the purchaser is the "delivered price." A seller who makes the "mill price" identical for all purchasers of like amount and quality simply delivers his goods at the same place (his mill) and for the same price (price at the mill). He thus receives for all f.o.b. mill sales an identical net amount of money for like goods from all customers. But a "delivered price" system creates complications which may result in a seller's receiving different net returns from the sale of like goods. The cost of transporting 500 miles is almost always more than the cost of transporting 100 miles. Consequently if customers 100 and 500 miles away pay the same "delivered price," the seller's net return is less from the more distant customer. This difference in the producer's net return from sales to customers in different localities under a "delivered price" system is an important element in the charge under Count I of the complaint and is the crux of Count II.

The best known early example of a basing point price system was called "Pittsburgh plus." It related to the price of steel. The Pittsburgh price was the base price, Pittsburgh being therefore called a price basing point. In order for the system to work, sales had to be made only at delivered prices. Under this system, the delivered price of steel from anywhere in the United States to a point of delivery anywhere in the United States was in general the Pittsburgh price plus the railroad freight rate from Pittsburgh to the point of delivery. Take Chicago, Illinois, as an illustration of the operation and consequences of the system. A Chicago steel producer was not free to sell his steel at cost plus a reasonable profit. He must sell it at the Pittsburgh price plus the railroad freight rate from Pittsburgh to the point of delivery. Chicago Steel customers were by this pricing plan thus arbitrarily required to pay for Chicago produced steel the Pittsburgh base price plus what it would have cost to ship the steel by rail from Pittsburgh to Chicago had it been shipped. The theoretical cost of this fictitious shipment became known as "phantom freight." But had it been economically possible under this plan for a Chicago producer to ship his steel to Pittsburgh, his "delivered price" would have been merely the Pittsburgh price, although he actually would have been required to pay the freight from Chicago to Pittsburgh. Thus the "delivered price" under these latter circumstances required a Chicago (non-basing point) producer to "absorb" freight costs. That is, such a seller's net returns became smaller and smaller as his deliveries approached closer and closer to the basing point.

Several results obviously flow from use of a single basing point system such as "Pittsburgh plus" originally was. One is that the "delivered prices" of all producers in every locality where deliveries are made are always the same regardless of the producers' different freight costs. Another is that sales made by a non-base mill for delivery at different localities result in net receipts to the seller which vary in amounts equivalent to the "phantom freight" included in, or the "freight absorption" taken from the "delivered price."

As commonly employed by respondents, the basing point system is not single but multiple. That is, instead of one basing point, like that in

"Pittsburgh plus," a number of basing point localities are used. In the multiple basing point system, just as in the single basing point system, freight absorption or phantom freight is an element of the delivered price on all sales not governed by a basing point actually located at the seller's mill. And all sellers quote identical delivered prices in any given locality regardless of their different costs of production and their different freight expenses. Thus the multiple and single systems function in the same general manner and produce the same consequences—identity of prices and diversity of net returns.[2] Such differences as there are in matters here pertinent are therefore differences in degree only. . . .

Findings and Evidence. It is strongly urged that the Commission failed to find, as charged in both counts of the complaint, that the respondents had by combination, agreements, or understandings among themselves utilized the multiple basing point delivered price system as a restraint to accomplish uniform prices and terms of sale. A subsidiary contention is that assuming the Commission did so find, there is no substantial evidence to support such a finding. We think that adequate findings of combination were made and that the findings have support in the evidence.

The Commission's findings of fact set out at great length and with painstaking detail numerous concerted activities carried on in order to make the multiple basing point system work in such way that competition in quality, price and terms of sale of cement would be non-existent, and that uniform prices, job contracts, discounts, and terms of sale would be continuously maintained. . . . Among the collective methods used to accomplish these purposes, according to the findings, were boycotts; discharge of uncooperative employees, organized opposition to the erection of new cement plants; selling cement in a recalcitrant price cutter's sales territory at a price so low that the recalcitrant was forced to adhere to the established basing point prices; discouraging the shipment of cement by truck or barge; and preparing and distributing freight rate books which provided respondents with similar figures to use as actual or "phantom" freight factors, thus guaranteeing that their delivered prices (base prices

[2] The Commission in its findings explained . . . , "The formula used to make this system operative is that the delivered price at any location shall be the lowest combination of base price plus all-rail freight. Thus, if Mill *A* has a base price of $1.50 per barrel, its delivered price at each location where it sells cement will be $1.50 per barrel plus the all-rail freight from its mill to the point of delivery, except that when a sale is made for delivery at a location at which the combination of the base price all-rail freight from another mill is a lower figure, Mill *A* uses this lower combination so that its delivered price at such location will be the same as the delivered price of the other mill. At all locations where the base price of Mill *A* plus freight is the lowest combination, Mill *A* recovers $1.50 net at the mill, and at locations where the combination of base price plus freight of another mill is lower, Mill *A* shrinks its mill net sufficiently to equal that price. Under these conditions it is obvious that the highest mill net which can be recovered by Mill *A* is $1.50 per barrel, and on sales where it has been necessary to shrink its mill net in order to match the delivered price of another mill, its net recovery at the mill is less than $1.50."

plus freight factors) would be identical on all sales whether made to individual purchasers under open bids or to governmental agencies under sealed bids. These are but a few of the many activities of respondents which the Commission found to have been done in combination to reduce or destroy price competition in cement. . . .

Thus we have a complaint which charged collective action by respondents designed to maintain a sales technique that restrained competition, detailed findings of collective activities by groups of respondents to achieve that end, then a general finding that respondents maintained the combination, and finally an order prohibiting the continuance of the combination. It seems impossible to conceive that anyone reading these findings in their entirety could doubt that the Commission found that respondents, collectively maintained a multiple basing point delivered price system for the purpose of suppressing competition in cement sales. The findings are sufficient. The contention that they are not is without substance. . . .

Although there is much more evidence to which reference could be made, we think that the following facts shown by evidence in the record, some of which are in dispute, are sufficient to warrant the Commission's finding of concerted action.

When the Commission rendered its decision there were about 80 cement manufacturing companies in the United States operating about 150 mills. Ten companies controlled more than half of the mills and there were substantial corporate affiliations among many of the others. This concentration of productive capacity made concerted action far less difficult than it would otherwise have been. The belief is prevalent in the industry that because of the standardized nature of cement, among other reasons, price competition is wholly unsuited to it. That belief is historic. It has resulted in concerted activities to devise means and measures to do away with competition in the industry. Out of those activities came the multiple basing point delivered price system. Evidence shows it to be a handy instrument to bring about elimination of any kind of price competition. The use of the multiple basing point delivered price system by the cement producers has been coincident with a situation whereby for many years, with rare exceptions, cement has been offered for sale in every given locality at identical prices and terms by all producers. Thousands of secret sealed bids have been received by public agencies which corresponded in prices of cement down to a fractional part of a penny.[3]

Occasionally foreign cement has been imported, and cement dealers have sold it below the delivered price of the domestic product. Dealers who persisted in selling foreign cement were boycotted by the domestic producers. Officers of the Institute took the lead in securing pledges by

[3] A footnote table pointed out that each of eleven companies, bidding for a 6,000 barrel United States Government order in 1936, entered sealed bids of $3.286854 per barrel. IMS.

producers not to permit sales f.o.b. mill to purchasers who furnished their own trucks, a practice regarded as seriously disruptive of the entire delivered price structure of the industry.

During the depression in the 1930's, slow business prompted some producers to deviate from the prices fixed by the delivered price system. Meetings were held by other producers; an effective plan was devised to punish the recalcitrants and bring them into line. The plan was simple but successful. Other producers made the recalcitrant's plant an involuntary base point. The base price was driven down with relatively insignificant losses to the producers who imposed the punitive basing point, but with heavy losses to the recalcitrant who had to make all its sales on this basis. In one instance, where a producer had made a low public bid, a punitive base point price was put on its plant and cement was reduced 10¢ per barrel; further reductions quickly followed until the base price at which this recalcitrant had to sell its cement dropped to 75¢ per barrel, scarcely one-half of its former base price of $1.45. Within six weeks after the base price hit 75¢ capitulation occurred and the recalcitrant joined a Portland cement association. Cement in that locality then bounced back to $1.15, later to $1.35, and finally to $1.75.

The foregoing are but illustrations of the practices shown to have been utilized to maintain the basing point price system. Respondents offered testimony that cement is a standardized product, that "cement is cement," that no differences existed in quality or usefulness, and that purchasers demanded delivered price quotations because of the high cost of transportation from mill to dealer. There was evidence, however, that the Institute and its members had, in the interest of eliminating competition, suppressed information as to the variations in quality that sometimes exist in different cements. Respondents introduced the testimony of economists to the effect that competition alone could lead to the evolution of a multiple basing point system of uniform delivered prices and terms of sale for an industry with a standardized product and with relatively high freight costs. These economists testified that for the above reasons no inferences of collusion, agreement, or understanding could be drawn from the admitted fact that cement prices of all United States producers had for many years almost invariably been the same in every given locality in the country. There was also considerable testimony by other economic experts that the multiple basing point system of delivered prices as employed by respondents contravened accepted economic principles and could only have been maintained through collusion.

The Commission did not adopt the views of the economists produced by the respondents. It decided that even though competition might tend to drive the price of standardized products to a uniform level, such a tendency alone could not account for the almost perfect identity in prices, discounts, and cement containers which had prevailed for so long a time in the cement industry. The Commission held that the uniformity and absence of competition in the industry were the results of understandings or agreements entered into or carried out by concert of the Institute and the other respondents. It may possibly be true, as respondents' economists testified, that cement producers will, without agreement express or implied and without understanding explicit or tacit, always and at all times (for such has been substantially the case here) charge for their cement precisely, to the fractional part of a penny, the price their competitors charge. Certainly it runs counter to what many people have believed, namely, that without agreement, prices will vary—that the desire to sell will sometimes be so strong that a seller will be willing to lower his prices and take his chances. We therefore hold that the Commission was not compelled to accept the views of respondents' economist-witnesses that active competition was bound to produce uniform cement prices. The Commission was authorized to find understanding, express or implied, from evidence that the industry's Institute actively worked, in cooperation with various of its members, to maintain the multiple basing point delivered price system; that this pricing system is calculated to produce, and has produced, uniform prices and terms of sale throughout the country; and that all of the respondents have sold their cement substantially in accord with the pattern required by the multiple basing point system. . . .

Unfair Methods of Competition. We sustain the Commission's holding that concerted maintenance of the basing point delivered price system is an unfair method of competition prohibited by the Federal Trade Commission Act. . . .

We cannot say that the Commission is wrong in concluding that the delivered-price system as here used provides an effective instrument which, if left free for use of the respondents, would result in complete destruction of competition and the establishment of monopoly in the cement industry. . . . We uphold the Commission's conclusion that the basing point delivered price system employed by respondents is an unfair trade practice which the Trade Commission may suppress.[4]

The Price Discrimination Charge in Count Two. The Commission found that respondents' combination to use the multiple basing point delivered price system had affected systematic price discrimination in violation of Section 2 of the Clayton Act as amended by the Robinson-Patman Act. . . .

The Commission held that the varying mill nets received by respondents on sales between customers in different localities constituted a "discrimination in price between different purchasers" within the prohibition of Section 2(a) and that the effect of this discrimination was the substantial lessening of competition between respondents. The Circuit Court of Appeals reversed the Commission on this count. It agreed that respondents' prices were unlawful insofar as they involved the collection of phan-

[4] While we hold that the Commission's findings of combination were supported by evidence, that does not mean that existence of a "combination" is an indispensable ingredient of an "unfair method of competition" under the Trade Commission Act. . . ."

tom freight, but it held that prices involving only freight absorption came within the "good faith" proviso of Section 2(*b*).

The respondents contend that the differences in their net returns from sales in different localities which result from use of the multiple basing point delivered price system are not price discriminations within the meaning of Section 2(*a*). If held that these net return differences are price discriminations prohibited by Section 2(*a*), they contend that the discriminations were justified under Section 2(*b*) because "made in good faith to meet an equally low price of a competitor." Practically all the arguments presented by respondents in support of their contentions were considered by this Court and rejected in 1945 in Corn Products Co. *v.* Federal Trade Comm'n . . . , and in the related case of Federal Trade Comm'n *v.* Staley Co. . . . Consequently, we see no reason for again reviewing the questions that were there decided.

In the Corn Products case the Court, in holding illegal a single basing point system, specifically reserved decision upon the legality under the Clayton Act of a multiple basing point price system, but only in view of the "good faith" proviso of Section 2(*b*), and referred at that point to the companion Staley opinion. . . . The latter case held that a seller could not justify the adoption of a competitor's basing point price system under Section 2(*b*) as a good faith attempt to meet the latter's equally low price. Thus the combined effect of the two cases was to forbid the adoption for sales purposes of any basing point pricing system. . . .

Section 2(*b*) permits a single company to sell one customer at a lower price than it sells to another if the price is "made in good faith to meet an equally low price of a competitor." But this does not mean that Section 2(*b*) permits a seller to use a sales system which constantly results in his getting more money for like goods from some customers than he does from others. We held to the contrary in the Staley case. . . . Each of the respondents, whether all its mills were basing points or not, sold some cement at prices determined by the basing point formula and governed by other base mills. Thus, all respondents to this extent adopted a discriminatory pricing system condemned by Section 2. As this in itself was evidence of the employment of the multiple basing point system by the respondents as a practice rather than as a good faith effort to meet "individual competitive situations," we think the Federal Trade Commission correctly concluded that the use of this cement basing point system violated the Act. Nor can we discern under these circumstances any distinction between the "good faith" proviso as applied to a situation involving only phantom freight and one involving only freight absorption. Neither comes within its terms. . . .

The Order. There are several objections to the Commission's cease and desist order. We consider the objections, having in mind that the language of its prohibitions should be clear and precise in order that they may be understood by those against whom they are directed. . . . But we also have in mind that the Commission has a wide discretion generally in the choice of remedies to cope with trade problems entrusted to it by the Commission Act.

There is a special reason, however, why courts should not lightly modify the Commission's orders made in efforts to safeguard a competitive economy. . . .

In the present proceeding the Commission has exhibited the familiarity with the competitive problems before it which Congress originally anticipated the Commission would achieve from its experience. The order it has prepared is we think clear and comprehensive. At the same time the prohibitions in the order forbid no activities except those which if continued would directly aid in perpetuating the same old unlawful practices. Nor do we find merit to the charges of surplusage in the order's terms.

Most of the objections to the order appear to rest on the premise that its terms will bar an individual cement producer from selling cement at delivered prices such that its net return from one customer will be less than from another, even if the particular sale be made in good faith to meet the lower price of a competitor. The Commission disclaims that the order can possibly be so understood. Nor do we so understand it. As we read the order, all of its separate prohibiting paragraphs and subparagraphs, which need not here be set out, are modified and limited by a preamble. This preamble directs that all of the respondents "do forthwith cease and desist from entering into, continuing, cooperating in, or carrying out any planned common course of action, understanding or agreement, combination or conspiracy, between and among any two or more of said respondents, or between any one or more of said respondents and others not parties hereto, to do or perform any of the following things. . . ." Then follow the prohibitory sentences. It is thus apparent that the order by its terms is directed solely at concerted, not individual activity on the part of the respondents. . . .

The Commission's order should not have been set aside by the Circuit Court of Appeals. Its judgment is reversed and the cause is remanded to that court with directions to enforce the order. It is so ordered.

Mr. Justice Douglas and Mr. Justice Jackson took no part in the consideration or decision of these cases.

Mr. Justice Burton dissented.

Triangle Conduit and Cable Company et al. v. *Federal Trade Commission*

168 F.2d 175 (1948)[5]

Before Sparks, Kerner, and Minton, Circuit Judges.

Kerner, Circuit Judge. Petitioners, fourteen corporate manufacturers

[5] On April 25, 1949 the Supreme Court upheld the Federal Trade Commission order—affirmed in this lower court decision—under Count II of the complaint by a four-to-four tie vote. Clayton Mark et al. *v.* Federal Trade Commission, 336 U.S. 956 (1949) consists of a 23-word order. Mr. Justice Jackson took no part in the case. IMS.

of rigid steel conduit,[6] and five representatives of these corporations ask us to review and set aside a cease and desist order of the Federal Trade Commission, upon a complaint in two counts, charging that petitioners collectively have violated Section 5 of the Federal Trade Commission Act . . . , which declares unlawful "unfair methods of competition in commerce."

In substance the first count alleged the existence and continuance of a conspiracy for the purpose and with the effect of substantially restricting and suppressing actual and potential competition in the distribution and sale of rigid steel conduit in commerce, effectuated by the adoption and use of a basing point method of quoting prices for rigid steel conduit. The second count did not rest upon an agreement or combination. It charged that each corporate petitioner and others violated Section 5 of the Federal Trade Commission Act "through their concurrent use of a formula method of making delivered price quotations with the knowledge that each did likewise, with the result that price competition between and among them was unreasonably restrained." It alleged that nearby customers were deprived of price advantages which they would have naturally enjoyed by reason of their proximity to points of production, and that such course of action created in said conduit sellers a monopolistic control over price in the sale and distribution of rigid steel conduit.

Petitioners answered the complaint. They denied any agreement or combination. After extensive hearings before a trial examiner, the Commission made its findings of fact and conclusions of law therefrom. It found the charges to be fully substantiated by the evidence. . . .

The argument [of defendants] is that there is no direct evidence of any conspiracy; that if the Commission made such a finding, it is based upon a series of inferences; and that the general use of the basing point method of pricing and the uniformity of prices does not justify an inference of conspiracy. We think there was direct proof of the conspiracy, but whether there was or not, in determining if such a finding is supported it is not necessary that there be direct proof of an agreement. Such an agreement may be shown by circumstantial evidence. . . .

In this case there was evidence showing collective action to eliminate the Evanston basing point, and collective activities in promoting the general use of the formula presently to be noted. The record clearly established the fact that conduit manufacturers controlling 93% of the industry use a system under which they quote only delivered prices, which are determined in accordance with a formula consisting of a base price at Pittsburgh or Chicago plus rail freight, depending upon which basing point controls at any particular destination or in any particular section of the United States; that as a result of using that formula the conduit pro-

---

[6] Rigid steel conduit is a steel pipe, used primarily in the roughing-in stage of building construction where electrical wiring is necessary in order to furnish a container for the wiring. It is a standard commodity made from standard steel pipe. IMS.

ducers were enabled to match their delivered price quotations, and purchasers everywhere were unable to find price advantages anywhere; and that purchasers at or near a place of production could not buy more cheaply from their nearby producer than from producers located at greater distances, and producers located at great distances from any given purchaser quoted as low a delivered price as that quoted by the nearest producer.

. . . Not only did petitioners match their bids when submitted under seal to agencies of public bodies, but each, with the knowledge of the others, did likewise—used the formula for the purpose of presenting to prospective private purchasers conditions of matched price quotations.

. . . Our study of this record and of applicable law has convinced us that the Commission was justified in drawing the inference that the petitioners acted in concert in a price-fixing conspiracy.

We now turn to consider petitioners' contention that the individual use of the basing point method, with knowledge that other sellers use it, does not constitute an unfair method of competition. This contention embodies the theory of the second count of the complaint. . . .

Briefly, the argument is that individual freight absorption is not illegal *per se*, and that the Commission's order is a denial of the right to meet competition. More specifically, petitioners say that conduit is a homogeneous product; that no buyer will pay more for the product of one seller than he will for that of another; that the buyer is not interested in the seller's cost of transportation or in any other factor of the seller's cost; that effective competition requires that traders have large freedom of action when conducting their own affairs; that in any particular market, the seller must adjust his own price to meet the market price or retire from that market altogether; that it has always been the custom of merchants to send their goods to distant markets to be sold at the prices there prevailing; that there is no lessening of competition, or injury to competitors, when a seller absorbs freight traffic to meet lawful competition; and that is for the court to decide as a matter of law what constitutes an unfair method of competition under Section 5 of the Act. . . .

On the other hand, the Commission contends that unfair methods of competition include not only methods that involve deception, bad faith, and fraud, but methods that involve oppression or such as are against public policy because of their dangerous tendency unduly to hinder competition or create monopoly.

As already noted, each conduit seller knows that each of the other sellers is using the basing point formula; each knows that by using it he will be able to quote identical delivered prices and thus present a condition of matched prices under which purchasers are isolated and deprived of choice among sellers so far as price advantage is concerned. Each seller must systematically increase or decrease his mill net price for customers at numerous destinations in order to match the delivered prices of his competitors. Each seller consciously intends not to attempt the exclusion of any competition from his natural freight advantage territory by reducing the price, and in effect invites the others to share the available business at matched prices in his natural market in return for a reciprocal invitation.

In this situation, and indeed all parties to these proceedings agree, the legal question presented is identical with the one the Supreme Court considered in the Federal Trade Commission *v.* The Cement Institute case. . . .

In the light of that opinion, we cannot say that the Commission was wrong in concluding that the individual use of the basing point method as here used does constitute an unfair method of competition. . . .

The Commission's order is affirmed and an enforcement decree will be entered. It is so ordered.

PART III

Trade Practices

Chapter 6

EXCLUSIVE DEALING ARRANGEMENTS

The problems involved in exclusive dealing cases are several. First and foremost is that of separating those arrangements which improve the workability of competition from those which foreclose competitors from a substantial market. Subsidiary to this is the problem of determining just what constitutes a "substantial" market. It may safely be said that what the Court attempts to do in these cases is to strike down exclusive arrangements which, resulting from the exercise of appreciable market power, tend to exclude competitors from a substantial market, while sanctioning those exclusive dealing arrangements which were freely entered into by both parties to serve a legitimate economic need.

The Standard Fashion case sets forth the Court's view that the qualifying clause of Sections 2 and 3 of the Clayton Act, ("where the effect . . . may be to substantially lessen competition or tend to . . . create a monopoly . . .") is satisfied when it is shown that a contract would *probably* lessen competition. The effect of the Corn Products case, reported in Chapter 5 below, was to change the requirement of proof from one of *probable* lessening of competition to a *reasonable possibility* of a weakening of competitive forces. To this was added the Standard Stations decision, in which the Court explicitly refused to consider the possible economic justifications of California Standard's exclusive dealing and full requirements contracts. That the Court did not outlaw all exclusive dealing, however, is shown by the later J. I. Case decision, in which Case's contracts were upheld as necessary business arrangements which had neither resulted from coercion of independent dealers, nor produced demonstrably deleterious effects on competition.

A fuller understanding of these cases will follow from reading them in conjunction with those presented in the following two chapters.

Standard Fashion Company v. *Magrane-Houston Company*

258 U.S. 346 (1922)

Mr. Justice Day delivered the opinion of the Court. . . .

Petitioner is a New York corporation engaged in the manufacture and distribution of patterns. Respondent conducted a retail dry goods business . . . in the city of Boston. On November 14, 1914, the parties entered into a contract by which the petitioner granted to the respondent an agency for the sale of Standard patterns at respondent's store, for a term of two years from the date of the contract, and from term to term thereafter until the agreement should be terminated as thereinafter provided. Petitioner agreed to sell to respondent Standard patterns at a discount of 50 percent from retail prices, with advertising matter and publication upon terms stated. . . . Respondent agreed not to assign or transfer the agency, or to remove it from its original location, without the written consent of the petitioner, and not to sell or permit to be sold on its premises during the term of the contract any other make of patterns, and not to sell Standard patterns except at labeled prices. . . .

The principal question in the case, and the one upon which the writ of certiorari was granted, involves the construction of Section 3 of the Clayton Act. . . .

The real question is: Does the contract of sale come within the third section of the Clayton Act, because the [effect of the] covenant not to sell the patterns of others "may be to substantially lessen competition or tend to create a monopoly"?

The Clayton Act, as its title and the history of its enactment discloses, was intended to supplement the purpose and effect of other antitrust legislation, principally the Sherman Act of 1890. . . .

The Clayton Act sought to reach the agreements embraced within its sphere in their incipiency, and in the section under consideration to determine their legality by specific tests of its own which declared illegal contracts of sale made upon the agreement or understanding that the purchaser shall not deal in the goods of a competitor or competitors of the seller, which "may substantially lessen competition or tend to create a monopoly.". . .

Section 3 condemns sales or agreements where the effect of such sale or contract of sale "may" be to substantially lessen competition or tend to create a monopoly. It thus deals with consequences to follow the making of the restrictive covenant limiting the right of the purchaser to deal in the goods of the seller only. But we do not think that the purpose in using the word "may" was to prohibit the mere possibility of the consequences described. It was intended to prevent such agreements as would under the circumstances disclosed probably lessen competition, or create an actual tendency to monopoly. That it was not intended to reach every remote lessening of competition is shown in the requirement that such lessening must be substantial.

Both courts below found that the contract interpreted in the light of the circumstances surrounding the making of it was within the provisions of the Clayton Act as one which substantially lessened competition or tended to create monopoly. These courts put special stress upon the fact found that of 52,000 so-called pattern agencies in the entire country, the petitioner, or its holding company controlling it and two other pattern companies, approximately controlled two-fifths of such agencies. As the Circuit Court of Appeals, summarizing the matter, pertinently observed:

The restriction of each merchant to one pattern manufacturer must in hundreds, perhaps in thousands, of small communities amount to giving such single pattern manufacturer a monopoly of the business in such community. Even in the larger cities, to limit to a single pattern maker the pattern business of dealers most resorted to by customers whose purchases tend to give fashions their vogue, may tend to facilitate further combinations; so that plaintiff, or some other aggressive concern, instead of controlling two-fifths, will shortly have almost, if not quite, all the pattern business.

We agree with these conclusions, and have no doubt that the contract, properly interpreted, with its restrictive covenant, brings it fairly within the section of the Clayton Act under consideration.

Affirmed.

Standard Oil of California and Standard Stations, Inc. v. *United States*

337 U.S. 293 (1949)

Mr. Justice Frankfurter delivered the opinion of the Court.

This is an appeal to review a decree enjoining the Standard Oil Company of California and its wholly-owned subsidiary, Standard Stations, Inc., from enforcing or entering exclusive supply contracts with any independent dealer in petroleum products and automobile accessories. The use of such contracts was successfully assailed by the United States as violative of Section 1 of the Sherman Act and Section 3 of the Clayton Act.

The Standard Oil Company of California . . . owns petroleum-producing resources and refining plants in California and sells petroleum products in what has been termed in these proceedings the "Western area.". . . It sells through its own service stations, to the operators of independent service stations, and to industrial users. It is the largest seller of gasoline in the area. In 1946 its combined sales amounted to 23% of the total taxable gallonage sold there in that year; sales by company-owned service stations constituted 6.8% of the total, sales under exclusive dealing contracts with independent stations, 6.7% of the total; the remainder were sales to industrial users. Retail service-station sales by Standard's six leading competitors absorbed 42.5% of the total taxable gallonage; the remaining retail sales were divided between more than seventy small companies. It is undisputed that Standard's major competitors employ similar exclusive dealing arrangements. In 1948 only 1.6% of retail outlets were what is known as "split-pump" stations, that is, sold the gasoline of more than one supplier.

Exclusive supply contracts with Standard had been entered, as of

March 12, 1947, by the operators of 5,937 independent stations, or 16% of the retail gasoline outlets in the Western area, which purchased from Standard in 1947 $57,646,233 worth of gasoline and $8,200,089.21 worth of other products. Some outlets are covered by more than one contract so that in all about 8,000 exclusive supply contracts are here in issue. These are of several types, but a feature common to each is the dealer's undertaking to purchase from Standard all his requirements of one or more products. Two types, covering 2,777 outlets, bind the dealer to purchase of Standard all his requirements of gasoline and other petroleum products as well as tires, tubes, and batteries. The remaining written agreements, 4,368 in number, bind the dealer to purchase of Standard all his requirements of petroleum products only. It was also found that independent dealers had entered 742 oral contracts by which they agreed to sell only Standard's gasoline. . . .

Between 1936 and 1946 Standard's sales of gasoline through independent dealers remained at a practically constant proportion of the area's total sales; its sales of lubricating oil declined slightly during that period from 6.2% to 5% of the total. Its proportionate sales of tires and batteries for 1946 were slightly higher than they were in 1936, though somewhat lower than for some intervening years; they have never, as to either of these products, exceeded 2% of the total sales in the Western area.

Since Section 3 of the Clayton Act was directed to prohibiting specific practices even though not covered by the broad terms of the Sherman Act, it is appropriate to consider first whether the enjoined contracts fall within the prohibition of the narrower Act. . . .

The District Court held that the requirement of showing an actual or potential lessening of competition or a tendency to establish monopoly was adequately met by proof that the contracts covered "a substantial number of outlets and a substantial amount of products, whether considered comparatively or not." Given such quantitative substantiality, the substantial lessening of competition—so the court reasoned—is an automatic result, for the very existence of such contracts denies dealers opportunity to deal in the products of competing suppliers and excludes suppliers from access to the outlets controlled by those dealers. . . .

The issue before us, therefore, is whether the requirement of showing that the effect of the agreements "may be to substantially lessen competition" may be met simply by proof that a substantial portion of commerce is affected or whether it must also be demonstrated that competitive activity has actually diminished or probably will diminish. . . .

It is . . . apparent that none of these [earlier] cases[1] controls the dis-

---

[1] The Court had summarized its opinions in the five earlier cases in which it had found violations of Section 3. These were: United Shoe Machinery Corp. *v.* United States, 258 U.S. 451; International Business Machine Corp. *v.* United States, 298 U.S. 131; International Salt Company *v.* United States, 332 U.S. 392; Standard Fashion Co. *v.* Magrane-Houston Co., 258 U.S. 364; and Fashion Originators' Guild *v.* Federal Trade Commission, 312 U.S. 457. IMS.

position of the present appeal, for Standard's share of the retail market for gasoline, even including sales through company-owned stations, is hardly large enough to conclude as a matter of law that it occupies a dominant position, nor did the trial court so find. The cases do indicate, however, that some sort of showing as to actual or probable economic consequences of the agreements, if only the inferences to be drawn from the fact of dominant power, is important, and to that extent they tend to support appellant's position.

Two of the three cases decided by this Court which have held Section 3 inapplicable also lend support to the view that such a showing is necessary. These are, Federal Trade Commission *v.* Sinclair Oil Co., 261 U.S. 463 . . . , and Pick Mfg. Co. *v.* General Motors Corp., 299 U.S. 3. . . . The third . . . is of no present relevance. . . .

But then came International Salt Co. *v.* United States, 332 U.S. 392. . . . That decision, at least as to contracts tying the sale of a nonpatented to a patented product, rejected the necessity of demonstrating economic consequences once it has been established that "the volume of business affected" is not "insignificant or insubstantial" and that the effect of the contracts is to "foreclose competitors from [a] substantial market.". . . Upon that basis we affirmed a summary judgment granting an injunction against the leasing of machines for the utilization of salt products on the condition that the lessee use in them only salt supplied by defendant. . . . It is clear, therefore, that unless a distinction is to be drawn for purposes of the applicability of Section 3 between requirements contracts and contracts tying the sale of a nonpatented to a patented product, the showing that Standard's requirements contracts affected a gross business of $58,-000,000 comprising 6.7% of the total in the area goes far toward supporting the inference that competition has been or probably will be substantially lessened.

In favor of confining the standard laid down by the International Salt case to tying agreements, important economic differences may be noted. Tying agreements serve hardly any purpose beyond the suppression of competition. The justification most often advanced in their defense— the protection of the good will of the manufacturer of the tying device— fails in the usual situation because specification of the type and quality of the product to be used in connection with the tying device is protection enough. If the manufacturer's brand of the tied product is in fact superior to that of competitors, the buyer will presumably choose it anyway. The only situation, indeed, in which the protection of good will may necessitate the use of tying clauses is where specifications for a substitute would be so detailed that they could not practicably be supplied. In the usual case only the prospect of reducing competition would persuade a seller to adopt such a contract and only his control of the supply of the tying device, whether conferred by patent monopoly or otherwise obtained, could induce a buyer to enter one. . . . The existence of market control of the tying device, therefore, affords a strong foundation for the presumption that it has been or probably will be used to limit competition in the tied product also.

Requirements contracts, on the other hand, may well be of economic advantage to buyers as well as to sellers, and thus indirectly of advantage to the consuming public. In the case of the buyer, they may assure supply, afford protection against rises in price, enable long-term planning on the basis of known costs, and obviate the expense and risk of storage in the quantity necessary for a commodity having a fluctuating demand. From the seller's point of view, requirements contracts may make possible the substantial reduction of selling expenses, give protection against price fluctuations, and—of particular advantage to a newcomer to the field to whom it is important to know what capital expenditures are justified—offer the possibility of a predictable market. . . . They may be useful, moreover, to a seller trying to establish a foothold against the counterattacks of entrenched competitors. . . . Since these advantages of requirements contracts may often be sufficient to account for their use, the coverage by such contracts of a substantial amount of business affords a weaker basis for the inference that competition may be lessened than would similar coverage by tying clauses, especially where use of the latter is combined with market control of the tying device. A patent, moreover, although in fact there may be many competing substitutes for the patented article, is at least *prima facie* evidence of such control. And so we could not dispose of this case merely by citing International Salt Co. *v.* United States. . . .

Thus, even though the qualifying clause of Section 3 is appended without distinction of terms equally to the prohibition of tying clauses and of requirements contracts, pertinent considerations support, certainly as a matter of economic reasoning, varying standards as to each for the proof necessary to fulfill the conditions of that clause. If this distinction were accepted, various tests of the economic usefulness or restrictive effect of requirements contracts would become relevant. Among them would be evidence that competition has flourished despite use of the contracts, and under this test much of the evidence tendered by appellant in this case would be important. . . . Likewise bearing on whether or not the contracts were being used to suppress competition, would be the conformity of the length of their term to the reasonable requirements of the field of commerce in which they were used. . . . Still another test would be the status of the defendant as a struggling newcomer or an established competitor. Perhaps most important, however, would be the defendant's degree of market control, for the greater the dominance of his position, the stronger the inference that an important factor in attaining and maintaining that position had been the use of requirements contracts to stifle competition rather than to serve legitimate economic needs. . . .

Yet serious difficulties would attend the attempt to apply these tests.

We may assume, as did the court below, that no improvement of Standard's competitive position has coincided with the period during which the requirements-contract system of distribution has been in effect. We may assume further that the duration of the contracts is not excessive and that Standard does not by itself dominate the market. But Standard was a major competitor when the present system was adopted, and it is possible that its position would have deteriorated but for the adoption of that system. When it is remembered that all other major suppliers have also been using requirements contracts, and when it is noted that the relative share of the business which fell to each has remained about the same during the period of their use, it would not be farfetched to infer that their effect has been to enable the established suppliers individually to maintain their own standing and at the same time collectively, even though not collusively, to prevent a late arrival from wresting away more than an insignificant portion of the market. If, indeed, this were a result of the system, it would seem unimportant that a short-run by-product of stability may have been greater efficiency and lower costs, for it is the theory of the antitrust laws that the long-run advantage of the community depends upon the removal of restraints upon competition. . . .

Moreover, to demand that bare inference be supported by evidence as to what would have happened but for the adoption of the practice that was in fact adopted or to require firm prediction of an increase in competition as a probable result of ordering the abandonment of the practice, would be a standard of proof if not virtually impossible to meet, at least most ill-suited for ascertainment by courts. . . .

Though it may be that such an alternative to the present system as buying out independent dealers and making them dependent employees of Standard Stations, Inc., would be a greater detriment to the public interest than perpetuation of the system, that is an issue, like the choice between greater efficiency and freer competition, that has not been submitted to our decision. We are faced, not with a broadly phrased expression of general policy, but merely a broadly phrased qualification of an otherwise narrowly directed statutory provision. . . .

We conclude, therefore, that the qualifying clause of Section 3 is satisfied by proof that competition has been foreclosed in a substantial share of the line of commerce affected. It cannot be gainsaid that observance by a dealer of his requirements contract with Standard does effectively foreclose whatever opportunity there might be for competing suppliers to attract his patronage, and it is clear that the affected proportion of retail sales of petroleum products is substantial. In the view of the widespread adoption of such contracts by Standard's competitors and the availability of alternative ways of obtaining an assured market, evidence that competitive activity has not actually declined is inconclusive. Standard's use of the contracts creates just such a potential clog on competition as it was the purpose of Section 3 to remove wherever, were it to become

buld impede a substantial amount of competitive activity.
decree below is sustained by our interpretation of Section 3
on Act, we need not go on to consider whether it might also
by Section 1 of the Sherman Act. . . .
ment below is affirmed.

Mr. Justice Jackson, with whom The Chief Justice and Mr. Justice Burton joined, dissented. . . . Mr. Justice Douglas separately dissented. . . .

United States v. J. I. Case Company

101 F.Supp. 856 (1951)

Nordbye, Chief Judge.

The J. I. Case Company . . . is a manufacturer and distributor of farm machinery. . . . Its business is nation-wide. . . . It manufactures and sells a complete line of farm machinery and is considered a long-line producer of farm machinery, that is, one which manufactures and sells a relatively complete line of farm machinery. . . .

The farm machinery distributed by Case is sold through a dealership organization. Those dealers are independent owners of and operators of farm machinery businesses in various towns and cities throughout the Nation. There were some 3,738 Case dealers in 1948. . . .

Plaintiff charges that . . . Case, in violation of Section 1 of the Sherman Act and Section 3 of the Clayton Act, . . . "executed, entered into and is operating under written and oral contracts with a substantial number of its dealers which require said dealers to confine their purchase and sale of farm machinery exclusively to the farm machinery manufactured and sold by Case, . . . which . . . contracts are in unreasonable restraint of, and substantially lessen competition, in . . . interstate trade and commerce in farm machinery.". . .

Plaintiff points out that in 1948 the sales of Case were third largest of the long-line companies in the Nation, and that during that year the amount of sales of the long-line companies and the percentage of such sales to the total sales of farm machinery in the United States was as follows:

International Harvester Co.	$351,511,000	22.79%
Deere Co.	235,339,000	15.26%
Case Co.	107,941,000	7. %[2]
Allis-Chalmers	104,423,000	6.77%
Oliver Corporation	64,446,000	4.18%
Minneapolis-Moline	55,741,000	3.63%
Massey-Harris	58,645,000	3.80%

[2] This represented an increase from 3.68% in 1944. IMS.

The acts of alleged coercion and pressure to bring about exclusivity in Case sales, upon which the plaintiff relies, are to be found in the dealings between Case representatives in the field, principally the territory supervisors and branch managers, and the dealers. The territory supervisors call upon the dealers frequently to observe the progress in their business methods, their facilities for service and the type of their establishments, and no doubt to aid them in putting into operation sound business policies so that they may be successful dealers for Case. When the contract with the dealer is to be renewed, it is generally the territory supervisor who recommends to the branch manager whether the contract should be renewed or whether Case should look for another dealer. . . . In addition to the alleged general policy of Case to obtain exclusive dealers, as reflected in correspondence and bulletins issued by the executives of the company and branch managers, plaintiff's testimony is directed primarily to instances involving some 108 dealers located in 13 of the 23 branches maintained by the defendant and as to which it is contended that there were certain acts and conduct of the territory supervisors and the branch managers which indicate coercion and pressure, all designed to obtain exclusivity in Case dealerships and in pursuance of the general policy allegedly adopted by Case. . . .

At the outset, it should be made clear that there is an absence of any evidence from any long- or short-line farm machinery manufacturer that its outlets have been restricted by Case's policy with its dealers, and further, there is no evidence that available outlets to the farmers for the purchase of farm machinery have been narrowed in any way thereby. On the contrary, the evidence discloses that there are farm machinery dealers representing nearly every full-line manufacturer and many short-line manufacturers in most towns in agricultural areas within a reasonable shopping radius of the farmer. And while there are a substantial number of Case dealers who handle either long- or short-lines of competing companies, it is alleged that the potential power of Case to eliminate competitors from access to its dealers as outlets for the distribution of competing farm machinery justifies the granting of relief prayed for herein. . . .

It is evident that Case has been intent throughout the years in question on obtaining dealers who will devote the major part of their activities to the Case line where the market in any particular area justifies it, and to have such dealers handle a full line of Case farm implements. . . .

But the company's policy regarding any attempt on the part of its representatives to coerce or dictate to a dealer as to the other lines he could handle was evidenced from a bulletin circulated as early as 1939 and recirculated in 1946 and sent to all managers and branch managers, stating in part:

It is the Company's policy to secure in each community the best possible dealers to represent it. . . . Whenever the dealer fails for any reason to fairly represent the Case line, then it is of course our privilege to endeavor to secure a better representative and we should exercise that privilege in building up and strengthening our dealer organization.

Occasionally an over-zealous salesman may attempt to use tactics other than well recognized salesmanship principles in building up a dealer organization. . . . In the long run this type of activity . . . is unsound and poor salesmanship. . . .

We, therefore, repeat: . . . it is neither good business nor good salesmanship to attempt to dictate or coerce any dealer with respect to lines of goods that he may be handling. . . .

Plaintiff contends that the policies thus enunciated are only "paper instructions.". . . But this contention is not fairly sustained by the evidence. . . .

During the last World War . . . many dealers in farm machinery handling competing lines were induced by Case to take on its line. . . . And when the war ended . . . Case recognized that it would have to make a survey of all of its dealers, and where inadequate representation was had, new dealers would have to be obtained. And where a dealer was handling another full line with Case and could not do justice to both lines, he was given in many instances a choice as to which line he preferred to handle, and if the competing line was chosen, Case looked for another dealer. . . . Generally, the result . . . would be that there became a Case dealer and the competitive dealer in the community. Therefore, not only did competition continue, but the free flow of farm machinery rather than being impeded was usually increased. There is no showing that any farm machinery manufacturer had difficulty in obtaining dealers as outlets for its particular line under such circumstances. . . .

The advent of power-drawn machinery on the farms . . . has entirely changed the farm machinery business. . . . A full supply of parts for the machinery handled is required to be kept by the dealer. Service men who can promptly respond to the farmer's call when machines break down in the field are indispensable to a successful dealer, and a progressive dealer in farm machinery generally recognizes that, if he is identified in a community as the representative of one of the major lines of farm machinery, he assumes a certain standing and reputation in the community as a dealer with adequate parts and personnel for servicing the particular line which he handles. Just as an automobile owner prefers to go to the agency for service which handles his car for sale and specializes in that car for service, the tractor owner naturally prefers to go to the farm machinery dealer who sells and specializes in that particular line.

It cannot be gainsaid that, in pursuit of a bona fide business policy, Case has the right to select its own customers in absence of any scheme or purpose to effect a monopoly. . . .

A farm machinery manufacturer must have independent discretion as to any person or concern which it will designate as a dealer. If a dealer is handling competitive lines to the detriment of Case, for instance, sound business permits it to withdraw and look for another dealer. The suggestion was made in argument by plaintiff's counsel that a dealer has the inherent right to handle as many lines as he desires regardless of the consequences to him business-wise. Granted, but he has no right to require the manufacturer to fail with him. Surely, where a dealer is so wedded to a competitive line that Case is a mere step-child in the dealer's family, there can be no restriction upon the right of Case to look for another business home in the community. But, with these observations, it must also be emphasized that Case cannot, by direct or indirect methods of coercion or pressure or business policy, obtain any understanding or condition in granting a dealer's contract that the latter will refrain from handling competitive lines if competition may be lessened substantially, or if its acts and conduct in this regard tend to create a monopoly in the farm machinery business.

This brings me to a consideration of the instances with reference to the 108 dealers, upon which plaintiff relies primarily in support of its bill. . . .

The problem which confronted Case after the war with a more or less hybrid group of dealers handling so many side lines, including competitive lines, may well have occasioned some supervisors and branch managers to over-step the bounds of bona fide salesmanship in selling the Case merchandise. However, after a careful consideration of the 108 dealer instances and an analysis of all the evidence bearing thereon, written and oral, it appears that, as to the bulk of them, they do not sustain plaintiff's inference of an understanding or agreement that the Case contracts were granted upon the condition that no competitive goods would be handled, or plaintiff's contention that the contract was not renewed in furtherance of pressure tactics to require a dealer to give up competing lines. . . . The contracts as to a substantial number of such dealers were not renewed due to the non-progressiveness of the dealer, rather than in the furtherance of any policy of competitive restraint. . . .

Moreover, there were only seven dealers out of the 3,738 Case dealers in the United States who were called to testify that any attempt had been made to convince them that they should drop competing lines during the years 1946 and 1947 [when the abnormal wartime situation was easing]. And of these 3,738 dealers, some 2,600 were handling competing lines, either long or short. . . . These circumstances tend to negative plaintiff's contention that Case is pursuing a pattern or policy of imposing competitive restrictions on its dealers.

Section 3 of the Clayton Act is directed to the preserving of a free flow of goods to the ultimate market—here, the users of farm machinery. If there are agreements . . . made with dealers that they shall not handle competitive lines, . . . competition may be lessened or there may be a tendency to create a monopoly. The potential power thus obtained to lessen competition would be sufficient if, were it to become actual, "it would impede a substantial amount of competitive activity." Standard Oil Co. [of California] *v.* United States. . . . But, here there is an absence of any sufficient showing that a substantial amount of competition in the farm machinery industry has been lessened thereby, either actually or potentially. . . .

Realistically considered, it is difficult to understand from the evidence how Case's acts and conduct would have any tendency to lessen competition substantially, or that the outlet for farm machinery has been, or would be, narrowed or endangered thereby. There are some 20,000 farm equipment dealers in the United States and of these dealers the Government relies upon evidence which pertains to 108—less than ½ of one percent of the entire number of farm equipment dealers. Moreover, generally when a Case contract was not renewed as to any one of its dealers, the merchandise of both Case and the competitor continued to flow in commerce as before—the competitor's through the former Case dealer, and Case's through another dealer established by it. . . . Not only is there failure in the evidence to establish any substantial restrictions on outlets for the retail distribution of farm machinery, but the evidence reflects that there is healthy competition among all farm machinery manufacturers. . . .

Attention is directed by the Government to what it terms "full line forcing." That is, it is contended that Case requires its dealer to handle a full line of Case merchandise as a condition of receiving the Case contract. And it is asserted that this practice tends to exclude the dealer as an outlet for competitive goods. . . . So far as the evidence indicates herein, the full line dealerships of Case mean nothing more than that the pattern of the industry has been followed by mutual agreements between the manufacturer and the dealers. The handling by a dealer of a few items of several full-line manufacturers might tend to discourage competition rather than to stimulate it. . . .

The instances of coercion and pressure among the 3,738 dealers of defendant, upon which the Government relies, largely abated prior to January 15, 1946. In fact, the number of Case dealers handling competitive lines increased percentage-wise slightly between 1944 and 1948. . . . Here, no appreciable segment of commerce has been affected or threatened. Here, there is no unreasonable restraint of trade or potential obstruction of competition. The few competitors who may have been foreclosed from dealing with a Case dealer were only temporarily without an outlet for their lines. And such instances are not only relatively few in number, but the amount of commerce actually affected by such restraint is wholly uncertain and speculative. The attempt to spell out any right to injunctive relief to restrain alleged violations of either the Sherman Act or the Clayton Act, on the present showing, is without sufficient persuasive support. . . . The bill, therefore, must be dismissed. . . .

Chapter 7

TYING DEVICES

As the Supreme Court itself noted in the Standard Stations case, *supra*, "Tying agreements serve hardly any purpose beyond
the suppression of competition." Yet, because of the possibility that such
agreements might occasionally be economically justified and legally un-
exceptionable, neither Congress nor the Courts has declared them to be
unlawful *per se*. Once again, it becomes necessary to examine a trade
practice—in this instance tying devices—on a case-by-case basis. The
selections presented below indicate that the crucial test in these cases is
whether the tie-in involves one product or service in which the company
enjoys substantial market power. In other words, the Court attempts to
discover whether the tie-in represents an attempt by a firm to exert leverage so that its monopoly power in one area may be extended into another.
In the American Can case the Court concluded that the tying arrangement was being used by American to extend its dominance of can-closing
machinery into canmaking. This, combined with American's other trade
practices, led the Court to find violations of Sections 1 and 2 of the Sherman Act as well as Section 3 of the Clayton Act. In the Times-Picayune
case, on the other hand, the Court found that the defendants did not
enjoy a dominant market position in either of the markets which it tied
together by its unit rule, and therefore was unable to discover the use
of monopoly leverage.[1] These two opinions might profitably be read in
connection with the International Salt case, presented in Chapter 9.

United States v. American Can Company

87 F.Supp. 18 (1949)

Harris, District Judge.

This action was instituted by the government under the Sherman Act,
Sections 1 and 2 . . . , and the Clayton Act, Section 3 . . . , seeking to
enjoin the American Can Company from unlawful practices, allegedly in

[1] For an extremely illuminating discussion of this case see Dirlam and Kahn, *Fair
Competition: The Law and Economics of Antitrust Policy* (Ithaca: Cornell University Press, 1955), pp. 105–8.

violation of both acts. The primary question for determination is whether defendant's requirements contracts and closing machine leases are illegal in the particulars specified. . . .

The facts are not in serious dispute save with respect to a conspiracy charged against American Can Company and Continental Can Company. . . .

Plaintiff attacks defendant's contracts under which it sells its metal and fiber containers; plaintiff also challenges the legality of defendant's closing machine leases under which it lets its can closing machines which complete the metal and fiber containers. Plaintiff contends that the can contracts and closing machine leases constitute unreasonable restraints of trade and commerce and, in addition, that such contracts and leases, together with certain specified devices, means, methods which will be discussed below, constitute a violation of Section 3 of the Clayton Act. Plaintiff further contends that defendant's contracts and closing machine leases constitute a mode of operation which gives rise to an attempt to monopolize trade and commerce and has effectuated such a monopoly in certain parts of the trade and commerce in canning, in violation of Sections 1 and 2 of the Sherman Act.

The ultimate remedy sought by the government is sweeping: it asks for elimination of requirements contracts and complete divestiture of the closing machine phase of the business. In connection with the requirements contracts, American contends that, if the relief sought is granted, the user-customer will be relegated to an uncertain mode of supply and demand not based upon contracts giving rise to enforceable obligations. . . .

Incorporated in New Jersey in 1902, defendant has long been foremost in the can manufacturing business of the United States. At its inception . . . defendant acquired sufficient plants to enable it to make ninety percent of the cans used in the country.

At the time of the [company's first] trial in 1913, American then consumed approximately one-third of the total tin plate used for domestic consumption in the can manufacturing business in the United States. It will be seen . . . that defendant has more than maintained its position in the industry. . . . On the basis of tin plate consumed [in 1946], American's percentage of the whole was somewhat in excess of 40 percent.

Viewed from the standpoint of competitive sales as against total output of cans, American's percentage is even more impressive. Some canning concerns manufacture their own cans and are thus not in the buying market. Among the can manufacturers who sell on a competitive basis, the total received for cans in 1946 was $433,621,729. American's percentage of the total was 46.4 percent.

What does the evidence disclose as to the business conducted by American's competitors? It shows that of not more than 125 manufacturers of cans, up to 25 make tin containers for their own use; of the competitive can companies only five manufacture what are known as packers' and general line cans. . . .

By graphical representation and statistical supporting data, the trial record is convincing, clear, and complete, that the defendant's domination of the industry has grown over the intervening years; that Continental and American manufacture about 80 percent of all cans made for sale; that there are six companies in the United States, making both packers' and general line cans, and they manufacture 93.6 percent of all cans made for sale. . . .

From the above recital of facts, it is clear that from a national standpoint, defendant is the leader in the manufacture of cans, although it has competition in its business and is not in a position of complete monopoly. From a regional standpoint, the story of control is different. Thus, in such an area as Utah, defendant has the only plant which serves the needs of the packers in that state. A similar monopoly exists in Hawaii, while in Alaska defendant has 80 percent of the can business. As might be expected American is the dominant influence in specific sections of the United States.

Viewed from another standpoint—type of container manufactured—defendant far outdistances its competitors in several lines. . . .

The foregoing should suffice to indicate the dominant position of American in the industry.

With respect to closing machines: Since the canning industry progressed from the hole and cap cans, which were used at the turn of the century, to the sanitary or packers' cans which are closed by machines, American has moved into leadership in the manufacture and leasing of closing machines. Today it makes and leases to its customers substantially all of their closing machines. The leasing practice by American is followed by its competitors, with Continental also making its own closing machines for this purpose. The number of independent concerns engaged in the manufacture of closing machines is limited to two—Max Ams Company and The Angelus.

In terms of the closing machines leased to canners, American controls 54 percent of all such machines. . . . Continental [controls] . . . approximately 36 percent of the total machines on lease. The independent can-closing machine makers are thus limited in their sales to a market of 12 percent of the closing machine business.

It is the fixed and uniform policy of American to lease rather than sell its closing machines. The only exceptions to this policy arise in the few instances in which American sells machines abroad or sells a few single spindle semi-automatic machines in the Ozarks. Other canmaking concerns follow American's policy. Therefore, the two independent can-closing machine makers, Angelus and Max Ams, have a market limited to the small canmakers, for the ordinary canner will not purchase a can-closing machine as long as he can lease it from his can supplier. An important factor which induces canners to lease their machines has been the low rentals charged for such machines. The defendant admits that low rentals provide an effective "sales tool."

. . . [P]resent rentals are insufficient to cover the complete cost of furnishing and servicing the machines. Other canmakers, on a competitive basis have followed American's policy of imposing low or nominal rentals on their closing machines. Rental figures appear to have been purely arbitrary, depending upon the exigencies and the desirability of the customer's business.

The present case is not directed toward American in its capacity as manufacturer of closing machines. However, it should be noted that the practices of defendant in leasing at below cost figures has tended to restrict the market for closing machine manufacturers and has limited the number of concerns engaged in this business. The record disclosed that others would engage in the manufacture of closing machines if there were a free market in which sellers might compete on an equal basis with the canmakers who now lease their machines. . . .

With respect to the requirements contracts: The Government contends that defendant's contracts are the major tool by which it is able to exclude or limit competition in the canning business and, hence, is able to maintain its dominant position. American now has a standard form of contract which the plaintiff chooses to call "total requirements contract." . . . Over the years defendant has handled only minute portions of its sales on an open order basis. . . .

Throughout its business life American has entered into requirements contracts of varied duration. These have ranged from three to twenty years. Recently, defendant prepared a standardized contract of uniform length for five years. For various reasons, defendant believes that a contract of such duration best serves the interest of both canner and canmaker.

American offers an attractive discount on quantity purchases. The scale serves as an inducement for canners to purchase all of their needs from a single manufacturer. . . . [R]equirements contract customers enjoy a price differential in discounts which are not granted to open order customers. . . .

The defendant's degree of market control: The statistical data in this case is voluminous. So that we may appreciate the impact of "bigness" as it relates to the canning industry, we must advert to the earlier [1916] remarks of Judge Rose in United States *v.* American Can Company, 230 F. at page 902. . . . The jurist said that American, although conceived in sin was leading a rather unblemished life and that the earlier transgression should be forgiven and forgotten as a result of its benign attitude. . . .

A decree of dissolution was not ordered. . . .

[From the defendant's history it] is clear an attempt was made both to restrain and monopolize the interstate trade in tin cans.

The closing machine Leases executed by customers with the defendant are violative of Section 3 of the Clayton Act: In the light of Standard Oil Company *v.* United States, 337 U.S. 293 . . . , this phase of the case is reduced to comparative simplicity. In reaching the conclusion that the leasing practices must be proscribed, we must trace briefly the practices of American since the "tying provision" was admittedly removed from the lease contracts covering closing machines.

In May 1917, in the course of an investigation of American by the Federal Trade Commission, the defendant agreed to eliminate from its forms of contract and lease . . . the offending "tying clause.". . .

The Government contends that the provision, although eliminated from the lease forms, has been kept alive and in effect as a result of the practices engaged in by American of a "subtle and refined" character. The practices, in substance, are as follows:

Defendant leases closing machines only to customers who purchase their cans from it, and closing machine leases run for terms concurrent with the can contracts. Sales policies, as contained in memoranda and directives from the executive officers, bear out the Government's contentions that the "tying provision" for all practical purposes has remained in the contract negotiations. The evidence introduced by the Government in this connection abundantly supports this contention. . . .

That the closing machines represent a most valuable sales tool becomes increasingly manifest when it is considered that defendant has in excess of 9,000 machines on lease of an approximate value of 12 million dollars, many of which have been rented at nominal or low rental values in order to foreclose competition. The evidence herein discloses that American owns and controls more closing machines than the rest of the industry together, and demonstrates that defendant effectively ties the leasing of such machines to the sales of its cans. Defendant owns approximately 54 percent of all closing machines available for lease to the industry.

It may be noted that the closing machines manufactured by American, with slight adjustment, may be used to close the cans of the other can manufacturers; that there are no basic patent rights involved as was the case in the International Salt controversy. . . .

It is manifest to this Court from the record herein that abundant proof has been supplied by the Government, and the Court accordingly finds that the leasing practices of can closing machines violate the said Act for they affect injuriously a sizable part of interstate commerce, i.e., an appreciable segment of interstate commerce.

The devices, means and methods used by defendant in accomplishing the monopoly: Much of the trial, which consumed approximately 117 days and embraced more than 7,000 pages of testimony, concerned the

Government's charge that for years American has, by various devices, means and methods, persuaded and induced canners to enter into the requirements contracts. Defendant describes this conduct in many instances as "commercial massage"; the Government counsel refers to the same as "commercial bribery" and other inelegant terms of comparable import.

Suffice it to say, that no useful purpose could be served by recounting herein the details of all the transactions spread over a period of years from 1930. They represent a saga of American business—so-called "big business." Taken alone, or disassociated from the general configuration or picture, many of the transactions would appear to be without probative value. However, as a composite they set a pattern of operations evidencing the extremes defendant saw fit to go in perpetuating the contractual relationship between defendant and the customer-user. The devices took many forms: defendant provided discounts in ancillary contracts; defendant paid large sums of money to obtain business of its customers; defendant furnished equipment, in addition to closing machines, at nominal rentals; defendant paid large claims when it appeared propitious and good policy; defendant purchased canmaking equipment from its customers for inflated values in order to obtain can business. The foregoing represent only part of the claims set up by the Government under the "inducements" phase of the case. . . .

Certain practices, as defendant claims, represent no more nor less than "ordinary business practices . . . in which competitors are seeking to serve the needs of their customers and keep their good will."

The incidents, when examined realistically and not as mere abstractions, are deeper than the typical run-of-the-mill, day-to-day business transactions. They represent a studied, methodical and effective method of retaining and acquiring by refined, gentlemanly and suave means, plus an occasional "commercial massage," the dominant position which American has had and maintained for at least a generation on and over the canning industry. A detailed analysis of this phase of the Government's case convinces that there is little room left in a competitive sense, for the independent small business man. As a competitive influence, he has slowly and sadly been relegated into the limbo of American enterprise.

The evidence establishes violations of Sections 1 and 2 of the Sherman Act: The proof in this case compels the conclusion that the five year requirements contracts and closing machine leases unreasonably restrain trade in violation of the Sherman Act. The evidence discloses that competitors have been foreclosed from a substantial market by the contracts and leases. . . .

With the premise established that American is in a dominant role and a position of preeminent power in the industry, we may then examine the record to determine whether: (*a*) competition has been foreclosed; (*b*) from any substantial market. . . .

Apart from the inevitable conclusion reached that the requirements contracts and closing machine leases, backgrounded by the configuration of the devices and practices, offend against the Sherman Act, Sections 1 and 2 thereof, there is the problem of the user-consumer which must be approached not as a legal abstraction, but realistically. He should not be left without a source of supply. The canners are subject in many instances to the whims of nature over which they have no control. They are, therefore, required to have available a supply of tin containers, fluid in amount, and appropriate from the technological and marketing viewpoints. . . .

In finding the five year requirements contract illegal, we are not thereby compelled to declare void any and all requirements contracts. We *cannot* ignore the testimony of countless witnesses who indicated the vital necessity of some sort of supply contract. . . .

Mindful that requirements contracts are not *per se* unlawful, and that one of the elements which should be considered is the length thereof, it is only fair to conclude after a careful review of the evidence, that a contract for a period of one year would permit competitive influences to operate at the expiration of said period of time, and the vice which is now present in the five year requirements contracts, would be removed. Under a contract limited to one year, the user-consumer would be guaranteed an assured supply and protected by a definite obligation on the part of American to meet the totality of needs of the canner, while he, in turn, would have a fixed obligation to purchase his seasonal needs from American, thus making for mutuality of contract and obligation. . . .

The Government contends that the requirements contracts also offend against Section 3 of the Clayton Act. From a review of the record, the Court perceived that these contracts properly fall within the proscription of Sections 1 and 2 of the Sherman Act and that their provisions must be dealt with accordingly. Defendant's requirements contracts do not come within either the language or the intent of Section 3 of the Clayton Act.

The agreement to fix prices between American and Continental: . . . It becomes unnecessary, under the issues as framed in this case, to make any finding with respect to a so-called conspiracy or to otherwise allude thereto. The conspiracy, or its absence, cannot serve as a premise in any logical reasoning leading to a conclusion with respect to the practices that are at issue. However, we do find that American and Continental, through their officers, agents, and servants, did directly agree to fix prices. This is manifest from the evidence, as well as the pattern of the price lists which appeared in the exhibits. . . .

The remedies sought by the Government: . . . The Court's conclusion being that there has been a violation of the Sherman Act as well as the Clayton Act, the final question is one of determining the equitable relief to be had. . . .

With respect to the ultimate remedies or relief, ruling will be deferred until further hearing and upon notice.

Times-Picayune Publishing Company v. United States

345 U.S. 594 (1953)

Mr. Justice Clark delivered the opinion of the Court.

At issue is the legality under the Sherman Act of the Times-Picayune Publishing Company's contracts for the sale of newspaper classified and general display advertising space. The Company in New Orleans owns and publishes the morning Times-Picayune and the evening States. Buyers of space for general display and classified advertising in its publications may purchase only combined insertions appearing in both the morning and evening papers, and not in either separately. The United States filed a civil suit under the Sherman Act, challenging these "unit" or "forced combination" contracts as unreasonable restraints of interstate trade, banned by Section 1, and as tools in an attempt to monopolize a segment of interstate commerce, in violation of Section 2. After intensive trial of the facts, the District Court found violations of both sections of the law and entered a decree enjoining the Publishing Company's use of these unit contracts and related arrangements for the marketing of advertising space. . . .

Testimony in a voluminous record retraces a history of over twenty-five years. Prior to 1933, four daily newspapers served New Orleans. The Item Company, Ltd., published the Morning Tribune and the evening Item. The morning Times-Picayune was published by its present owners, and the Daily States Publishing Company, Ltd., an independent organization, distributed the evening States. In 1933, the Times-Picayune Publishing Company purchased the name, good will, circulation, and advertising contracts of the States, and continued to publish it evenings. The Morning Tribune of the Item Co., Ltd., suspended publication in 1941. Today the Times-Picayune, Item, and States remain the sole significant newspaper media for the dissemination of news and advertising to the residents of New Orleans.

The Times-Picayune Publishing Company distributes the leading newspaper in the area, the Times-Picayune. The 1933 acquisition of the States did not include its plant and other physical assets; since the States' absorption the Publishing Company has utilized facilities at a single plant for printing and distributing the Times-Picayune and the States. Unified financial, purchasing, and sales administration, in addition to a substantial segment of personnel servicing both publications, results in further joint operation. Although both publications adhere to a single general editorial policy, distinct features and format differentiate the morning Times-Picayune from the evening States. 1950 data reveal a daily average circulation of 188,402 for the Times-Picayune, 114,660 for the Item, and 105,235 for the States. The Times-Picayune thus sold nearly as many copies as the circulation of the Item and States together.

Each of these New Orleans publications sells advertising in various forms. Three principal classes of advertising space are sold: classified, general, and local display. . . . After the Times-Picayune Publishing Company acquired the States . . . it adopted the unit plan of its competitor, the Item Co., Ltd. in selling space for classified ads. . . . In 1950 . . . the Publishing Company eliminated all optional plans for general advertisers, and instituted the unit plan theretofore applied solely to classified ads. As a result, since 1950 general and classified advertisers cannot buy space in either the Times-Picayune or the States alone, but must insert identical copy in both or none. Against that practice the Government levels its attack grounded on Sections 1 and 2 of the Sherman Act. . . .

The daily newspaper, though essential to the effective functioning of our political system, has in recent years suffered drastic economic decline. A vigorous and dauntless press is a chief source feeding the flow of democratic expression and controversy which maintains the institutions of a free society. . . . Yet today, despite the vital task that in our society the press performs, the number of daily newspapers in the United States is at its lowest point since the century's turn. . . . Concurrently, daily newspaper competition within individual cities has grown nearly extinct: in 1951, 81% of all daily newspaper cities had only one daily paper; 11% more had two or more publications, but a single publisher controlled both or all. In that year, therefore, only 8% of daily newspaper cities enjoyed the clash of opinion which competition among publishers of their daily press could provide.

Advertising is the economic mainstay of the newspaper business. Generally, more than two-thirds of a newspaper's total revenues flow from the sale of advertising space. . . . Of the 598 daily newspapers which broke into publication between 1929 and 1950, 38% still published when that period closed. Forty-six of these entering dailies, however, encountered the competition of established dailies which utilized unit rates; significantly, by 1950, of these 46, 41 had collapsed. Thus a newcomer in the daily newspaper business could calculate his chances of survival as 11% in cities where unit plans had taken hold. Viewed against the background of rapidly declining competition in the daily newspaper business, such a trade practice becomes suspect under the Sherman Act.

Tying arrangements, we may readily agree, flout the Sherman Act's policy that competition rule the marts of trade. Basic to the faith that a free economy best promotes the public weal is that goods must stand the cold test of competition; that the public, acting through the market's impersonal judgment, shall allocate the Nation's resources and thus direct the course its economic development will take. . . . By conditioning his sale of one commodity on the purchase of another, a seller coerces the abdication of buyers' independent judgment as to the "tied" product's merits and insulates it from the competitive stresses of the open market. But any intrinsic superiority of the "tied" product would convince freely choosing buyers to select it over others, anyway. Thus "[i]n the usual case only the prospect of reducing competition would persuade a seller to adopt such a contract and only his control of the supply of the tying device, whether conferred by patent monopoly or otherwise obtained, could induce a buyer to enter one.". . . [Standard Oil Co. of Cal. *v.* United States, 337 U.S. at page 306.] . . . Conversely, the effect on competing sellers attempting to rival the "tied" product is drastic: to the extent the enforcer of the tying arrangement enjoys market control, other existing or potential sellers are foreclosed from offering up their goods to a free competitive judgment; they are effectively excluded from the marketplace.

For that reason, tying agreements fare harshly under the laws forbidding restraints of trade. . . .

When the seller enjoys a monopolistic position in the market for the "tying" product, *or* if a substantial volume of commerce in the "tied" product is restrained, a tying arrangement violates the narrower standards expressed in Section 3 of the Clayton Act because from either factor the requisite potential lessening of competition is inferred. And because for even a lawful monopolist it is "unreasonable, *per se,* to foreclose competitors from any substantial market," a tying arrangement is banned by Section 1 of the Sherman Act whenever *both* conditions are met. In either case, the arrangement transgresses Section 5 of the Federal Trade Commission Act, since minimally that section registers violations of the Clayton and Sherman Acts. . . .

In this case, the rule of International Salt can apply only if both its ingredients are met. The Government at the outset elected to proceed not under the Clayton but the Sherman Act. While the Clayton Act's more specific standards illuminate the public policy which the Sherman Act was designed to subserve, . . . the Government here must measure up to the criteria of the more stringent law. . . .

Once granted that the volume of commerce affected was not "insignificant or insubstantial," the Times-Picayune's market position becomes critical to the case. The District Court found that the Times-Picayune occupied a "dominant position" in New Orleans; the sole morning daily in the area, it led its competitors in circulation, number of pages and advertising linage. . . .

But the essence of illegality in tying agreements is the wielding of monopolistic leverage; a seller exploits his dominant position in one market to expand his empire into the next. Solely for testing the strength of that lever, the whole and not part of a relevant market must be assigned controlling weight. . . .

We do not think that the Times-Picayune occupied a "dominant" position in the newspaper advertising market in New Orleans. Unlike other "tying" cases where patents or copyrights supplied the requisite market control, any equivalent market "dominance" in this case must rest on comparative marketing data. Excluding advertising placed through other communications media and including general and classified linage inserted in all New Orleans dailies, as we must since the record contains no evidence which could circumscribe a broader or narrower "market" defined by buyers' habits or mobility of demand, the Times-Picayune's sales of both general and classified linage over the years hovered around 40%. . . . If each of the New Orleans publications shared equally in the total volume of linage, the Times-Picayune would have sold 33½%; in the absence of patent or copyright control, the small existing increment in the circumstances here disclosed cannot confer that market "dominance" which, in conjunction with a "not insubstantial" volume of trade in the "tied" product, would result in a Sherman Act offense under the rule of International Salt.

Yet another consideration vitiates the applicability of International Salt. . . .

The common core of the adjudicated unlawful tying arrangements is the forced purchase of a second distinct commodity with the desired purchase of a dominant "tying" product, resulting in economic harm to competition in the "tied" market. Here, however, two newspapers under single ownership at the same place, time, and terms sell indistinguishable products to advertisers; no dominant "tying" product exists (in fact, since space in neither the Times-Picayune nor the States can be bought alone, one may be viewed as "tying" as the other); no leverage in one market excludes sellers in the second, because for present purposes the products are identical and the market the same. . . . In short, neither the rationale nor the doctrines evolved by the "tying" cases can dispose of the Publishing Company's arrangements challenged here.

The Publishing Company's advertising contracts must thus be tested under the Sherman Act's general prohibition on unreasonable restraints of trade. . . . [T]he contracts may yet be banned by Section 1 if unreasonable restraint was either their object or effect. Although these unit contracts do not in express terms preclude buyers from purchasing additional space in competing newspapers, the Act deals with competitive realities, not words. . . .

Classified. The Item Company, then publishing the Morning Tribune and the evening Item, utilized unit rates for classified advertising in its papers in the year the Times-Picayune Company absorbed the evening States. . . . While thus evenly matched, the Times-Picayune over the years steadily increased its lead. . . .

At the end of that year [1940] the Item Company's Morning Tribune suspended publication; a new local competitive structure took form. In that first year the Item . . . accounted for roughly 23% of the total [classified linage]. Ten years later the Item's share had declined to approximately 20%. . . . Measured against the evening States alone, the

Item's percentage attrition is comparable. In 1941 it sold 37% of the two evening papers' total linage; by 1950 that share had declined to 32%. Thus, over a period of ten years' competition while facing its morning-evening rival's compulsory unit rate the New Orleans Item's share of the New Orleans classified linage market declined 3%; viewed solely in relation to its evening competitor, its percentage loss amounted to 5%.

General Display. Because the unit rate applicable to general display linage was instituted to become effective 1950, only one year's comparative data are in the record. In 1949 . . . the Publishing Company ran 73% of the total. One year's experience with the unit rate for general display advertising showed . . . the Publishing Company's share had risen to 75%. Compared with the States alone, the Item in 1949 accounted for 49% of the two evening papers' total; in 1950, that had declined to 42%. . . .

On the other hand, . . . while in 1949 only 51.6% of general display accounts utilized the Item either exclusively or in conjunction with other New Orleans dailies, one year later 52.8% of the accounts so patronized the Item.

The record's factual data, in sum, do not demonstrate that the Publishing Company's advertising contracts unduly handicapped its extant competitor, the Item. . . .

In effect, the Publishing Company's unit plan merely reallocated the linage sold by its two constituent papers. . . . Apparently it also led more advertisers to insert in the Item, which sold general display space to a proportionately greater number of accounts in 1950 than in 1949.

Meanwhile the Item flourishes. The ten years preceding this trial marked its more than 75% growth in classified linage. Between 1946 and 1950 its general display volume increased almost 25%. . . . [T]he demonstrated diminution of its New Orleans market shares in these advertising classes might well not have resulted in revenue losses exceeding 1%. Moreover, between 1943 and 1949 the Item earned over $1.4 million net before taxes. . . . The Item, the alleged victim of the Times-Picayune Company's challenged trade practices, appeared, in short, to be doing well.

The record in this case thus does not disclose evidence from which demonstrably deleterious effects on competition may be inferred. To be sure, . . . [it] may well be that any enhancement of the Times-Picayune's market position during the period of the assailed arrangements resulted from better service or lower prices, or was due to superior planning initiative or managerial skills; conversely, it is equally possible that but for the adoption of the unit contracts its market position might have turned for the worse. Nor can we be certain that the challenged practice, though not destructive of existing competition, did not abort yet unborn competitors equally within the concern of the Sherman Act. . . . Under the broad general policy directed by Section 1 against unreasonable trade restraints, [however], guilt cannot rest on speculation; the Government here has proved neither actual unlawful effects nor facts which radiate a potential for future harm.

While even otherwise reasonable trade arrangements must fall if conceived to achieve forbidden ends, legitimate business aims predominantly motivated the Publishing Company's adoption of the unit plan. Because the antitrust laws strike equally at nascent and accomplished restraints of trade, monopolistic designs as well as results are reached by the prohibitions of the Sherman Act. . . . The unit rate for classified advertising, however, was adopted in 1935 obviously to counteract the competition of the Item and Morning Tribune which confronted the Times-Picayune Publishing Company with an established unit rate. To be sure, an unlawful trade practice may not be justified as an emulation of another's illegal plan. . . . But . . . uncontradicted testimony suggests that unit insertions of classified ads substantially reduce the publisher's overhead costs. . . .

Similarly, competitive business considerations apparently actuated the adoption of the unit rate for general display linage in 1950. At that time about 180 other publishers, the vast majority of morning-evening owners, had previously instituted similar unit plans. Doubtless, long-tolerated trade arrangements acquire no vested immunity under the Sherman Act; no prescriptive rights accrue by the prosecutor's delay. . . . That consideration, however, is not wholly irrelevant when monopolistic purpose rather than effect remains to be gauged. . . . [T]he unit rate was viewed as a competitive weapon in the rivalry for national advertising accounts. . . . In summary, neither unlawful effects nor aims are shown by the record.

Consequently, no Sherman Act violation has occurred unless the Publishing Company's refusal to sell advertising space except *en bloc*, viewed alone, constitutes a violation of the Act. Refusals to sell, without more, do not violate the law. . . . [T]his Court's decisions have recognized individual refusals to sell as a general right, though "neither absolute nor exempt from regulation.". . .

With the advertising contracts in this proceeding viewed as in themselves lawful and no further elements of combination apparent in the case, Section 2 criteria must become dispositive here.

An insufficient showing of specific intent vitiates this part of the Government's case. While the completed offense of monopolization under Section 2 demands only a general intent to do the act, "for no monopolist monopolizes unconscious of what he is doing," a specific intent to destroy competition or build monopoly is essential to guilt for the mere attempt now charged. . . .

The District Court, and much evidence supports its conclusions, determined that the 1933 purchase of the States then seemed a legitimate means of business expansion; assumed that the Company's cost and revenue allocations between its two publications were mere bookkeeping transactions without economic significance; and concluded that the Company rather than obstruct street sales of the Item merely sought to assure equal treatment by news vendors of the Item and States. Because these pillars of the Government's Section 2 case thus collapsed in the District Court, only the adoption of the unit rates remains to support the alleged violation of Section 2 of the Sherman Act. Since we have viewed that step as predominantly motivated by legitimate business aims, this record cannot bear out the specific intent essential to sustain an attempt to monopolize under Section 2.

We conclude, therefore, that this record does not establish the charged violations of Section 1 and Section 2 of the Sherman Act. We do not determine that unit advertising arrangements are lawful in other circumstances or in other proceedings. Our decision adjudicates solely that this record cannot substantiate the Government's view of this case. Accordingly, the District Court's judgment must be reversed.

Reversed.

Mr. Justice Burton, with whom Mr. Justice Black, Mr. Justice Douglas, and Mr. Justice Minton joined, dissented. . . .

<table>
<tr><td>Chapter
8</td><td># PRICE DISCRIMINATION</td></tr>
</table>

Although many of the legal and economic issues involved in price discrimination were discussed in the delivered pricing cases presented in Chapter 5, *supra*, a few others remain to be considered. The first of these, discussed in the Morton Salt decision, relates to the extent to which the Federal Trade Commission, in enforcing the Robinson-Patman Act, must go to prove that a given discrimination "may" injure competition. The second, and perhaps more complex issue concerns the so-called "good faith defense," and is discussed in the Standard of Indiana case. The importance attached to this latter issue stems partly from the fact that in recent years economists have emphasized that price discrimination, far from injuring competition, may actually make it more workable. The Federal Trade Commission, on the other hand, for some time seemed bent on severely limiting the ability of a firm to meet competition in good faith if any competitive injury might result. In the Standard of Indiana case the Court resolved this conflict in favor of the good faith defense.[1]

Federal Trade Commission v. *Morton Salt Company*

334 U.S. 37 (1948)

Mr. Justice Black delivered the opinion of the Court.

The Federal Trade Commission, after a hearing, found that the respondent, which manufactures and sells table salt in interstate commerce, had discriminated in price between different purchasers of like grades and qualities, and concluded that such discriminations were in violation of Section 2 of the Clayton Act . . . , as amended by the Robinson-Patman Act. . . . It accordingly issued a cease and desist order. . . . Upon petition of the respondent the Circuit Court of Appeals, with one judge

---

[1] Good discussions of these issues may be found in Dirlam and Kahn, *Fair Competition: The Law and Economics of Antitrust Policy* (Ithaca: Cornell University Press, 1955), chapters 7 and 8; and Robert A. Wallace and Paul H. Douglas, "Antitrust Policies and the New Attack on the Federal Trade Commission," Vol. 19, *University of Chicago Law Review* (1952), pp. 1–40.

dissenting, set aside the Commission's findings and order, directed the Commission to dismiss its complaint against respondent, and denied a cross petition of the Commission for enforcement of its order. 162 F.2d 949. The Court's judgment rested on its construction of the Act, its holding that crucial findings of the Commission were either not supported by evidence or were contrary to the evidence, and its conclusion that the Commission's order was too broad. Since questions of importance in the construction and administration of the Act were presented, we granted certiorari. . . .

Respondent manufactures several different brands of table salt and sells them directly to (1) wholesalers or jobbers, who in turn resell to the retail trade, and (2) large retailers, including chain store retailers. Respondent sells its finest brand of table salt, known as Blue Label, on what it terms a standard quantity discount system available to all customers. Under this system the purchasers pay a delivered price and the cost to both wholesale and retail purchasers of this brand differs according to the quantities bought. These prices are as follows, after making allowance for rebates and discounts:

	Per Case
Less-than-carload purchases	$1.60
Carload purchases	1.50
5,000-case purchases in any consecutive 12 months	1.40
50,000-case purchases in any consecutive 12 months	1.35

Only five companies have ever bought sufficient quantities of respondent's salt to obtain the $1.35 per case price. These companies could buy in such quantities because they operate large chains of retail stores in various parts of the country. As a result of this low price these five companies have been able to sell Blue Label salt at retail cheaper than wholesale purchasers from respondent could reasonably sell the same brand of salt to independently operated retail stores, many of whom competed with the local outlets of the five chain stores. . . .

In addition to these standard quantity discounts, special allowances were granted certain favored customers who competed with other customers to whom they were denied.

First. Respondent's basic contention, which it argues this case hinges upon, is that its "standard quantity discounts, available to all on equal terms, as contrasted for example, to hidden or special rebates, allowances, prices or discounts, are not discriminatory, within the meaning of the Robinson-Patman Act." Theoretically, these discounts are equally available to all, but functionally they are not. For as the record indicates (if reference to it on this point were necessary) no single independent retail grocery store, and probably no single wholesaler, bought as many as 50,-000 cases or as much as $50,000 worth of table salt in one year. Furthermore, the record shows that, while certain purchasers were enjoying one or more of respondent's standard quantity discounts, some of their competitors made purchases in such small quantities that they could not qualify for any of respondent's discounts, even those based on carload shipments. The legislative history of the Robinson-Patman Act makes it abundantly clear that Congress considered it to be an evil that a large buyer could secure a competitive advantage over a small buyer solely because of the large buyer's quantity purchasing ability. The Robinson-Patman Act was passed to deprive a large buyer of such advantages except to the extent that a lower price could be justified by reason of a seller's diminished costs due to quantity manufacture, delivery or sale, or by reason of the seller's good faith effort to meet a competitor's equally low price.

Section 2 of the original Clayton Act had included a proviso that nothing contained in it should prevent "discrimination in price . . . on account of differences in the grade, quality or quantity of the commodity sold, or that makes only due allowance for difference in the cost of selling or transportation. . . ." That section has been construed as permitting quantity discounts, such as those here, without regard to the amount of the seller's actual savings in cost attributable to quantity sales or quantity deliveries. . . . The House Committee Report on the Robinson-Patman Act considered that the Clayton Act's proviso allowing quantity discounts so weakened Section 2 "as to render it inadequate, if not almost a nullity.". . . And it was . . . to protect competition from all price differentials except those based in full on cost savings that Section 2(*a*) of the amendment provided "That nothing herein contained shall prevent differentials which make only due allowance for differences in the cost of manufacture, sale, or delivery resulting from the differing methods or quantities in which such commodities are to such purchasers sold or delivered."

The foregoing references, without regard to others which could be mentioned, establish that respondent's standard quantity discounts are discriminatory within the meaning of the Act, and are prohibited by it whenever they have the defined effect on competition.

Second. The Government interprets the opinion of the Circuit Court of Appeals as having held that in order to establish "discrimination in price" under the Act the burden rested on the Commission to prove that respondent's quantity discount differentials were not justified by its cost savings. Respondent does not so understand the Court of Appeals decision, and furthermore admits that no such burden rests on the Commission. We agree that it does not. . . . [S]ection 2(*b*) of the Act specifically imposes the burden of showing justification upon one who is shown to have discriminated in prices. . . .

Third. It is argued that the findings fail to show that respondent's discriminatory discounts had in fact caused injury to competition. There are specific findings that such injuries had resulted from respondent's discounts, although the statute does not require the Commission to find that injury has actually resulted. The statute requires no more than that the effect of the prohibited price discriminations "may be substantially to lessen competition . . . or to injure, destroy or prevent competition." After a careful consideration of this provision of the Robinson-Patman Act, we have said that "the statute does not require that the discriminations must in fact have harmed competition, but only that there is a reasonable possibility that they 'may' have such an effect." Corn Products Co. *v.* Federal Trade Comm'n, 324 U.S. 726, 742. Here the Commission found what would appear to be obvious, that the competitive opportunities of certain merchants were injured when they had to pay respondent substantially more for their goods than their competitors had to pay. The findings are adequate.

Fourth. It is urged that the evidence is inadequate to support the Commission's findings of injury to competition. As we have pointed out, however, the Commission is authorized by the Act to bar discriminatory prices upon the "reasonable possibility" that different prices for like goods to competing purchasers may have the defined effect on competition. That respondent's quantity discounts did result in price differentials between competing purchasers sufficient to influence their resale price of salt was shown by evidence. This showing in itself is adequate to support the Commission's appropriate findings that the effect of such price discriminations "may be substantially to lessen competition . . . and to injure, destroy and prevent competition."

The adequacy of the evidence to support the Commission's findings of reasonably possible injury to competition from respondent's price differentials between competing carload and less-than-carload purchasers is singled out for special attacks here. . . . The argument is that there is an obvious saving to a seller who delivers goods in carload lots. Assuming this to be true, that fact would not tend to disprove injury to the merchant compelled to pay the less-than-carload price. For a ten-cent carload price differential against a merchant would injure him competitively just as much as a ten-cent differential under any other name. However relevant the separate carload argument might be to the question of justifying a differential by cost savings, it has no relevancy in determining whether the differential works an injury to a competitor. Since Congress has not seen fit to give carload discounts any favored classification we cannot do so. Such discounts, like all others, can be justified by a seller who proves that the full amount of the discount is based on his actual savings in cost. The trouble with this phase of respondent's case is that it has thus far failed to make such proof.

It is also argued that respondent's less-than-carload sales are very small in comparison with the total volume of its business and for that reason we should reject the Commission's finding that the effect of the carload discrimination may substantially lessen competition and may injure competition between purchasers who are granted and those who are denied this discriminatory discount. To support this argument, reference is made to the fact that salt is a small item in most wholesale and retail businesses and in consumers' budgets. For several reasons we cannot accept this contention.

There are many articles in a grocery store that, considered separately, are comparatively small parts of a merchant's stock. Congress intended to protect a merchant from competitive injury attributable to discriminatory prices on any or all goods sold in interstate commerce, whether the particular goods constituted a major or minor portion of his stock. Since a grocery store consists of many comparatively small articles, there is no possible way effectively to protect a grocer from discriminatory prices except by applying the prohibitions of the Act to each individual article in the store.

Furthermore, in enacting the Robinson-Patman Act Congress was especially concerned with protecting small businesses which were unable to buy in quantities, such as the merchants here who purchased in less-than-carload lots. To this end it undertook to strengthen this very phase of the old Clayton Act. . . . Since there was evidence sufficient to show that the less-than-carload purchasers might have been handicapped in competing with the more favored carload purchasers by the differential in price established by respondent, the Commission was justified in finding that competition might have thereby been substantially lessened or have been injured within the meaning of the Act.

Apprehension is expressed in this Court that enforcement of the Commission's order against respondent's continued violations of the Robinson-Patman Act might lead respondent to raise table salt prices to its carload purchasers. Such a conceivable, though, we think, highly improbable contingency, could afford us no reason for upsetting the Commission's findings and declining to direct compliance with a statute passed by Congress.

The Commission here went much further in receiving evidence than the statute requires. It heard testimony from many witnesses in various parts of the country to show that they had suffered actual financial losses on account of respondent's discriminatory prices. Experts were offered to prove the tendency of injury from such prices. The evidence covers about two thousand pages, largely devoted to this single issue—injury to competition. It would greatly handicap effective enforcement of the Act to require testimony to show that which we believe to be self-evident, namely, that there is a "reasonable possibility" that competition may be adversely affected by a practice under which manufacturers and producers sell their goods to some customers substantially cheaper than they sell like goods to the competitors of these customers. This showing in itself is sufficient to justify our conclusion that the Commission's findings of injury to competition were adequately supported by evidence.

Fifth. The Circuit Court of Appeals held, and respondent here contends, that the order was too sweeping. . . .

True, the Commission did not merely prohibit future discounts, rebates, and allowances in the exact mathematical percentages previously utilized by respondent. Had the order done no more than that, respondent could have continued substantially the same unlawful practices despite the order by simply altering the discount percentages and the quantities of salt to which the percentages applied. . . .

The judgment of the Circuit Court of Appeals is reversed and the proceedings are remanded to that court to be disposed of in conformity with this opinion. Reversed.

Mr. Justice Jackson with whom Mr. Justice Frankfurter joined, dissented in part. . . .

Standard Oil Company v. Federal Trade Commission

340 U.S. 231 (1951)

Mr. Justice Burton delivered the opinion of the Court.

In this case the Federal Trade Commission challenged the right of the Standard Oil Company, under the Robinson-Patman Act, to sell gasoline to four comparatively large "jobber" customers in Detroit at a less price per gallon than it sold like gasoline to many comparatively small service station customers in the same area. The Company's defenses were that (1) the sales involved were not in interstate commerce and (2) its lower price to the jobbers was justified because made to retain them as customers and in good faith to meet an equally low price of a competitor. The Commission, with one member dissenting, ordered the company to cease and desist from making such a price differential. 43 F.T.C. 56. The Court of Appeals slightly modified the order and required its enforcement as modified. 173 F.2d 210. We granted certiorari on petition of the company because the case presents an important issue under the Robinson-Patman Act which has not been settled by this Court. . . .

For the reasons hereinafter stated, we agree with the court below that the sales were made in interstate commerce but we agree with petitioner that, under the Act, the lower price to the jobbers was justified if it was made to retain each of them as a customer and in good faith to meet an equally low price of a competitor.

. . . [T]he material facts are summarized here on the basis of the Commission's findings. The sales described are those of Red Crown gasoline because those sales raise all of the material issues and constitute about 90% of petitioner's sales in the Detroit area.

Since the effective date of the Robinson-Patman Act, June 19, 1936, petitioner has sold its Red Crown Gasoline to its "jobber" customers at its tank-car prices. Those prices have been 1½¢ per gallon less than its tank-wagon prices to service station customers for identical gasoline in the same area. In practice, the service stations have resold the gasoline at the prevailing retail service station prices. Each of petitioner's so-called "jobber" customers has been free to resell its gasoline at retail or wholesale. Each, at some time, has resold some of it at retail. One now resells it only at retail. The others now resell it largely at wholesale. As to resale prices, two of the "jobbers" have resold their gasoline only at the prevailing wholesale or retail rates. The other two, however, have reflected, in varying degrees, petitioner's reductions in the cost of the gasoline to them by reducing their resale prices of that gasoline below the prevailing rates. The effect of these reductions has thus reached competing retail service stations in part through retail stations operated by the "jobbers" and in part through retail stations which purchased gasoline from the "jobbers" at less than the prevailing tank-wagon prices. The Commission found that such reduced resale prices "have resulted in injuring, destroying, and preventing competition between said favored dealers and retail dealers in respondent's [petitioner's] gasoline and other major brands of gasoline. . . ." The distinctive characteristics of these "jobbers" are that each (1) maintains sufficient bulk storage to take delivery of gasoline in tank-car quantities (of 8,000 to 12,000 gallons) rather than in tank-wagon quantities (or 700 to 800 gallons) as is customary for service stations; (2) owns and operates tank wagons and other facilities for delivery of gasoline to service stations; (3) has an established business sufficient to insure purchases of from one to two million gallons a year; and (4) has adequate credit responsibility. While the cost of petitioner's sales and deliveries of gasoline to each of these four "jobbers" is no doubt less, per gallon, than the cost of its sales and deliveries of like gasoline to its service station customers in the same area, there is no finding that such difference accounts for the entire reduction in price made by petitioner to these "jobbers," and we proceed on the assumption that it does not entirely account for that difference.

Petitioner placed its reliance upon evidence offered to show that its lower price to each jobber was made in order to retain that jobber as a customer and in good faith to meet an equally low price offered by one or more competitors. The Commission, however, treated such evidence as not relevant. [The Commission stated:] . . .

. . . [E]ven though the lower prices in question may have been made by respondent in good faith to meet the lower prices of competitors, this does not constitute a defense in the face of affirmative proof that the effect of the discrimination was to injure, destroy and prevent competition with the retail stations operated by the said named dealers and with stations operated by their retailer-customers. . . .

In its opinion in the instant case, the Commission recognizes that it is an absolute defense to a charge of price discrimination for a seller to prove, under Section 2(*a*) that its price differential makes only due allowances for differences in cost or for price changes made in response to changing market conditions. 41 F.T.C. at 283. Each of these three defenses is introduced by the same phrase, "nothing . . . shall prevent," and all are embraced in the same word "justification" in the first sentence of Section 2(*b*). It is natural, therefore, to conclude that each of these defenses is entitled to the same effect, without regard to whether there also appears an affirmative showing of actual or potential injury to competition at the same or a lower level traceable to the price differential made by the seller. The Commission says, however, that the proviso in Section 2(*b*) as to a seller meeting in good faith a lower competitive price is not an absolute defense if an injury to competition may result from such price reduction. We find no basis for such a distinction between the defense in Section 2(*a*) and (*b*).

The defense in subsection (*b*), now before us, is limited to a price reduction made to meet in good faith an equally low price of a competitor. . . . [But] . . . the actual core of the defense . . . still consists of the provision that wherever a lawful lower price of a competitor threatens to deprive a seller of a customer, the seller, to retain that customer, may in good faith meet that lower price. Actual competition, at least in this elemental form, is thus preserved. . . .

This right of a seller, under Section 2(*b*), to meet in good faith an equally low price of a competitor has been considered here before. Both in Corn Products Refining Co. *v.* Federal Trade Comm'n, 324 U.S. 726, and in Federal Trade Comm'n *v.* Staley Mfg. Co., 324 U.S. 746, evidence in support of this defense was reviewed at length. There would have been no occasion thus to review it under the theory now contended for by the Commission. While this Court did not sustain the seller's defense in either case, it did unquestionably recognize the relevance of the evidence in support of that defense. The decision in each case was based upon the insufficiency of the seller's evidence to establish its defense, not upon the inadequacy of its defense as a matter of law. . . .

In the Staley case . . . , most of the Court's opinion is devoted to the consideration of the evidence introduced in support of the seller's defense under Section 2(*b*). The discussion proceeds upon the assumption, applicable here, that if a competitor's "lower price" is a lawful individual price offered to any of the seller's customers, then the seller is protected, under Section 2(*b*), in making a counteroffer provided the seller proves that its counteroffer is made to meet in good faith its competitor's equally low price.

. . . All that petitioner asks in the instant case is that its evidence be considered and that findings be made by the Commission as to the sufficiency of that evidence to support petitioner's defense under Section 2(*b*).

In addition, there has been widespread understanding that, under the

Robinson-Patman Act, it is a complete defense to a charge of price discrimination for the seller to show that its price differential has been made in good faith to meet a lawful and equally low price of a competitor. This understanding is reflected in actions and statements of members and counsel of the Federal Trade Commission. Representatives of the Department of Justice have testified to the effectiveness and value of the defense under the Robinson-Patman Act. We see no reason to depart now from that interpretation.

The heart of our national economic policy long has been faith in the value of competition. In the Sherman and Clayton Acts, as well as in the Robinson-Patman Act, "Congress was dealing with competition, which it sought to protect, and monopoly, which it sought to prevent.". . . We need not now reconcile, in its entirety, the economic theory which underlies the Robinson-Patman Act with that of the Sherman and Clayton Acts. It is enough to say that Congress did not seek by the Robinson-Patman Act either to abolish competition or so radically to curtail it that a seller would have no substantial right of self-defense against a price raid by a competitor. . . . There is . . . plain language and established practice which permits a seller, through Section 2(b), to retain a customer by realistically meeting in good faith the price offered to that customer, without necessarily changing the sellers price to its other customers.

In a case where a seller sustains the burden of proof placed upon it to establish its defense under Section 2(b), we find no reason to destroy that defense indirectly, merely because it also appears that the beneficiaries of the seller's price reductions may derive a competitive advantage from them or may, in a natural course of events, reduce their own resale prices to their customers. It must have been obvious to Congress that any price reduction to any dealer may always affect competition at that dealer's level as well as at the dealer's resale level, whether or not the reduction to the dealer is discriminatory. Likewise, it must have been obvious to Congress that any price reductions initiated by a seller's competitor would, if not met by the seller, affect competition at the beneficiary's level or among the beneficiary's customers just as much as if those reductions had been met by the seller. The proviso in Section 2(b), as interpreted by the Commission, would not be available when there was or might be an injury to competition at a resale level. So interpreted the proviso would have such little, if any, applicability as to be practically meaningless. We may, therefore, conclude that Congress meant to permit the natural consequences to follow the seller's action in meeting in good faith a lawful and equally low price of its competitor.

In its argument here, the Commission suggests that there may be some situations in which it might recognize the proviso in Section 2(b) as a complete defense, even though the seller's differential in price did injure competition. In support of this, the Commission indicates that in each case it must weigh the potentially injurious effect of a seller's price reduction upon competition at all lower levels against its beneficial effect in permitting the seller to meet competition at its own level. In the absence of more explicit requirements and more specific standards of comparison than we have here, it is difficult to see how an injury to competition at a level below that of the seller can thus be balanced fairly against a justification for meeting the competition at the seller's level. We hesitate to accept Section 2(b) as establishing such a dubious defense. . . .

The judgment of the Court of Appeals, accordingly, is reversed and the case is remanded to that court with instructions to remand it to the Federal Trade Commission to make findings, in conformity with this opinion. It is so ordered.

Mr. Justice Minton took no part in the consideration or decision of this case.

Mr. Justice Reed, with whom the Chief Justice and Mr. Justice Black joined, dissented. . . .

PART IV

Legal Monopolies under Federal Antitrust

| Chapter | PATENTS—THE RIGHT AND |
| 9 | ITS LIMITS |

Our patent laws are predicated upon the assumption that progress in the sciences and in the useful arts will best be promoted by granting to the inventor a legal monopoly of his discovery. Thus, in a sense, the patent laws may be viewed as exceptions to our antitrust policy of preserving competition. In another sense, however, the patent laws appear as instruments which are designed to accelerate technological progress by granting short-term monopoly privileges as offsets to the risks involved in introducing a new product or process; i.e., they may stimulate competition in the long-run, Schumpeterian sense of that word. In any event, conflict between the patent and antitrust laws has arisen only when the holder of the patent right oversteps the bounds of his lawful monopoly in an attempt to suppress competition. This may occur when, as in the Hartford-Empire case, patent cross-licensing is used, not to promote competition by making technological information more widely available in the industry,[1] but to monopolize an entire industry. A patentee may violate the antitrust laws when, as in the International Salt case, he uses the patent monopoly as a lever to gain dominance in another and totally different market. These cases provide at least a partial understanding of the varied and complex public policy issues involved in antitrust suits of this type.[2] In addition, the Hartford-Empire case illustrates perhaps more clearly than any other in this general area the problem of framing an adequate decree—one which prevents future antitrust violations without unnecessarily impinging on the patent right.

Further insight into the antitrust implications of patents may be obtained by reading Judge Rifkind's decision in the National Lead case, presented in Chapter 11.

[1] See, for example, D. A. Moore, "The Automobile Industry," *The Structure of American Industry*, ed. Walter Adams (New York: Macmillan, 1954).

[2] For a fuller treatment see Clair Wilcox, *Public Policies Toward Business* (Homewood, Ill.: Richard D. Irwin, 1955), chapter 6; S. C. Oppenheim, *Cases on Federal Antitrust Laws* (St. Paul: West Publishing Co., 1948), chapter 11; Alfred E. Kahn, "Deficiencies of American Patent Law," *American Economic Review*, Vol. XXX, No. 3 (September, 1940); Fritz Machlup, *The Political Economy of Monopoly* (Baltimore: Johns Hopkins Press, 1952), pp. 280–86; Vernon Mund, *Government and Business* (New York: Harper, 1955) chapter 14.

Hartford-Empire Company v. United States

323 U.S. 386 (1945)

Mr. Justice Roberts delivered the opinion of the Court.

These are appeals from a decree awarding an injunction against violations of Sections 1 and 2 of the Sherman Act, as amended, and Section 3
of the Clayton Act. Two questions are presented. Were violations proved?
If so, are the provisions of the decree right?

The complaint named as defendants . . . the leaders in automatic
glassmaking machinery and in the glassware industry. The charge is that
all the defendants agreed, conspired, and combined to monopolize, and
did monopolize and restrain interstate and foreign commerce by acquiring patents covering the manufacture of glass-making machinery, and by
excluding others from a fair opportunity freely to engage in commerce in
such machinery and in the manufacture and distribution of glass products.
The gravamen of the case is that the defendants have cooperated in obtaining and licensing patents covering glass-making machinery, have limited and restricted the use of the patented machinery by a network of
agreements, and have maintained prices for unpatented glassware. . . .

In 1919 the Glass Container Association of America was formed. . . .
The court below, on sufficient evidence, has found that the association,
through its statistical committee, assigned production quotas to its members and that they and Hartford were zealous in seeing that these were
observed.

In summary, the situation brought about in the glass industry, and existing in 1938, was this: Hartford, with the technical and financial aid of
others in the conspiracy, had acquired, by issue to it or assignment from
the owners, more than 600 patents. These, with over 100 Corning controlled patents, over 60 Owens patents, over 70 Hazel patents, and some
12 Lynch patents, had been, by cross-licensing agreements, merged into a
pool which effectually controlled the industry. This control was exercised
to allot production in Corning's field[3] to Corning, and that in restricted
classes within the general container field to Owens, Hazel, Thatcher, Ball,
and such other smaller manufacturers as the group agreed should be
licensed. The result was that 94% of the glass containers manufactured
in this country on feeders and formers were made on machinery licensed
under the pooled patents.

The district court found that invention of glass-making machinery
had been discouraged, that competition in the manufacture and sale or
licensing of such machinery had been suppressed, and that the system of
restricted licensing had been employed to suppress competition in the
manufacture of unpatented glassware and to maintain prices of the manufactured product. The findings are full and adequate and are supported

[3] The pressed and blown glass, or non-container field. IMS.

by evidence, much of it contemporary writings of corporate defendants or their officers and agents. . . .

We affirm the District Court's findings and conclusions that the corporate appellants combined in violation of the Sherman Act, that Hartford and Lynch contracted in violation of the Clayton Act, and that the individual appellants with exceptions to be noted participated in the violations in their capacities as officers and directors of the corporations. . . .

I. Little need be said concerning the legal principles which vindicate the District Court's findings and conclusions. . . .

It is clear that, by cooperative arrangements and binding agreements, the appellant corporations, over a period of years, regulated and suppressed competition in the use of glass making machinery and employed their joint patent position to allocate fields of manufacture and to maintain prices of unpatented glassware.

The explanations offered by the appellants are unconvincing. It is said, on behalf of Hartford, that its business, in its inception, was lawful and within the patent laws; and that, in order to protect its legitimate interests as holder of patents for automatic glass machinery, it was justified in buying up and fencing off improvement patents, the grant of which, while leaving the fundamental inventions untouched, would hamper their use unless tribute were paid to the owners of the so-called improvements which, of themselves, had only a nuisance value.

The explanation fails to account for the offensive and defensive alliance of patent owners with its concomitant stifling of initiative, invention and competition.

Nor can Owens' contention prevail that it long ago abandoned any cooperation with the other corporate defendants and has been free of any trammel to unrestricted competition either in the machinery or glass field. Owens remained active in the association. It remained dominant in the suction field. It continued in close touch with Hartford and with other large manufacturers of glassware who were parties to the conspiracy. The District Court was justified in finding that the mere cancellation of the written word was not enough, in the light of subsequent conduct, to acquit Owens of further participation in the conspiracy. . . .

II. The Government sought the dissolution of Hartford. The court, however, decided that a continuance of certain of Hartford's activities would be of advantage to the glass industry and denied, for the time being, that form of relief. The court was of opinion, however, that the long series of transactions and the persistent manifestations of a purpose to violate the antitrust statutes required the entry of a decree which would preclude the resumption of unlawful practices. It was faced, therefore, with the difficult problem of awarding an injunction which would insure the desired end without imposing punishments or other sanctions for past misconduct, a problem especially difficult in view of the status and relationship of the parties.

At the trial the Government stated that in this suit it was not attacking the validity of any patent or claiming any patent had been awarded an improper priority.

At the time of the District Court's decision, Hartford had reduced the royalties of all its licensees to its then schedule of standard royalties so that all stood on an equal basis so far as license fees were concerned. Government counsel did not assert, or attempt to prove, that these royalties were not reasonable in amount.

Owens, as respects suction invention licenses, had removed all restrictive clauses; Hartford had done the same with respect to all its glass machinery licenses and so had Hartford and Lynch with respect to forming machine licenses. . . .

The association had ceased to allot quotas amongst the glass manufacturers or to furnish advance information or make recommendations to its members. The licensing system of Hartford remained that of leasing machinery built for it embodying the patented inventions. Rentals consisted of standard royalties on production. Under this system Hartford rendered a service in the repair, maintenance, and protection of the machines, which is valuable, if not essential, to the users. This was the status with which the court had to deal.

The applicable principles are not doubtful. The Sherman Act provides criminal penalties for its violation, and authorizes the recovery of a penal sum in addition to damages in a civil suit by one injured by violation. It also authorizes an injunction to prevent continuing violations by those acting contrary to its prescriptions. The present suit is in the last named category and we may not impose penalties in the guise of preventing future violations. This is not to say that a decree need deal only with the exact type of acts found to have been committed or that the court should not, in framing its decree, resolve all doubts in favor of the Government, or may not prohibit acts which in another setting would be unobjectionable. But, even so, the court may not create, as to the defendants, new duties, prescription of which is the function of Congress, or place the defendants, for the future, "in a different class than the other people," as the Government has suggested. The decree must not be "so vague as to put the whole conduct of the defendants' business at the peril of a summons for contempt"; or cause the defendants hereafter not "to be under the protection of the law of the land." With these principles in mind we proceed to examine the terms of the decree entered. . . .

The court appointed a receiver for Hartford *pendente lite*. By paragraphs 10 to 20 of the final decree it continued him in office and gave directions as to his administration of Hartford's affairs, including certain actions to be taken to effectuate features of the decree affecting Hartford's business and licenses, which will later be described, and meantime to continue the receipt of royalties under existing licenses, these to be repaid to the licensees on the decree bcoming final. . . .

[T]he receivership and the impounding of funds were not necessary to the prescription of appropriate relief. The receivership should be wound up and the business returned to Hartford. The royalties paid to the receiver by Harford's lessees may, unless the District Court finds that Hartford has, since the entry of the receivership decree, violated the anti-trust laws, or acted contrary to the terms of the final decree as modified by this opinion, be paid over to Hartford. . . .

Paragraphs 21, 22, and 23 . . . forbid any disposition or transfer of possession of such machinery by any means other than an outright sale, and require Hartford to offer in writing to sell each of the present lessees all the machinery now under lease to such lessee at a reasonable price. . . .

All of the appellants attack these provisions. . . . The Government replies that the injunction is intended only to prevent them from again setting up a patent pool and monopolizing the patented inventions. . . . But the decree as entered requires that each of the defendants must here-after forever abstain from leasing a patented machine, no matter what the date of the invention and compels each of them if he desires to distribute patented machinery to sell the machine which embodies the patent to ev-eryone who applies, at a price to be fixed by the court. The injunction as drawn is not directed at any combination, agreement or conspiracy. It binds every defendant forever irrespective of his connection with any other or of the independence of his action. . . .

[Paragraph 24 requires defendants to license all present and future pat-ents on a royalty-free basis.]

Since the provisions of paragraphs 21 to 24 inclusive, in effect confis-cate considerable portions of the appellants' property, we think they go beyond what is required to dissolve the combination and prevent future combinations of like character. It is to be borne in mind that the Govern-ment has not, in this litigation, attacked the validity of any patent or the priority ascribed to any by the patent office, nor has it attacked, as exces-sive or unreasonable, the standard royalties heretofore exacted by Hart-ford. Hartford has reduced all of its royalties to a uniform scale and has waived and abolished and agreed to waive and abolish all restrictions and limitations in its outstanding leases so that every licensee shall be at liberty to use the machinery for the manufacture of any kind or quantity of glassware comprehended within the decree. Moreover, if licenses or as-signments by any one of the corporate defendants to any other still con-tain any offensive provision, such provision can, by appropriate injunc-tion, be cancelled, so that the owner of each patent will have unrestricted freedom to use and to license, and every licensee equally with every other will be free of restriction as to the use of the leased or licensed machinery, method or process, or the articles manufactured thereon or thereunder.

It is suggested that there is not confiscation since Hartford might, with later consent of the court, sell its patents. Under the decree as entered be-low nothing can be obtained by Hartford for the use of its patents and we cannot speculate as to what might be the ultimate adjustments made by the trial court in the decree.

If, as suggested, some of Hartford's patents were improperly obtained, or if some of them were awarded a priority to which the invention was not entitled, avenues are open to the Government to raise these questions and to have the patents cancelled. But if, as we must assume on this record, a defendant owns valid patents, it is difficult to say that, however much in the past such defendant has abused the rights thereby conferred, it must now dedicate them to the public.

That a patent is property, protected against appropriation both by individuals and by government, has long been settled. In recognition of this quality of a patent the courts, in enjoining violations of the Sherman Act arising from the use of patent licenses, agreements, and leases have abstained from action which amounted to a forfeiture of the patents. . . .

Since paragraphs 21 to 24(*a*) inclusive are to be eliminated this paragraph, which is ancillary to them should also be deleted from the decree, but in view of the nature of the conspiracy found, an injunction should go against the further prosecution of all infringement suits pending at the date this suit was brought. Hartford and the other corporate defendants mentioned in paragraph 24 should be required to lease or license glass making machinery of the classes each now manufactures to any who may desire to take licenses, (under patents on such machinery or on improvements, methods or processes applicable thereto) at standard royalties and without discrimination or restriction, and if at the time of entry of the decree there are any alleged infringers who are willing to take such licenses they should be released, and the patent owner deprived of all damages and profits which it might have claimed for past infringement. The decree should, however, be without prejudice to the future institution of any suit or suits for asserted infringements against persons refusing to take licenses under any of the presently licensed inventions arising out of their use after the date of the decree. The decree should not forbid any defendant from seeking recovery for infringement, occurring after the date of the final decree, of patents not covering feeders, formers, stackers, lehrs, or processes or methods applicable to any of them.

Paragraph 27 cancels all outstanding agreements between corporate appellants. . . .

In view of what we have already said about these earlier paragraphs, the license agreements as modified by the parties and in accordance with the views here expressed, should be allowed to stand. . . .

Paragraph 28 orders cancellation of all Hartford machinery leases now outstanding and requires that each lessee be offered a new license (without royalty, pursuant to paragraph 24) and offered the right to purchase all of the machinery now held under lease (as required by paragraph 23). In view of what has been said this provision should not stand.

Paragraph 29 enjoins the insertion or enforcement of any provision in any agreement heretofore or hereafter made by any of the appellants which (a) directly or indirectly limits or restricts (1) the type or kind of product, whether glassware or any other, which can be produced on machines or equipment or by processes embodying inventions licensed under patents or patent applications, (2) the use of the product so produced, (3) the character, weight, color, capacity, or composition of the product, (4) the quantity, (5) the market, either as to territory or customers in or to which the product may be sold or distributed, (6) the price or terms of sale or other disposition of the product, or (7) the use of the machinery or equipment distributed or the inventions licensed in connection with any other machinery or equipment, or the use of it in any specified plant or locality; (b) authorizes termination of the license for unauthorized use; (c) provides that the licensee shall not contest the validity of any patent or patents of the licensor; (d) provides that improvements by the licensee on machinery leased and sold shall become the property of the lessor; (e) provides that rights to improvements and inventions covering licensed machinery or processes or methods shall become the exclusive property of the lessor or vendor; or (f) grants to any licensee a preferential position by lower rates of royalty, by different provisions of licensing, leasing, or sale, by exclusive licensing, rebate, discounts or requiring a share in net or gross income, or by any other means.

The paragraph now covers every kind of invention and every patent, present or future, in any field if owned or controlled or distributed by an appellant.

The injunction will stop all inventions or acquirement of patents in any field by any appellant unless for its own use in its business, for it sets such limitations upon the reward of a patent as to make it practically worthless except for use by the owner. It is unlimited in time. It is not limited to any joint action or conspiracy violative of the antitrust laws; it covers inventions in every conceivable field.

The Government now agrees that this injunction should be limited to glass making machinery and glassware as defined in paragraph 1 of the decree of the District Court. . . .

Paragraph 31 requires court approval of "any agreement between any of the defendants" and "of any license agreement made pursuant to this judgment." This is too sweeping. The provision is without limit of time and not terminable upon fulfilment of any condition. . . . This paragraph, if retained, should be restricted in application to lease or license agreements and agreements respecting patents and trade practices, production and trade relations.

By paragraph 33 each of the individual defendants is enjoined from "holding, controlling, directly or indirectly, or through corporations, agents, trustees, representatives, or nominees, any of the issued and outstanding capital stock, bonds or other evidences of indebtedness of more than one corporation engaged either in the manufacture and sale of glassware or in the manufacture or distribution of machinery used in the manufacture of glassware or in both. . . ." The purpose of dealing with stock ownership is to prevent aggregation of control to the end of establishing a monopoly or stifling competition. The ownership of a few, or even a few hundred, shares of stock of a glass manufacturing company not in competition with the company of which a defendant happens to be a director can have no tendency towards such a result. . . .

Moreover, the injunction is against ownership of bonds of any such company. It is difficult to see how such ownership in any reasonable amount by any of the individuals in question could tend towards a violation of the Sherman Act. . . .

The decree should be modified to prohibit acquisition of stocks or bonds of any corporate appellant by any other such appellant, and to prohibit only the acquisition of a measure of control through ownership of stocks or bonds or otherwise, by any individual in a company competing with that with which he is officially connected or a subsidiary or affiliate of such competing company. . . .

Paragraphs 37 to 39 are directed at the glass container association. . . .

The injunctions entered in paragraphs 37 to 39, inclusive, compel the association to abolish its statistical committee and to refrain from establishing any committee with similar functions. . . .

We think the injunction as respects the association, while leaving it in existence, practically destroys its functioning, even as an innocent trade association for what have been held lawful ends. The association has undoubtedly been an important instrument of restraint and monopoly. It may be made such again, and detection and prevention and punishment for such resumption of violations of law may be difficult if not impossible. In the light of the record, we think it better to order its dissolution, and to provide that the corporate defendants be restrained for a period of five years from forming or joining any such trade association. . . .

Paragraph 52 deals with the problem of suppressed or unworked patents. Much is said in the opinion below, and in the briefs, about the practice of the appellants in applying for patents to "block off" or "fence in" competing inventions. In the cooperative effort of certain of the appellants to obtain dominance in the field of patented glass-making machinery, many patents were applied for to prevent others from obtaining patents on improvements which might, to some extent, limit the return in the way of royalty on original or fundamental inventions. The decree should restrain agreements and combinations with this object. But it is another matter to restrain every defendant, for the indefinite future, from attempting to patent improvements of machines or processes previously patented and then owned by such defendant. This paragraph, is, in our judgment, too broad. In effect it prohibits several of the corporate defendants from applying for patents covering their own inventions in the

art of glassmaking. For reasons elsewhere elaborated it can
tained. . . .

A patent owner is not in the position of a quasi-trustee for
or under any obligation to see that the public acquires the free
use the invention. He has no obligation either to use it or to gran
to others. If he discloses the invention in his application so that
come into the public domain at the end of the 17 year period of exclusive
right he has fulfilled the only obligation imposed by the statute. . . .

Reversed in part, affirmed in part and decree vacated and remanded.

Mr. Justice Douglas, Mr. Justice Murphy and Mr. Justice Jackson
took no part in the consideration or decision of this case.

Mr. Justice Black and Mr. Justice Rutledge separately dissented in
part. . . .

International Salt Co., Inc. v. United States

332 U.S. 392 (1947)

Mr. Justice Jackson delivered the opinion of the Court.

The Government brought this civil action to enjoin the International
Salt Company, appellant here, from carrying out provisions of the leases
of its patented machines to the effect that lessees would use therein only
International's salt products. The restriction is alleged to violate Section 1
of the Sherman Act, and Section 3 of the Clayton Act. . . .

It was established . . . that the International Salt Company is engaged
in interstate commerce in salt, of which it is the country's largest producer for industrial uses. It also owns patents on two machines for utilization of salt products. . . . The principal distribution of each of these machines is under leases which, among other things, require the lessees to
purchase from appellant all unpatented salt and salt tablets consumed in
the leased machines. . . .

In 1944, appellant sold approximately 119,000 tons of salt, for about
$500,000, for use in these machines.

The appellant's patents confer a limited monopoly of the invention
they reward. From them appellant derives a right to restrain others from
making, vending or using the patented machines. But the patents confer
no right to restrain use of, or trade in, unpatented salt. By contracting to
close this market for salt against competition, International has engaged in
a restraint of trade for which its patents afford no immunity from the
antitrust laws. . . .

Appellant contends, however, that summary judgment was unauthorized because it precluded trial of alleged issues of fact as to whether the
restraint was unreasonable within the Sherman Act or substantially lessened competition or tended to create a monopoly in salt within the Clay-

ton Act. We think the admitted facts left no genuine issue. Not only is price-fixing unreasonable, *per se*, United States *v.* Socony-Vacuum Oil Co. . . . ; United States *v.* Trenton Potteries Co. . . . , but it is also unreasonable, *per se*, to foreclose competitors from any substantial market. . . . The volume of business affected by these contracts cannot be said to be insignificant or insubstantial and the tendency of the arrangement to accomplishment of monopoly seems obvious. Under the law, agreements are forbidden which "tend to create a monopoly," and it is immaterial that the tendency is a creeping one rather than one that proceeds at full gallop; nor does the law await arrival at the goal before condemning the direction of the movement. . . .

Appellant also urges that since under the leases it remained under an obligation to repair and maintain the machines, it was reasonable to confine their use to its own salt because its high quality assured satisfactory functioning and low maintenance cost. . . .

Of course, a lessor may impose on a lessee reasonable restrictions designed in good faith to minimize maintenance burdens and to assure satisfactory operation. . . . But it is not pleaded, nor is it argued, that the machine is allergic to salt of equal quality produced by anyone except International. If others cannot produce salt equal to reasonable specifications for machine use, it is one thing; but it is admitted that, at times, at least, competitors do offer such a product. They are, however, shut out of the market by a provision that limits it, not in terms of quality, but in terms of a particular vendor. Rules for use of leased machinery must not be disguised restraints of free competition, though they may set reasonable standards which all suppliers must meet. . . .

Judgment affirmed.

Mr. Justice Frankfurter, joined by Mr. Justice Reed and Mr. Justice Burton, dissented in part. . . .

Chapter 10

COPYRIGHTS AND
TRADEMARKS

The antitrust problems created by copyrights and trademarks are quite similar.[1] Hence, all that need be said about the following cases is that the Interstate Circuit decision is important not only for its discussion of the relation of the Copyright Act to the Sherman Act, but for its use of the implied conspiracy doctrine. It might, in fact, be contended that that doctrine, as expounded in this case, borders on the "conscious parallelism" doctrine later set forth in the Rigid Steel Conduit case (see Chapter 5, above).

Interstate Circuit, Inc. v. United States

306 U.S. 208 (1939)

Mr. Justice Stone delivered the opinion of the Court.

The case is here on appeal . . . from a final decree of the District Court for northern Texas restraining appellants from continuing in a combination and conspiracy condemned by the court as a violation of Section 1 of the Sherman Antitrust Act . . . , and from enforcing or renewing certain contracts found by the court to have been entered into in pursuance of the conspiracy. . . .

Appellants comprise the two groups of defendants in the District Court. The members of one group of eight corporations which are distributors of motion picture films, and the Texas agents of two of them, are appellants in No. 270. . . . The distributor appellants are engaged in the business of distributing in interstate commerce motion picture films, copyrights on which they own or control, for exhibition in theatres throughout the United States. They distribute about 75 percent of all first-class feature films exhibited in the United States. . . .

The exhibitor group of appellants consists of Interstate Circuit, Inc., and Texas Consolidated Theatres, Inc., and Hoblitzelle and O'Donnell, who are respectively president and general manager of both and in ac-

[1] See Clair Wilcox, *Public Policies Toward Business* (Homewood, Ill.: Richard D. Irwin, Inc., 1955), chapter 6.

tive charge of their business operations. The two corporations are affiliated with each other and with Paramount Pictures Distributing Co., Inc., one of the distributor appellants.

Interstate operates forty-three first-run and second-run motion picture theatres, located in six Texas cities. It has a complete monopoly of first-run theatres in these cities, except for one in Houston operated by one distributor's Texas agent. In most of these theatres the admission price for adults for the better seats at night is 40 cents or more. Interstate also operates several subsequent-run theatres in each of these cities, twenty-two in all, but in all but Galveston there are other subsequent-run theatres which compete with both its first- and subsequent-run theatres in those cities.

Texas Consolidated operates sixty-six theatres, some first- and some subsequent-run houses, in various cities and towns in the Rio Grande Valley and elsewhere in Texas and New Mexico. In some of these cities there are no competing theatres, and in six leading cities there are no competing first-run theatres. It has no theatres in the six Texas cities in which Interstate operates. That Interstate and Texas Consolidated dominate the motion picture business in the cities where their theatres are located is indicated by the fact that at the time of the contracts in question Interstate and Consolidated each contributed more than 74 percent of all the license fees paid by the motion picture theatres in their respective territories to the distributor appellants.

On July 11, 1934 . . . , O'Donnell, the manager of Interstate and Consolidated, sent to each of them [the distributors] a letter on the letterhead of Interstate, each letter naming all of them as addressees, in which he asked compliance with two demands as a condition of Interstate's continued exhibition of the distributors' films in its "A" or first-run theatres at a night admission of 40 cents or more. One demand was that the distributors "agree that in selling their product to subsequent runs, that this 'A' product will never be exhibited at any time or in any theatre at a smaller admission price than 25¢ for adults in the evening." The other was that "on 'A' pictures which are exhibited at a night admission of 40¢ or more—they shall never be exhibited in conjunction with another feature picture under the so-called policy of double features.". . .

The admission price customarily charged for preferred seats at night in independently operated subsequent-run theatres in Texas at the time of these letters was less than 25 cents. . . . In most of them the admission was 15 cents or less. It was also the general practice in those theatres to provide double bills either on certain days of the week or with any feature picture which was weak in drawing power. . . .

. . . [E]ach distributor agreed with Interstate for the 1934–35 season to impose both the demanded restrictions upon their subsequent-run licensees in the six Texas cities served by Interstate, except Austin and Galveston. . . .

The [lower] court concluded as matters of law that the agreement of the distributors with each other and those with Interstate to impose restrictions upon subsequent-run exhibitors . . . constituted a combination and conspiracy in restraint of interstate commerce in violation of the Sherman Act. . . .

Appellants assail the decree of the District Court upon three principal grounds: (*a*) that the finding of agreement and conspiracy among the distributor appellants . . . is not supported by . . . the evidence; (*b*) that the several separate contracts entered into by Interstate with the distributors are within the protection of the Copyright Act and consequently are not violations of the Sherman Act; and (*c*) that the restrictions do not unreasonably restrain interstate commerce within the provisions of the Sherman Act.

The Agreement Among the Distributors. . . . As is usual in cases of alleged unlawful agreements to restrain commerce, the government is without the aid of direct testimony that the distributors entered into any agreement with each other to impose the restrictions upon subsequent-run exhibitors. In order to establish agreement it is compelled to rely on inferences drawn from the course of conduct of the alleged conspirators.

The trial court drew the inference of agreement from the nature of the proposals made on behalf of Interstate and Consolidated; from the manner in which they were made; from the substantial unanimity of action taken upon them by the distributors; and from the fact that appellants did not call as witnesses any of the superior officials who negotiated the contracts. . . . This conclusion is challenged by appellants because not supported by subsidiary findings or by the evidence. We think this inference of the trial court was rightly drawn from the evidence. . . .

The O'Donnell letter named on its face as addressees the eight local representatives of the distributors, and so from the beginning each of the distributors knew that the proposals were under consideration by the others. Each was aware that all were in active competition and that without substantially unanimous action with respect to the restrictions for any given territory there was risk of a substantial loss of the business and good will of the subsequent-run and independent exhibitors, but that with it there was the prospect of increased profits. There was, therefore, strong motive for concerted action, full advantage of which was taken by Interstate and Consolidated in presenting their demands to all in a single document.

There was risk, too, that without agreement diversity of action would follow. Compliance with the proposals involved a radical departure from the previous business practices of the industry and a drastic increase in admission prices of most of the subsequent-run theatres. . . .

It taxes credulity to believe that the several distributors would, in the circumstances, have accepted and put into operation with substantial unanimity such far-reaching changes in their business methods without some understanding that all were to join, and we reject as beyond the range of probability that it was the result of mere chance. . . .

Taken together, the circumstances of the case which we have mentioned, when uncontradicted and with no more explanation than the record affords, justify the inference that the distributors acted in concert and in common agreement in imposing the restrictions upon their licensees in the four Texas cities.

The inference was supported and strengthened when the distributors, with like unanimity, failed to tender the testimony, at their command, of any officer or agent of a distributor who knew, or was in a position to know, whether in fact an agreement had been reached among them for concerted action. When the proof supported, as we think it did, the inferences of such conduct, the burden rested on appellants of going forward with the evidence to explain away or contradict it. . . .

It was enough that, knowing that concerted action was contemplated and invited, the distributors gave their adherence to the scheme and participated in it. Each distributor was advised that the others were asked to participate; each knew that cooperation was essential to successful operation of the plan. They knew that the plan, if carried out, would result in a restraint of commerce, which, we will presently point out, was unreasonable within the meaning of the Sherman Act, and knowing it, all participated in the plan. The evidence is persuasive that each distributor early became aware that others had joined. With that knowledge they renewed the arrangement and carried it into effect for the two successive years.

The Protection Afforded by the Copyright Act to the Contracts Between Interstate and the Distributors. The decree below enjoined enforcement and renewal of the separate agreements . . . imposing the restrictions upon later-run theatres in certain cities . . . , although the court found no conspiracy among the distributors to effect this latter restriction. Appellants assail this part of the decree on the ground that such separate agreements, if entered into without agreement or concert among the distributors, are a legitimate exercise of the monopoly secured to the distributors by their copyrights.

Under Section 1 of the Copyright Act . . . , the owners of the copyright of a motion picture film acquire the right to exhibit the picture and to grant an exclusive or restrictive license to others to exhibit it. . . .

The case is not one of the mere restriction of competition between the first showing of a copyrighted film by Interstate and a subsequent showing of the same film by a licensee of the copyright owner. . . .

A contract between a copyright owner and one who has no copyright, restraining the competitive distribution of the copyrighted articles in the open market in order to protect the latter from the competition, can no more be valid than a like agreement between two copyright owners or patentees. . . . In either case if the contract is effective, as it was here, competition is suppressed and the possibility of its resumption precluded by force of the contract. An agreement illegal because it suppresses competition is not any less so because the competitive article is copyrighted. The fact that the restraint is made easier or more effective by making the copyright subservient to the contract does not relieve it of illegality. . . .

Unreasonableness of the Restraint. The restrictions imposed on the subsequent-run exhibitors were harsh and arbitrary. . . . Compliance with the restrictions was a uniform condition of exhibition of the films by subsequent-run theatres. There were wide differences in the location and character of the subsequent-run houses. . . . Despite these differences which normally affect the admission price that could be charged by subsequent-run theatres, the 25 cents admission price was to be required of all alike, forcing increases in admission prices ranging from 25 percent to 150 percent.

The trial court found that practically all of the later-run exhibitors who bowed to the restrictions would not have done so but for the compulsion of their need of showing the restricted pictures, and that the result was to increase the income of the distributors and Interstate and diminish that of the exhibitors who accepted the restrictions, by deflecting attendance from subsequent-run theatres to Interstate's first-run theatres. . . . The effect was a drastic suppression of competition and an oppressive price maintenance, of benefit to Interstate and the distributors but injurious alike to Interstate's subsequent-run competitors and to the public.

The benefit, at such a cost, does not justify the restraint. . . . It does not appear that the competition at which they were aimed was unfair or abnormal. Cf. Appalachian Coals, Inc. *v.* United States, 288 U.S. 344. . . .

We think the conclusion is unavoidable that the conspiracy and each contract between Interstate and the distributors by which those consequences were affected are violations of the Sherman Act and that the District Court rightly enjoined enforcement and renewal of these agreements, as well as of the conspiracy among the distributors.

Affirmed.

Mr. Justice Frankfurter took no part in the consideration or decision of this case.

Mr. Justice Roberts, with whom Mr. Justice McReynolds and Mr. Justice Butler joined, dissented. . . .

United States v. Paramount Pictures, Inc. et al.

334 U.S. 131 (1948)

[The major portion of this decision is presented in Chapter 1 in connection with cases involving close-knit combinations and monopoly. Only that portion relevant to the copyright is presented below.]

Mr. Justice Douglas delivered the opinion of the Court. . . .

Block-booking is the practice of licensing, or offering for license, one feature [film] or group of features on condition that the exhibitor will also license another feature or group of features released by the distributors during a given period. The films are licensed in blocks before they are actually produced. All the defendants, except United Artists, have engaged in the practice. Block-booking prevents competitors from bidding for single features on their individual merits. The District Court . . . held it illegal for that reason and for the reason that it "adds to the monopoly of a single copyrighted picture that of another copyrighted picture which must be taken and exhibited in order to secure the first." That enlargement of the monopoly of the copyright was condemned below in reliance on the principle which forbids the owner of a patent to condition its use on the purchase or use of patented or unpatented materials. . . . The court enjoined defendants from performing or entering into any license in which the right to exhibit one feature is conditioned upon the licensee's taking one or more other features.

We approve that restriction. The copyright law, like the patent statutes, makes reward to the owner a secondary consideration. In Fox Film Corp. *v.* Doyal . . . Chief Justice Hughes spoke as follows respecting the copyright monopoly granted by Congress, "The sole interest of the United States and the primary object in conferring the monopoly lie in the general benefits derived by the public from the labors of authors." It is said that reward to the author or artist serves to induce release to the public of the products of his creative genius. But the reward does not serve its public purpose if it is not related to the quality of the copyright. Where a high quality film greatly desired is licensed only if an inferior one is taken, the latter borrows quality from the former and strengthens its monopoly by drawing on the other. The practice tends to equalize rather than differentiate the reward for the individual copyrights. Even where all the films included in the package are of equal quality, the requirement that all be taken if one is desired increases the market for some. Each stands not on its own footing but in whole or in part on the appeal which another film may have. As the District Court said, the result is to add to the monopoly of the copyright in violation of the principal of the patent cases involving tying clauses. . . .

Columbia pictures makes an earnest argument that enforcement of the restriction as to block-booking will be very disadvantageous to it and will greatly impair its ability to operate profitably. But the policy of the antitrust laws is not qualified or conditioned by the convenience of those whose conduct is regulated. Nor can a vested interest, in a practice which contravenes the policy of the antitrust laws, receive judicial sanction.

We do not suggest that films may not be sold in blocks or groups when there is no requirement, express or implied, for the purchase of more than one film. All we hold to be illegal is a refusal to license one or more copyrights unless another copyright is accepted. . . .

[The block-booking portion of the lower court decision was thereby affirmed.]

PART V

Foreign Commerce and International

Agreements

Chapter 11

CARTELS[1]

Relatively few cartel cases have been brought under our antitrust laws. The first case presented in this chapter—United States v. International Lead—might equally well have been placed in Chapter 9, as one of interest for its ruling concerning the use of patents. The international scope of the various patent agreements, however, makes it of interest to students of cartel problems as well. The Timken case also raises problems of some importance. Not only was the Court called upon to rule on the increasingly difficult problem of the legality of so-called joint ventures; it had to decide whether the realities of international trade conditions required the adoption of some rule of reason in cartel cases. The difficulty involved in reaching a decision which condemned Timken for eliminating competition in world markets is highlighted by Mr. Justice Jackson's dissent, reported below.

United States v. National Lead Company et al.

63 F.Supp. 513 (1945)[2]

Rifkind, District Judge.

By its complaint the United States alleges a cause of action under Sections 1 and 2 of the Sherman Act. Its prayer is for an injunction to re

[1] The economic, political, and social problems involved in the cartel issue are so numerous that cursory discussion would be valueless. The interested reader is referred to Clair Wilcox, *Public Policies Toward Business* (Homewood, Ill.: Richard D. Irwin, Inc., 1955), chapter 27; Joel Dirlam and Alfred E. Kahn, *Fair Competition: The Law and Economics of Antitrust Policy* (Ithaca: Cornell University Press, 1955), pp. 272–75; George W. Stocking and Myron W. Watkins, *Cartels in Action* and *Cartels or Competition?* (New York: Twentieth Century Fund, 1946); Joseph Borkin and Charles A. Welsh, *Germany's Master Plan* (New York: Duell, Sloan and Pearce, 1943); *Joint Oil Producing Ventures in the Middle East, Their Status Under United States Antitrust Laws*, a Submittal by Standard Oil Co., (New Jersey) to the Attorney General's National Committee to Study the Antitrust Laws, 1953.

[2] In 1947 the Supreme Court upheld this lower court decision, 332 U.S. 319. In his opinion Mr. Justice Burton relied so heavily on Judge Rifkind's decision that the latter is presented here. In the Supreme Court Mr. Justice Black and Mr. Justice Jackson took no part in the consideration or decision of the case; Mr. Justice Douglas, with whom Mr. Justice Murphy and Mr. Justice Rutledge concurred, dissented in part. IMS.

strain the alleged violations of the statute and for ancillary remedies to make the court's mandate effective.

The defendants are National Lead Company and E. I. duPont de Nemours & Company, Inc., the two principal producers of titanium pigments in the United States and the two largest producers thereof in the world; and Titan Company, Inc. wholly owned by NL and in turn the owner of substantial stock interests in the following corporations, producers of, dealers in titanium pigments: BTP, TG, SIT, TAS and TK.[3]

The complaint charges that:

"Beginning on or about July 30, 1920, . . . defendants . . . have been continuously engaged in a combination by the means and methods hereinafter set forth; in restraint of, and to monopolize, the aforesaid trade and commerce in titanium compounds among the several states of the United States and with foreign nations and have been and are now parties to contracts, agreements, and understandings in restraint of such trade and commerce, all in violation of Sections 1 and 2" of the Sherman Act.

The evidence supports the allegation in every material respect.

Titanium is a very abundant element. The principal ores which yield titanium in commercial concentration are ilmenite and rutile. Titanium compounds and particularly titanium dioxide possess the characteristics of opacity, great hiding power, high tinting strength and chemical inertness. These properties make it superlatively suitable for the manufacture of white paint and valuable in the production of rubber, glass, paper and several additional materials.

The commercial development of titanium compounds is founded largely upon the work of three groups of chemists working independently at and about the time of the first World War. In the United States, at Niagara Falls, New York, Messrs. Barton and Rossi developed a process for the manufacture of titanium compounds. Patents were issued to them; and these they assigned to TP, a corporation formed for the purpose. In Norway, Gustav Jebsen and his associates interested in the utilization of a large ilmenite deposit, developed another process. The patents which were granted thereon were assigned to TAS, organized for the purpose of exploiting them.

In France, Joseph Blumenfeld invented and procured patents for a third process. Terres Rares acquired these patents.

In 1920 NL held 10% of the stock of TP and had an option to acquire up to 50% of its stock. NL thereupon negotiated an agreement with TAS which was executed and went into effect on July 30, 1920. This agreement became the basic charter for the world-wide regulation of production and commerce in titanium compounds.

It marked the birth of a new industry. In the course of the ensuing

[3] British Titan Products, Ltd.; Titangesellschaft, m.b.H.; Société Industrielle du Titane; Titan Co. A/S; and Titan Kogyo Kabushiki Kaisha, respectively. Tinc represents Titanium Co., Ltd. IMS.

twenty years titanium pigments outstripped the production and sale of lithopone and white lead. . . .

Throughout this period prices were repeatedly reduced and only once, in 1941, increased.

At or about the time of the outbreak of World War II . . . we find this industry predominantly occupied in the United States by two producers, NL and DP, who supplied, in 1939, 73,645 tons out of a total of 82,940 tons. The balance of 9,295 tons is produced by American Zirconium, a licensee of both NL and DP and by Virginia Chemical, a licensee of DP. We further find a complete absence of imports of titanium products from abroad, and complete absence of exports from the United States, except to the countries of the Western Hemisphere.

In order to understand how the condition of affairs came to be, it is necessary to review the provisions of the mentioned contract of 1920 and briefly to relate the history of the persistence of its principles in more than 60 agreements subsequently executed. . . .

It is manifest that by the terms of this agreement the parties had divided the world into two trade areas or territories; that each party agreed not to trespass into the territory allotted to the other; and that all commerce between the two territories in titanium products was, as far as these parties were concerned, interdicted and could proceed only by the grace of their mutual consent. The suppression of this commerce was not limited to patented articles or to articles produced by patented processes but extended to all products within the "licensed field."

The objects of this arrangement have not been left unstated, to be ascertained by inference and deduction. They are disclosed by a large volume of written correspondence, uninhibited by any respect for, or indeed any apparent awareness of, the prohibitions of the antitrust laws.

The explicitly stated objects are: (1) the elimination of competition; (2) the advancement of the art through the exchange of technology. It was the belief of the architects of this foundation of the industrial structure they hoped to build thereon, that the second object could not be attained except in a climate of cooperation engendered by the achievement of the first object. And it was their intention that the advance in the art, accelerated by the exchange of patents, patent applications and "know-how," constitute their shield and weapon against outsiders.

This intention was carried into effect.

An examination of the evidence reveals the perpetuation of what the parties called the principles of the 1920 contract by a network of agreements which have confined the international trade in titanium products within the preordained channels where through it moves only by the grace and under the regulations of NL and its foreign associates. It is unnecessary to rehearse the history and detail of that development. . . .

In detail, the elapsed quarter century is crowded with negotiations, conferences, correspondence and agreements. The men who participated in these were all articulate, literate and, with the exception of DP's Rupprecht, recorded what they saw, heard, said and thought with Boswellian fidelity. When the story is seen as a whole, there is no blinking the fact that there is no free commerce in titanium. Every pound of it is trammelled by privately imposed regulation. The channels of this commerce have not been formed by the winds and currents of competition. They are, in large measure, artificial canals privately constructed. The borders of the private domain in titanium are guarded by hundreds of patents, procured without opposition, and maintained without litigation. The accumulated power of this private empire, at the outbreak of World War II, was tremendous. It was more difficult for the independent outsider to enter this business than for the camel to make its proverbial passage through the eye of a needle.

For the purpose of the discussion which follows, it is convenient to segregate DP's relation with NL and the foreign producers from NL's relations with the foreign producers.

The Case Against NL and Tinc

At the outbreak of World War II we find that NL and Tinc are, by virtue of agreements, members of a world-wide combination. . . . Territories are allocated; patents and patent applications are interchanged and cross licensed; technological information or "know-how" of one is promptly made available to the others. . . . Each operates in its own exclusive territory. When there is suspicion that a customer of one is shipping into the territory of another, investigation is promptly made with a view to suppressing the "illicit" traffic. Competition among them is nonexistent. . . .

And all this is the product of agreements.

Clearly this combination affects the interstate and foreign commerce of the United States. No titanium pigments enter the United States except with the consent of NL. No foreign titanium pigments move in interstate commerce except with like approval. No titanium pigment produced by NL may leave the ports of the United States for points outside the Western Hemisphere.

One of the objects of the combination is to suppress competition. . . .

To have access to the patents of the combination, the stranger must not only have the consent of the member of the combination in whose "territory" he would operate, but he must adhere to the principles of the combination. The cornerstone of the system was the private regulation of international trade. The suppression of competition was the cement which held the superstructure in place.

Whether the form of association they created be called a cartel, an international cartel, a patent pool, or "a technical and commercial cooperation," is of little significance. It is a combination and conspiracy in restraint of trade; and the restraint is unreasonable. As such it is outlawed by Section 1 of the Sherman Act; and it is unimportant whether it also violated Section 2.

No citation of authority is any longer necessary to support the proposition that a combination of competitors, which by agreement divides the world into exclusive trade areas, and suppresses all competition among the members of the combination, offends the Sherman Act. Hence we need only consider the adequacy of the defenses asserted against the case established by the plaintiff.

The system of territorial allocation and suppression of trans-Atlantic traffic in titanium compounds and pigments cannot be justified as ancillary to the grant of a license under a patent. True, the network of agreements did involve cross-licensing of patents—but it was not limited thereto. The agreements applied to patents not yet issued and to inventions not yet imagined. They applied to commerce beyond the scope of any patents. They extended to a time beyond the duration of any then-existing patent. . . .

This is a case where if not the sole, at least one of the principal, objects was "to restrain trade in order to avoid the competition which it has always been the policy of the common law to foster.". . .

It is suggested that plaintiff has failed to establish injury to the public interest, Appalachian Coal, Inc., *v.* United States . . . ; and that the defendants have proved substantial public benefit. The latter proposition, defendants derive from two lines of evidence. The first is that during the regime of the combination, the art has rapidly advanced, production has increased enormously and prices have sharply declined. The evidence does show as much; but it does not follow that the public interest has not been abused. Indeed, the major premise of the Sherman Act is that the suppression of competition in international trade is in and of itself a public injury; or at any rate, that such suppression is a greater price than we want to pay for the benefits it sometimes secures. Nor does it necessarily follow that the advance of the art, the rise in production and the decline of prices are attributable to the effects of the combination. *Post hoc, propter hoc,* is an invalid argument whether used by the plaintiff or the defendant. Anyone is free to speculate whether, in the absence of the arrangement, the stimulus of competiton might not have produced far greater strides in these beneficial directions. The economic theory underlying the Sherman Act is that, in the long run, competition is a more effective prod to production and a more trustworthy regulator of prices than even an enlightened combination.

The second line of evidence is that American producers cannot do business successfully in a cartelized world except on cartel terms; and that, to abstain from such business, would amount to a greater restraint on trade than is involved in joining the cartel. . . . For the courts it is conclusive that Congress has not yet validated such a solution to the problem. Until it does, private agreement and combination and private regulation may not substitute for legislation. Only Congress, not the courts, may grant the required immunity. . . .

This branch of the case may be briefly summarized thus:

Agreements creating a world-wide patent pool of all present and future patents of the parties, covering an entire industry, and embracing a division of the world into exclusive territories within which each of the parties is to confine its business activities, with respect to patent protected commodities, as well as unpatented, for the purpose and with the effect of suppressing imports into and exports from the United States, are unlawful under the Sherman Act; they constitute an unreasonable restraint of trade.

My general summary of the evidence on this issue is that DP was a member of the combination—true, a special member, with a status, rights and obligations, different from that of the other members, but a member nonetheless.

At this point, DP advances the argument that it had no choice but to do business with the cartel unless it was content to stay out of the titanium field. . . .

Perhaps, the answer is that DP, having discovered the conspiracy, should have asked the Attorney General to break it up. Confessedly, the chances of DP getting NL's patents and know-how after such a hostile act would be, to say the least, dubious. But in any event the courts may not validate unlawful conduct because in a particular instance there may be social losses involved in enforcing the law. The paradox which DP discovers, even if it were a genuine one, would be of interest to Congress, not to the courts. But the paradox is not genuine. The conflict is a specious one. Judicial intervention to break up a combination in restraint of trade is not in itself a restraint of trade, although for a time the established channels of commerce may be disarranged. To prohibit adherence to conspiratorial trade restraints hampers trade in about the same way that the prohibition against the circulation of counterfeit money hampers it. It may prevent the consummation of a particular transaction but in the long run it frees business from private regimentation and secures it against those who would trammel it.

The case also presents the question whether the contract between NL and DP is offensive to the antitrust laws independently of the relation of that contract and the parties thereto to the foreign producers.

Here are two competing producers who, at the time their agreement is made, between them control 100% of the commerce in titanium products in the United States. They agree not only to settle their conflicting patent claims—which presumably they may do under the Gasoline Cracking case . . . —but they agree to exchange all future patents, patent applications and know-how. Though these exchanges are not on an exclusive basis, is it not clear, however, that the capacity of such a combination to dominate the market is vastly increased, that the capacity for the exclusion of outsiders from the industry is multiplied? In other words, was not Mr. Ewing, DP's London manager, (whose disavowal of authority to make the following statement I accept) saying no more than the obvious when he wrote in 1933, concerning the NL-DP agreement: "We look upon this patent pool as a definite advance in cooperation and the strengthening of both parties' position to the exclusion of outsiders"? I think so.

When the effect of an arrangement is obvious it is fair inference that the parties intended that effect. The accumulation of great power to restrain trade may in itself be an evil. . . . When the power thus acquired is exerted to accomplish unreasonable restraints of trade, it is surely an evil. A pertinent question is, therefore, how did NL and DP exercise the great power they acquired.

NL licensed one American producer, American Zirconium, and on conditions which required submission to the illegal 1920 contract. . . .

DP licensed both American Zirconium and Virginia Chemical. In both instances the licenses were subject to a severe tonnage limitation on the product made under the license and to a royalty on all titanium dioxide produced, whether under the licensed patents or not. . . .

Another inevitable consequence of the NL-DP agreement has been the proliferation of patents. . . . The result of that is that the newcomer is confronted by a veritable jungle of patents claims through which only the very powerful and stouthearted would venture, having a regard for the large initial investment which this business requires. These patents, through the agreements in which they are enmeshed and the manner in which they have been used, in fact, have been forged into instruments of domination of an entire industry. The net effect is that a business, originally founded upon patents which have long since expired, is today less accessible to free enterprise than when it was first launched. . . .

I need not consider whether an exchange of patents, present and future, between competitors, is violative of the Sherman Act. I assume that such an exchange standing alone is innocent. But in the context of the present case . . . this exchange between two corporations, who between them controlled the entire market, becomes an instrument of restraint, available for use and used, to continue the mastery of the market which NL and DP achieved by means of the illegal international agreements.

In order to give effect to the Sherman Act, plaintiff is entitled to a decree which will restore titanium to the system of free competition; the means of preventing such a development must be destroyed and the power to prevent it must be shorn from those who, by combination, have acquired it.

A decree will be entered for the plaintiff. . . .

Timken Roller Bearing Co. v. *United States*

341 U.S. 593 (1951)

Mr. Justice Black delivered the opinion of the Court.

The United States brought this action to prevent and restrain violations of the Sherman Act by appellant, Timken Roller Bearing Co. . . .

The complaint charged that appellant, in violation of Sections 1 and 3 of the Act, combined, conspired and acted with British Timken, Ltd. . . . and . . . French Timken to restrain interstate and foreign commerce by eliminating competition in the manufacture and sale of antifriction bearings in the markets of the world. . . .

As early as 1909 appellant and British Timken's predecessor had made comprehensive agreements for a territorial division of the world markets for antifriction bearings. . . . [I]n 1927 the agreements were substantially renewed in connection with a transaction by which appellant and one Dewar, an English businessman, cooperated in purchasing all the stock of British Timken. Later some British Timken stock was sold to the public with the result that appellant now holds about 30% of the outstanding shares while Dewar owns about 24%. In 1928 appellant and Dewar organized French Timken and since that date have together owned all the stock in the French Company. Beginning in that year . . . the three companies . . . have (1) allocated trade territories among themselves; (2) fixed prices on products of one sold in the territory of the others; (3) cooperated to protect each other's markets and to eliminate outside competition; (4) participated in cartels to restrict imports to, and exports from, the United States.

On these findings, the District Court concluded that appellant had violated the Sherman Act as charged, and entered a comprehensive decree designed to bar future violations. . . .

[T]he real grounds relied on for reversal are only a few in number. In the first place, appellant contends that most of the District Court's material findings of fact are without evidential support; . . . in effect, it is an invitation for us to try the case *de novo*. This Court must decline such an invitation just as it does when the Government makes the same request. United States *v.* Yellow Cab Co., 338 U.S. 338. . . . Since we cannot say the findings are "clearly erroneous," we accept them. . . .

Appellant next contends that the restraints of trade so clearly revealed by the District Court's findings can be justified as "reasonable," and therefore not in violation of the Sherman Act, because they are "ancillary" to allegedly "legal main transactions," namely, (1) a "joint venture" between appellant and Dewar, and (2) an exercise of appellant's right to license the trademark "Timken."

We cannot accept the "joint venture" contention. That the trade restraints were merely incidental to an otherwise legitimate "joint venture" is, to say the least, doubtful. The District Court found that the dominant purpose of the restrictive agreements into which appellant, British Timken and French Timken entered was to avoid all competition either among themselves or with others. Regardless of this, however, appellant's argument must be rejected. Our prior decisions plainly establish that agreements providing for an aggregation of trade restraints such as those existing in this case are illegal under the Act. . . . The fact that there is common ownership or control of the contracting corporations does not liberate them from the impact of the antitrust laws. . . . Nor do we find any support in reason or authority for the proposition that agreements between legally separate persons and companies to suppress competition among themselves and others can be justified as a "joint venture." Perhaps every agreement and combination to restrain trade could be so labeled.

Nor can the restraints of trade be justified as reasonable steps taken to implement a valid trademark licensing system . . . , [for] while a trademark merely affords protection to a name, the agreements in the present case went far beyond protection of the name "Timken" and provided for control of the manufacture and sale of antifriction bearings whether carrying the mark or not. A trademark cannot be legally used as a device for Sherman Act violation. . . .

We also reject the suggestion that the Sherman Act should not be enforced in this case because what appellant has done is reasonable in view of current foreign trade conditions. The argument in this regard seems to be that tariffs, quota restrictions and the like are now such that export and import of antifriction bearings can no longer be expected as a practical matter; that appellant cannot successfully sell its American-made goods abroad; and that the only way it can profit from business in England, France and other countries is through the ownership of stock in companies organized and manufacturing there. This position ignores the fact that the provisions of the Sherman Act against restraints of foreign trade are based on the assumption, and reflect the policy, that export and import trade in commodities is both possible and desirable. Those provisions of the Act are wholly inconsistent with appellant's argument that American business must be left free to participate in international cartels, that free foreign commerce in goods must be sacrificed in order to foster export of American dollars for investment in foreign factories which sell abroad. Acceptance of appellant's view would make the Sherman Act a dead letter insofar as it prohibits contracts and conspiracies in restraint of foreign trade. If such a drastic change is to be made in the statute, Congress is the one to do it.

Finally, appellant attacks the District Court's decree as being too broad in scope. The decree enjoins continuation or repetition of the conduct found illegal. This is clearly correct . . . because "relief, to be effective, must go beyond the narrow limits of the proven violation. . . ."

Mr. Justice Douglas, Mr. Justice Minton and I believe that the decree properly ordered divestiture. . . . Absent divestiture, it is difficult to see where other parts of the decree forbidding trade restraints would add much to what the Sherman Act by itself already prohibits. . . .

Nevertheless, a majority of the Court . . . believe that divestiture should not have been ordered. . . . As so modified, the judgment of the District Court is affirmed. . . .

Mr. Justice Burton and Mr. Justice Clark took no part in the consideration or decision of this case.

Mr. Justice Reed, with whom the Chief Justice joins concurred. . . .

Mr. Justice Frankfurter, dissented [basically on the same grounds as those set forth in the following dissent]. . . .

Mr. Justice Jackson, dissenting.

I doubt that it should be regarded as an unreasonable restraint of trade for an American industrial concern to organize foreign subsidiaries, each limited to serving a particular market area. If so, it seems to preclude the only practical means of reaching foreign markets by many American industries.

The fundamental issue here concerns a severely technical application to foreign commerce of the concept of conspiracy. It is admitted that if Timken had, within its own corporate organization, set up separate departments to operate plants in France and Great Britain, as well as in the United States, "that would not be a conspiracy; we must have two entities to have a conspiracy."[4] . . . The doctrine now applied to foreign commerce is that foreign subsidiaries organized by an American corporation are "separate persons," and any arrangement between them and the parent corporation to do that which is legal for the parent alone is an unlawful conspiracy. I think that result places too much weight on labels. . . .

[N]ot all agreements are conspiracies and not all restraints of trade are unlawful. In a world of tariffs, trade barriers, empire or domestic preferences, and various forms of parochialism from which we are by no means free, I think a rule that it is a restraint of trade to enter a foreign market through a separate subsidiary of limited scope is virtually to foreclose foreign commerce of many kinds. . . . I think this decision will restrain more trade than it will make free.

[4] Argument of Government counsel reported 19 L.W. 3291 *et seq.*

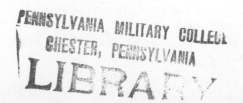

Appendix

APPENDIX:

EXCERPTS FROM ANTITRUST STATUTES

Sherman Act, 1890

SEC. 1. Every contract, combination in the form of trust or otherwise, or conspiracy, in restraint of trade or commerce among the several States, or with foreign nations, is hereby declared to be illegal. Every person who shall make any such contract or engage in any such combination or conspiracy, shall be deemed guilty of a misdemeanor, and, on conviction thereof, shall be punished by fine not exceeding five thousand dollars, or by imprisonment not exceeding one year, or by both said punishments, in the discretion of the court.

SEC. 2. Every person who shall monopolize, or attempt to monopolize, or combine or conspire with any other person or persons, to monopolize any part of the trade or commerce among the several States, or with foreign nations, shall be deemed guilty of a misdemeanor, and, on conviction thereof, shall be punished by fine not exceeding five thousand dollars, or by imprisonment not exceeding one year, or by both said punishments, in the discretion of the court.

Clayton Act, 1914

SEC. 2. That it shall be unlawful for any person engaged in commerce, in the course of such commerce, either directly or indirectly, to discriminate in price between different purchasers of commodities, which commodities are sold for use, consumption, or resale within the United States or any Territory thereof or the District of Columbia or any insular possession or other place under the jurisdiction of the United States, where the effect of such discrimination may be to substantially lessen competition or tend to create a monopoly in any line of commerce: *Provided*, That nothing herein contained shall prevent discrimination in price between purchasers of commodities on account of differences in the grade, quality, or quantity of the commodity sold, or that makes only due allowance for differences in the cost of selling or transportation, or discrimination in price in the same or different communities made in good faith to meet competition: *And provided further*, That nothing herein contained shall prevent persons engaged in selling goods, wares, or merchandise in commerce from selecting their own customers in bona fide transactions and not in restraint of trade.

SEC. 3. That it shall be unlawful for any person engaged in commerce, in the course of such commerce, to lease or make a sale or contract for sale of goods, wares, merchandise, machinery, supplies, or other commodities, whether patented or unpatented, for use, consumption, or resale within the United States or any Territory thereof or the District of Columbia or any insular possession or other place under the jurisdiction of the United States, or fix a price charged therefor, or discount from, or rebate upon, such price, on the condition, agreement, or understanding that the lessee or purchaser thereof shall not use or deal in the goods, wares, merchandise, machinery, supplies, or other commodity of a competitor or competitors of the lessor or seller, where the effect of such lease, sale, or contract for sale or such condition, agreement, or understanding may be to substantially lessen competition or tend to create a monopoly in any line of commerce.

Federal Trade Commission Act, 1914

SEC. 5. That unfair methods of competition in commerce are hereby declared unlawful.

Robinson–Patman Act, 1936, Amending Section 2 of the Clayton Act

SEC. 2. (*a*) That it shall be unlawful for any person engaged in commerce, in the course of such commerce, either directly or indirectly, to discriminate in price between different purchasers of commodities of like grade and quality, where either or any of the purchases involved in such discrimination are in commerce, where such commodities are sold for use, consumption, or resale within the United States or any Territory thereof or the District of Columbia or any insular possession or other place under the jurisdiction of the United States, and where the effect of such discrimination may be substantially to lessen competition or tend to create a monopoly in any line of commerce, or to injure, destroy, or prevent competition with any person who either grants or knowingly receives the benefit of such discrimination, or with customers of either of them: *Provided*, That nothing herein contained shall prevent differentials which make only due allowance for differences in the cost of manufacture, sale, or delivery resulting from the differing methods or quantities in which such commodities are to such purchasers sold or delivered: *Provided, however*, That the Federal Trade Commission may, after due investigation and hearing to all interested parties, fix and establish quantity limits, and revise the same as it finds necessary, as to particular commodities or classes of commodities, where it finds that available purchasers in greater quantities are so few as to render differentials on account thereof unjustly discriminatory or promotive of monopoly in any line of commerce; and the foregoing shall then not be construed to permit differentials based on differences in quantities greater than those so fixed and established: *And provided further*, That nothing herein contained shall prevent persons engaged in selling goods, wares, or merchandise in commerce from selecting their own customers in bona fide transactions and not in restraint of trade: *And provided further*, That nothing herein contained shall prevent price changes from time to time where in response to changing conditions affecting the market for or the marketability of the goods concerned, such as but not limited to actual or imminent deterioration of perishable goods, obsolescence of seasonal goods, distress sales under court process, or sales in good faith in discontinuance of business in the goods concerned.

(*b*) Upon proof being made, at any hearing on a complaint under this section, that there has been discrimination in price or services or facilities furnished, the burden of rebutting the prima-facie case thus made by showing justification shall be upon the person charged with a violation of this section, and unless justification shall be affirmatively shown, the Commission is authorized to issue an order terminating the discrimination: *Provided, however*, That nothing herein contained shall prevent a seller rebutting the prima-facie case thus made by showing that his lower price or the furnishing of services or facilities to any purchaser or purchasers was made in good faith to meet an equally low price of a competitor, or the services or facilities furnished by a competitor.

(*c*) That it shall be unlawful for any person engaged in commerce, in the course of such commerce, to pay or grant, or to receive or accept, anything of value as a commission, brokerage, or other compensation, or any allowance or discount in lieu thereof, except for services rendered in connection with the sale or purchase of goods, wares, or merchandise, either to the other party to such transaction or to an agent, representative, or other intermediary therein where such intermediary is acting in fact for or in behalf, or is subject to the direct or indirect control, of any party to such transaction other than the person by whom such compensation is so granted or paid.

(*d*) That it shall be unlawful for any person engaged in commerce to pay or contract for the payment of anything of value to or for the benefit of a customer of such person in the course of such commerce as compensation or in consideration for any services or facilities furnished by or through such customer in connection with the processing, handling, sale, or offering for sale of any products or commodities manufactured, sold, or offered for sale by such person, unless such payment or consideration is available on proportionally equal terms to all other customers competing in the distribution of such products or commodities.

(*e*) That it shall be unlawful for any person to discriminate in favor of one purchaser against another purchaser or purchasers of a commodity bought for resale, with or without processing, by contracting to furnish or furnishing, or by contributing to the furnishing of, any services or facilities connected with the processing, handling, sale, or offering for sale of such commodity so purchased upon terms not accorded to all purchasers on proportionally equal terms.

(*f*) That it shall be unlawful for any person engaged in commerce, in the course of such commerce, knowingly to induce or receive a discrimination in price which is prohibited by this section.

Celler-Kefauver Act, 1950, Amending Section 7 of the Clayton Act

SEC. 7. That no corporation engaged in commerce shall acquire, directly or indirectly, the whole or any part of the stock or other share capital and no corporation subject to the jurisdiction of the Federal Trade Commission shall acquire the whole or any part of the assets of another corporation engaged also in commerce, where in any line of commerce in any section of the country, the effect of such acquisition may be substantially to lessen competition, or to tend to create a monopoly.